A Good Year For Blossom

WOMEN WRITERS OF THE GUARDIAN COUNTRY DIARY

EDITED BY
MARTIN WAINWRIGHT

guardianbooks

A good year for blossom

This is a good year for blossom, the foam of wild cherry is retreating from the valleys now but upon the fells even ancient and storm-scarred trees shine white, as white as the snow which today lies on the mountain tops. All the garden bushes – currants, gooseberries and raspberries – are thick with flower or bud and this year, for the first time in many, the sparrows have left my cutleaf Japanese maple untouched. They usually take the buds almost as soon as they show but perhaps this damp spring has made the difference. Broom and gorse are yellow, sycamore is coming to flower and soon there will be apple blossom. Indeed, this is the time of year – the awakening – when I miss my bees, which I had kept for so long and parted with three years ago. I still feel a surge of excitement in a good blossom year and remember the contented hum of working hives just as I remember the kindliness of my fellow beekeepers. It seemed to me that bees, like other creatures, take after their owners – the over-careful, perhaps nervous ones have kittle or 'hot-footed' bees, while the happy, easy-going ones preside over quietly contented stocks. One jumpy beekeeper here kept a bottle of ammonia (much needed) in his hedge for his own and his neighbours' solace but one of the older bee-men by contrast went round the countryside to clover or to heather with teeming hives in his car boot and its interior humming with bees. But, as he said, he never went 'agin t'bees'; he did not (so far as I know) tell the bees of family events as beekeepers were reputed to do but he often said, 'Let t'bees tell you, go with them, not agin them.' That was, indeed, his philosophy of life – go with it, not 'agin it'.

Enid Wilson
May 1968

Contents

Introduction

I am sorry that I am not a woman, because without me this would be a man-free book, which would be a morsel of atonement for centuries of wasted talent. This is not a didactic or ranting collection. Quite the opposite. But while engrossed in many hundreds of these diaries by 11 women – only 11 – I have thought repeatedly of the *millions* of women who watched the same birds, grew the same plants or took the same walks, and yet were condemned, in Katherine Arnold Foster's chilling phrase, to see their nature study dismissed as the 'artless admiration of crinolines and ringlets'.

For centuries, women were excluded almost entirely from politics, business and everything else outside the home and family, so that the reader or viewer of Jane Austen bursts with frustration at the untapped virtues of her sparky characters. Why weren't they at least set to work to record the plants, birds, insects, soil – in today's buzzword the *environment* – of Mansfield Park or Northanger Abbey? And then have their findings published seriously and nationally, like our 11 here?

We would have learned so much science, so much sooner. History's catalogue of failed opportunities to use this skill is dumbfounding.

This failure lasted well beyond the mediaeval days when women who showed too much knowledge of medicinal plants risked death as witches, while churchmen debated absurdly whether they had souls. In 1614, a preacher in Peterborough who said that they did, but only in their shoes, was reported to the church authorities and disciplined. But by then there were other excuses for sidelining scientific knowledge shown by a studious daughter or wife.

The Linnaean system of classification, begun in 1735 and accepted in Britain within 30 years, inevitably laid emphasis on reproduction. Prudes considered it unsuitable, even licentious, for young ladies to study what they called the 'private parts' of vegetables and flowers. Serious botany fell into disfavour in many households, where it was deemed acceptable for women only to supervise the gardening. In 1657, an almanac of husbandry observed that 'Gentlewomen, if the ground be not too much wet, may do themselves much good by kneeling upon a cushion and weeding.' Enthusiasts who went further than this, such as Thomasin Tunstall, who sent unusual tubers from her garden to King James I's apothecary John Parkinson, were very much the exception. It was too risky for their social standing.

Consider the fate of Eleanor Glanville, the daughter of a quiet gentry couple who together perfected the celebrated Ribston Pippin apple on their Yorkshire estate in the mid-17th century. Raised in this enlightened home, Glanville became interested in butterflies and moths and in her middle age was one of the country's leading experts on them, albeit publicly unsung. It was the male scientists to whom she sent data and insects (three samples of which survive in the Natural History Museum in London) whose observations were published and taken seriously. Posthumously, Glanville has received her due in the naming of the rare and beautiful Glanville fritillary butterfly in her memory, but she got very short shrift from contemporaries. Her will was overthrown on the grounds of insanity, the main proof in the judge's mind being that she had 'chased flies without all necessary cloathes' and employed servant girls to beat hedges with poles so that 'wormes' (caterpillars) would fall on sheets that she had laid below, as any modern fieldworker would. The depositions of almost 100 witnesses are preserved at the Public Record Office, written horizontally, vertically and finally at an angle on the same few pages, because parchment was so rare and valuable.

They tell a sorry tale of prejudice, and if I were a woman, I would feel vengeful. But two wrongs do not make a right, and fortunately 21st-century women show little interest in getting their own back. Instead, we seem to be on the correct course to what surely must be the right arrangement: dividing everything roughly half-and-half, in proportion to the world's population. In the world of morsels, that includes the *Guardian*'s Country Diary and, as you will discover, its probable future authors.

So why take the path of the convent at this joyful moment, and publish a single-sex volume? Partly atonement, but much more because of the sheer pleasure of reading the work of these contributors and wanting to pass it on. Originally, this book came about because of just one of them, Gwen McBryde, whose Country Diaries especially appealed to me when I was choosing the *Guardian*'s centenary and wartime collections. She seemed to be perky, gallant, amusing, daffy. Her great friend Montagu James, the ghost story writer and provost of both King's College, Cambridge, and Eton school, called her 'a chirrupy sort of person' and I liked that. I Googled the lovely old farm of Dippersmoor Manor which she ran for years as a single mother (her husband died within a year of their marriage), and discovered it is now a B&B. I went to Kilpeck in Herefordshire to see it, with very high expectations, and they were not disappointed.

But McBryde was not A Harry Griffin, marching on for 53 years in the column, and she needed some companions in a new book. My researches had also introduced me to some impressive colleagues of hers: the suffragette leader Helena Swanwick who first broke the male monopoly of *Guardian* Country Diary writers. Janet Case, who taught Virginia Woolf Greek. Katherine Arnold Foster who, as Ka Cox, was the toast of pre-first world war Cambridge undergraduates and died after a confrontation with the Satanist Aleister Crowley (or his followers) who were dabbling in witchcraft close to her Cornish badger setts.

It is quite a cast, and one that has continued to attract lustrous recruits to this day, as I believe this collection shows. They leave no doubt in my mind about how much more rapidly we would have made scientific and social progress before the 20th century, if the army of female gardeners, naturalists and countryside observers had been taken seriously and encouraged to debate and publish alongside men. At the very least, some eminent chaps would surely have been corrected by commonsense wives.

Take Gilbert White. His *Natural History of Selborne* has, deservedly, never been out of print since it was first published in 1789, yet it includes his strange theory that swallows spent the winter in mudholes in river banks. 'Come along, Gilbert,' Mrs White would have said, had there been one (for he was a celibate priest). 'Let's just go down to the Test or the Itchen and check this one out.'

I make that suggestion, because practicality has been one distinctive attitude to emerge from these women's diaries. Mothers, some of them, farmers and gardeners, most of them, householders, all of them, every one of these writers has a down-to-earth side. They are true sisters of Beatrix Potter, not only through a shared skill with words but in parallels to her scientific expertise (her published work on fungi is masterly but eternally overshadowed by the bunnies), and to her other life as Mrs Heelis, farming Herdwick sheep and cannily buying land to give to the National Trust. They also share warmth, modesty, mastery of small worlds (while male diarists such as A Harry Griffin march over record-busting miles of mountain), and much more enthusiasm than the men for roaming about at night. Witches and moonshine, maybe? I don't think so; and I have had to work hard to find any flaws that might be described as feminine, if only as a debating point. Is there, for example, a habit of raising interesting questions in a vague way that doesn't seem to want an answer?

Helena Swanwick concludes a diary about robins invading her house by wondering why birds sleep on one leg, and whether they swap legs regularly so that neither gets tired. Fascinating, but she then drops the subject entirely. So as an experiment I asked a current *Guardian* Country Diarist for the answer – a man, Mark Cocker, one of the country's leading authorities on birds. He not only gave science's best answer to the question – tucking the leg beneath a wing keeps it warm and, yes, they do swap legs – but also consulted an even greater expert at Sheffield University, also a man, who bore him out. Does this suggest that men can go into excessive overdrive in a narrowly focused search for such solutions? Certainly, several of today's female diarists on whom I tested this example said (separately): 'men go in for the statistics; we prefer emotions'. But then, Swanwick takes trouble in another diary to explain why potatoes are sweeter after freezing. It is all good debating material, and that, I hope, will be one of the pleasures stimulated by these diaries.

I do not think, however, that many people of either sex will deny that women are generally much better than men at taking a back seat and being self-effacing and sitting quietly, which are two of the greatest skills any field naturalist must learn. It was admittedly a man, Lord Grey of Fallodon, who put this particularly well: 'If we sit down in some secluded spot, unobtrusive and still, we shall presently understand how much there is that as passers-by we never see.' But the *Guardian* Country Diarist Enid Wilson goes a telling step further by suggesting that even when she was spotted, her gender reassured shy creatures; and not only them, but interesting but reclusive local people as well. 'They sort of realise you're a fairly harmless person,' she said, explaining her technique. 'And that's it.'

By happy coincidence, my usual thanks for help this time go exclusively to women, starting with Lisa Darnell and her team of Amelia Hodsdon, Helen Brooks and Sara Montgomery in Guardian Books. Mariam Yamin in the paper's Newsroom archive and Caroline Corcoran helped me to use the new digital archive, which has hugely speeded up research although (because I like old libraries and crinkly microfilm) made it less fun. Elaine Moll, librarian of local studies in Hull, was instantly helpful on the youth of Gwen McBryde. Virginia Spiers took me for a lovely wander round the Tamar valley, Veronica Heath gave me tea in Northumberland and Audrey Insch was full of good conversation over lunch in Edinburgh. All the contemporary contributors could not have been more helpful, and their departed predecessors have taught me many things.

None of these diaries except the very first, the title piece by Enid Wilson, and two by Katherine Arnold Foster whose output was tiny, have been published in the previous three books and I have included at least one for every year since Helena Swanwick broke the male monopoly in December 1915. There is also one small mystery that I hope will entertain you. In The Year's Round that follows this introduction – a piece for each month by this book's diary writers – I was one short. Eleven diarists. Twelve months. Then I remembered 'MA', one of three *Guardian* Country Diary writers whose identity I failed to crack in the centenary and wartime collections. I am sure that the other two, BA and CDHA, were men, but MA's style and subjects – jam-making, wartime village food markets and outings with children – make me wonder. So she, if she she is, gets the missing month below, for one of the earliest references to bonsai I've come across. You can see if you agree.

The Year's Round

January

Around old Twelfth Night, James and Mary review their orchard of local varieties, plant more trees and collect graftwood of apples not yet established in their extensive collection.

Outside the apple-house door, soft, part-rotten fruit is strewn for blackbirds. Inside, wooden boxes are labelled with different names. Despite last year's poor growing season and the exceptionally mild, wet winter, Rough Pippin, Improved Keswick, Sawpit, Limberlimb and orange-flavoured Veitch's Perfection are still firm and juicy. At Luxulyan, old labels were found in a garden shed and, after several years of observation, the nearby Early Peach apple tree was identified; luckily the new owners had not chopped it down. Graftwood was also taken from a White Quarrenden/Quallender in Mevagissey, planted by the owner's grandfather 60 years ago. This tree thrives in a steep garden, alongside a spinney of Kea plums.

As well as named varieties, James grafts from a few chance seedlings with particularly valuable characteristics of hardiness and prolific fruiting. One gnarled old tree was found on boggy, tin-streaming land south of Redruth, its roots clinging to a huge boulder. The Boulder apple, grafted on to new rootstock two years ago, was feted on Wassail night, its smooth grey twigs hung with cider-soaked toast.

Virginia Spiers 1999

February

The beeches in the manor woods are silver-tipped as the brown buds' sheath withdraws. In the sunshine they were sprays of pearls on the soft blue sky. And the feathery tops of the larches which the sun caught were gold-dusted, and the cones at the top golden balls fit for a fairy tale. A birch's trunk gleamed dazzling white above through its fountain of reddish twigs and branches. And when the oak tops caught the magic they were transfigured to a golden filigree, gnarled and grey and rugged as they were below, with ivy clinging at the base and the hard-fern flourishing along the mossed branches and wisps of grey lichen hanging down like an old man's beard.

The sun struck full on a woodpecker's hole in one of these, last year's not this, though there were one or two tentative scrapings near that might be either. Cole-tits and long-tailed tits flitted through the high branches and a nuthatch called, and down below a pair of fighting chaffinches were a revolving wheel of feathers. You can feel the spring coming. Besides, you can easily see the little crimson flowers on the hazels now, and at the wood's end a missel-thrush was singing at last.

Janet Case 1931

March

I find something austere in the cold luminous haze of spring. The same impression was made on me this morning as I walked through the dim grey aisles of an old church, once a Cistercian abbey. It was founded in 1147, restored in 1634, and used as a parish church. There is hardly a trace left of the old monastic buildings. A mill stream runs nearby; it was diverted but once ran under the frater and the kitchen. Under ancient yew trees snowdrops linger, but only as a line of snow will stay on the north side of a wood. Already primroses take first place; they shine out of the rough grass.

Early lambs seem to have done very well this season; the only bother is that we are all having a struggle to feed stock, there are so few grass fields left. It is very worrying to see animals 'going back' for want of food. The small farmer finds it a regular Chinese puzzle making room for roots, kale, beans, and catch-crops, but they will manage it somehow.

Gwen McBryde 1943

April

Morning mist covered the sun-disc on Easter Sunday. For all we knew it might have been doing a slip-jig or a glissade! At noon it emerged, clothing coast and valley in golden sheen. It illuminated our 'ghost', a six-inch high daffodil of golden trumpet, palely fringed. We call it our 'ghost', our Bowen daffodil because it's an old species and four years ago we found, cast aside, its bulb with two others at Bowen's Court, Kildorrery, Co Cork, former home of the novelist Elizabeth Bowen. With care we planted them, the daffodils of one of our favourite writers. Each year only leaves appeared until this spring when, in this one bloom, Bowen's Court 'lives' again. Elizabeth

Bowen's last sentence in Bowen's Court catches our feeling, 'There is a sort of perpetuity about livingness, and it is part of the character of Bowen's Court to be, in sometimes its silent way, very much alive.' On March 26 another 'ghost' was added to our coast – Loop Head became an unmanned lighthouse, joining others on this western seaboard. It began in 1670 with a keeper who tended a coal-burning brazier to warn ships. In 1720 £1,000 was paid for three years to a woman lighthouse-keeper, Mary Wesby, to kindle the warning fire. I remember as a small child with short legs climbing, behind the keeper, the narrow spiral stairs of Hook Lighthouse, Co Wexford, to be shown the great lantern. The wonder of it never left me – the small light reflected and beamed out hundreds of feet the beauty of the very visible technology; the carefulness and caring attitude of the keepers; their bravery in isolation; their concern for the men 'that go down to the sea in ships … ' Their very hobbies, gardening, painting, music-making, poetry-writing, ship-modelling reveal their quality, their self-sufficiency. The automated light will be operated from Dun Laoghaire, Co Dublin. Now the tall towers will be empty, empty of men who dealt not in death but in life, who spread light upon the darkness of the waters.

Sarah Poyntz 1991

May

Watching badgers (or more truthfully, watching for badgers because to know that badgers are in a sett is no guarantee of

A young badger cub peeks from under a log

seeing them) is one of the most uncomfortable, time-consuming and fruitless occupations anyone could devise. Last night's gnat bites emphasise this all too persistently. Why, then, do it? Well – it is rather like fishing or beekeeping, the rewards can outweigh all discomforts and disappointments. One needs luck, too, as well as experience, like meeting four young badgers by chance as I did on one of the few warm May evenings recently when the world, after sunset, seemed to be breathing and expanding with a life of its own. The voice of grasshopper warblers reeling in the sedges and a woodcock riding overhead almost distracted my attention from a flicker of movement behind strands of honeysuckle on a shelf of earth above me, and there they were, four little badgers as oblivious of me as

I had been of them until a few seconds before – and so they remained for almost half an hour. This was obviously a very new world for them and to judge from their small size and their innocence, it was astonishing that their mother had allowed them out at all. Their round baby bodies were almost pinkish in colour, tailed by ridiculous stumps and topped by small black ears, white-edged, and already the shining black and white badger face blazon. They stayed close to the sett mouth, moving very gently, shoving a little at times but not, as yet, playing. One dug, experimentally, in the earth and dislodged a stone that bounced down, loud in the quietness, and this riveted all four with interest but none was afraid. Indeed, they were completely confident until a pair of late whooper swans flew in, barking sharply to one another and, in a flash, there were no badgers at all – nor have I seen them since.

Enid Wilson 1966

June

Last week I attended the annual general meeting of our county's branch of the Wildlife Trust, which is well supported here and has many enthusiastic volunteers. Wildlife projects already supported are tree-planting, building broad walks and bog-gripping – which means blocking drains to create wetlands. There are also family-orientated tasks involving help with pond creation and mini-beast hunting.

Returning to my garden last night after a day in the country, I saw a crow fly from a local farm plot with a small potato spiked on its bill. It paused while crossing my back lawn as though it seemed to be finding its burden unmanageable. Lowering its head, the bird transferred the potato to its feet and carried it like that, with legs dangling, for another 50 yards before pitching down in the field. I have never seen a crow do this before, but I believe that juggling with objects in midair is occasionally indulged in by rooks. Accompanying my father in a local wood we once saw a rook, followed by three companions, circling with a large dead leaf, which it kept repeatedly passing from its bill to its feet.

Probably due to the ban on hunting, foxes are now in abundance here. A friend saw one in the churchyard of our local market town. Walking down my field early one morning last week, I was halfway along the hedge when a fox loped past and then stopped a few yards in front of me. He stared past me as an unwelcome intruder on his premises and then ran off with a series of harsh yaps. My labrador is well trained and kept to heel while I watched the fox. But the animal had not forgiven us for being on his territory. He stopped after only a short run and, turning to watch us, lifted his nose to give a full-throated bark. I had better avoid that particular corner of the field until the mating season is over.

Veronica Heath 2007

July

These are the very green weeks of the year. Nearly all the threads and patches, the high lights and the shadows, have 'run' together into a cinnamon green covering the countryside. Here, on this treeless moor, the bracken floods over into every crease and fold of the ground. But at this green time plantings and groups of trees are often in one's mind; the hanging beech woods of Arundel or the heavy clumps on the Wiltshire and Berkshire downs; or, above all, those groups of sycamore or ash in the Lake District and the North Country, making as they so often do, so perfect a setting for some grey farm in a green secret valley. We have a few even here, near this house; sycamore and ash, wind-shorn and twisted but graceful still. What friendly trees they are!

And today on a hillside running down to a little south coast harbour, there hanging above, sharp against the July sky – ash and sycamore, sycamore and ash; the 'keys' of the ash and the sycamore's seed bunches still green too, but what a lovely difference of pattern against the water and the sky.

Katherine Arnold Foster 1931

August

Go down to the Nevern estuary, slip off your shoes, splurge over the mud. Your toes are already rejoicing. 'We've come to a health farm,' they sing in happy chorus. You're heading towards a bed of glasswort, at last a vegetable not festooned with slugs. Originally it was used to make glass. If you burn a pile of it you horrify epicures to create a sort of carbonate of soda, which mixed with sand will give you glass.

William Turner, in his 1568 *A New Herball*, called it

glaswede. When people started to eat it, the name marsh samphire became popular. It has a distinctive peppery taste and fibrous texture. Here it is only washed twice a day by salt water, so its salty flavour is not overpowering. You can use it in salads, or cook it like asparagus and gently tease the succulent flesh from the stems. It's an annual, but the flowers need to be searched for as they are so small. They nestle at the joints of the stalks – as edible as the rest of it.

The name samphire comes from the French 'herbe de St Pierre' originally describing the rock samphire, *Crithmum maritimum*. This grows on our cliffs, an umbellifer with linear fleshy leaves. It is King Lear's samphire, but I've never meddled with the dreadful trade of picking it.* Another samphire is *Inula crithmoides*, the golden samphire, which has a daisy flower.

Another type of inula is Nicholas Culpeper's 'robust and stately plant', the elecampane, *Inula helenium*, confirmed by modern medicine as holding a root helpful against chest infections. In some places it is called wild sunflower, but nowadays you can walk far enough without spotting it – apart from old cottage gardens, where its generous fecundity quickly fills the ground and delights, or daunts, the passerby. Long ago it came here from Asia for its medical qualities, and continued to America. This does not presage plant globalisation, simply recognition of medicinal properties. Certainly our bees and

---

* King Lear, Act 4, Scene 6. "half-way down/hangs one that gathers samphire;/dreadful trade!"

butterflies respond well to this eastern immigrant. The glasswort is an old island plant and looks it.

Audrey Insch 2001

September

Shetland is a place where the unexpected often turns up, but the shout of 'Grab your bins, there's something big going past the hippo!' would have sounded a touch unlikely to anyone who had overheard it. The said hippo is not a rare visitor, however, but a curiously shaped rock outcrop, and it provides one of our main reference points for anything of interest going past the house by land, sea or air.

We climbed rapidly over the gate into the field and scanned the unusually calm water while swatting at our accompanying cloud of midges, the bane of still days at this time of year. Then a streamlined head broke the surface just beneath us with a curiously gentle explosive sigh. A gleaming body with a thorn-like fin rose effortlessly upwards and then slipped smoothly beneath the surface again. A whale!

'Minke?' Elatedly, in unison. Our eyes never left the sea. Then another blow, a surfacing and an elegant, powerful curve culminating in a strong arch of the tail as the whale began its dive. Excitedly we waited for it to surface again, which it did, further away but still clearly visible.

Eventually resorting to the aforementioned 'bins' – binoculars – we watched it repeat this pattern of two breaths before a longer period below the surface as it made its stately circuit of the bay.

Occasionally in view at the same time, porpoises who average 1.2-1.8m in length appeared tiny compared to the more distant minke whale – a species that can reach 100m.

What is it about a whale, dolphin or the humbler porpoise that captures people so? Is it the sheer size, the powerful grace or a strange sense of kinship with another life lived almost entirely out of sight but sometimes close by? Is it the mass of myth, legend and history, or is it the sheer unlikeliness of the encounter that generates such a sense of excitement and privilege?

Christine Smith 2007

October

The countryside is changing colour: the hedgerows are bejewelled with rubies and strings of pearls and the trees are shimmering in the low sunlight with leaves of reds and gold. But very soon the autumn gales will have blown their leaves to the ground and some of the trees are already bare. Flocks of birds are starting to increase their numbers as they trawl across the countryside searching out the wealth of food that is available. As I watch the farmer work his land, seagulls are soaring and squealing around as they follow the plough, diving in for all the titbits turned over with those furrows of glistening chocolate-brown soil. Fat wood pigeons are pillaging anything they can find. The glint of goldfinches is a charm to see as they descend on the shaggy seed heads of thistles; long-tailed tits are whistling down the hedgerow and the migrant thrushes, redwing and fieldfares are seeking out all the hedgerow berries, of which there are an abundance. I have already taken my share of brambles and sloes, but there are many more berries on offer, a veritable larder for all the birds to survive the winter. Then there are the starlings that are increasing their numbers with migrant flocks. At first glance these are dull brown birds, but look closer and you discover that they are speckled with all the colours of the rainbow.

At dusk a whoosh passes over my head, surprising me and making me duck: it is a flock of starlings coming in to land. They rise again, increase their numbers with another flock arriving from a different direction, come down, rise yet again, and more and more appear from nowhere, circling above, swirling and swarming like bees, twitching this way and that way, making pictures in the sky. En masse they flop down to land, bedecking the skeletal trees with living leaves, and what a crescendo of noise as they roost. Without warning, they are up and away, swarming, into the greying sky, and I am left with an over-whelming silence.

Rosemary Roach 2007

November

Mitzi – my small Austrian friend – will not be three till Christmas, but she is robust and adventurous. When I am at work in my front garden she trundles up to the gate on her tricycle (babies abandon the art of walking nowadays almost as soon as they have acquired it) and calls peremptorily, 'I come in. I help you.' She does, and scrapes the leaves up with hands elegantly gloved in pale blue woollies. She clambers on to the stone seat and over the back, from which she crashes; but she knows that I am hard-hearted, so she does not cry. Then she must ascend the flight of five steps and terrify me by attempting to jump from the top; an impossible feat, for the steps spread over a length of six feet. Then she wants to climb the birdbath, which is a foot above her head and rather rickety. Finally she announces that she wants to see the goldfish.

So we pass into the back garden through the gate which is kept locked for good reasons, and I tell her to wait for me. But she runs ahead. When she is in view of the fish pool (ten feet across) she turns round to face me in laughing defiance and continues running backwards. A few steps and she is over the edge. Flinging her arms up with a frightened expression, she falls and the water closes over her. She turns her vigorous little body round and at once makes strokes like a puppy. I enter the water more sedately and haul her out by the armpits. She stands dripping, a much astonished child, but she only whimpers a little as we trot over to her long-suffering mother, who gives her a hot tub and puts her to bed. I had not thought of my little plots as so full of dangers. Mitzi is now busy drawing pools 'full of fishes and frogs', and desires nothing more than to renew acquaintance with them. But the gate remains locked. There is ice over the pool.

Helena Swanwick 1938

December

I have had two amusing Christmas gifts sent to me here in Surrey. One is a twisted veteran oak only three inches high and the other a gnarled palm tree, just a little higher, both of them growing in a varnished orange skin. My friend who specialises in these not unattractive oddities made them, with much patience, as follows:-

He cuts a hole about the size of a shilling in the side of an orange and, with skill, removes all the pith and juice without doing damage to the skin. This empty shell he fills with a mixture of coconut fibre, fine moss and charcoal, stiffened with a little loam. In this mixture and in the centre of the orange he places an acorn or a date stone. When complete the orange is placed in a shallow bowl on the window-sill and for some weeks the only attention needed is judicious and gentle watering through the hole and a sprinkling of wood ashes from time to time. At the end of the month the tiny trees appear, rather miraculously, through the hole and roots push their way through the orange peel. Every week these roots are cut off flush with the peel. After the plants have become four or five inches high they stop growing in height and become gnarled and twisted; the process of cutting off the roots, however, goes on for two years, after which time all growth seems to cease. Then comes the time to paint the end of the roots black and varnish the orange skin all over. My friend, who learned this 'accomplishment' in China, says he has seen trees 60 years old grown in this way. Our windows are now lined with orange shells, but so far nothing else!

MA 1938

Helena Breaks Through

Helena Swanwick is the bossy one, the great organiser and pioneer who broke the men's monopoly of the *Guardian* Country Diary. Lively, dauntless and a careful planner – of suffragette demonstrations and flowerbeds equally – she described her role in a speech to the National Union of Women's Suffrage Societies as 'beating at the closed doors of life'. She also pushed at open ones, including those at the *Guardian*'s famous offices in Cross Street, Manchester. In 1899 when she was 35 and settled in the city as the wife of a professor of maths at Manchester University, she wrote to the paper asking to review books. In 1915 she told the famous editor CP Scott: 'I should like to try my hand at a weekly note on gardening.' In 1922 she wanted to be one of the first contributors to the new Women's Page, which was to become a national journalistic institution. She was accepted every time.

Don't wait to be asked, was Swanwick's motto, an attitude forged by her youthful experience of Victorian male chauvinism. Her father, Oswald Sickert, although a modern-minded painter who had left his home in Germany to avoid his sons being conscripted into the Kaiser's army, was so angry at her decision to apply to university against his wishes that he refused to pay the fees. Helena only got to Girton College, Cambridge, with the help of a generous godmother. Her grandfather's shoddy treatment of her mother, Eleanor, which anticipated Oswald's pique, must also have influenced her upbringing. Eleanor Sickert was the illegitimate daughter of an Irish dancer and a fellow of Trinity College, Cambridge, the astronomer Richard Sheepshanks. He cut Eleanor out of his will, shortly before his death, out of resentment when she told him that she had fallen in love with Oswald. It transpired that he had been about to acknowledge for the first time publicly that he was her father – a solemn, if disgracefully belated, act whose thunder he accused her of stealing. Doubtless it was Eleanor who encouraged Helena to read *The Subjection of Women* by John Stuart Mill at Notting Hill high school when she was 14.

Swanwick was not just bright but robust and strong-minded, having to fight her corner against five brothers, one of them Walter Sickert, the English Impressionist who is also a candidate for Jack the Ripper. He certainly had raffish friends, including Oscar Wilde and Aubrey Beardsley, but they were not to be shared with Helena. When Walter offered to introduce her to the music hall star Ellen Terry, the Sickert parents forbade the meeting. Helena only really started to flourish at the age of 24 when she met Frederick Swanwick, a brilliant mathematician at Cambridge, and in spite of an age difference of 13 years accepted his offer of marriage.

'Until then, all my brothers had rights as persons; not I,' she recalled in 1935 in her autobiography *I Have Been Young*. 'But once I had a husband attitudes towards me changed and just as formerly I could do nothing right, so latterly, I could do nothing wrong.' It was complete hypocrisy but meant genuine freedom because Frederick was committed to women's rights. It also led to her writing the *Guardian* Country Diary. Frederick had been born and brought up in Manchester and when the offer of a senior lectureship at Owen's College – soon to become Manchester University – was offered in 1890, he accepted eagerly. The city was fizzing with ideas compared with Victorian Cambridge, and Frederick was also keen on cycling and fell-walking in the Lake District. His obituary in the *Manchester Guardian* in 1934 described him as 'an indefatigable cyclist in the palmy days of the sport'.

The most famous of Manchester's other indefatigable cyclists at the time was Charles Prestwich Scott, the editor of the *Guardian*, who pedalled into the Cross Street office every weekday carrying his unchanging packed lunch of an orange and a boiled egg. He and the Swanwicks shared radical Liberal views and became fast friends. At their homes in Didsbury and at Manesty on the shores of Derwentwater in the Lakes, they met regularly to talk about world peace, women's suffrage – and herbaceous borders. Helena Swanwick was a highly political animal, soon to become a leading suffragette, but she was also a devoted and knowledgeable gardener, with firm, indeed missionary views. She not only knew the right and wrong things to do with a phlox or an alstromeria, but she wanted to get the message across to others. She told Scott that she had written a short guide with the suggested title of *The Small Town Garden*. Through his contacts at the publishers Sherrett and Hughes, he got it into print.

He also got Swanwick into the *Manchester Guardian*, which was not as simple a matter as it might appear with all our years of hindsight. Women were new to journalism in any numbers and had made a poor start. In 1903 Alfred Harmsworth, later Lord Northcliffe, founded the *Daily Mirror* as 'a newspaper for gentlewomen produced by ladies of breeding' and it was a disaster. Sales collapsed and the ladies were all sacked; an experience described by the new editor, Henry Hamilton Fyfe, as 'a horrid experience – like drowning kittens. They begged to be allowed to stay. They left little presents on my desk. They waylaid me tearfully in the corridors.' Even CP Scott, recommending Swanwick to a colleague as one of only two suffragettes who were also good journalists, added: 'The ordinary run of women journalists in London, so far as my experience goes, are deplorably inefficient.'

Swanwick started regular work for the *Guardian* as resident expert on plants and vegetables in the Saturday edition (a modest, 14-page predecessor of today's vast equivalent) and then, from December 1915 at an increased salary of a guinea and a half a week (£130 today), as the fourth member of the Country Diary team. The column's sole writer for the first eight years, the retired textile bleacher and bird expert from Cheshire Thomas Coward, had – most unwillingly – learned to share in the previous three years with a Cheshire farmer, Arthur Nicholson, and then the literary critic Basil de Selincourt. Now he had a suffragette pacifist campaigner on his hands as well.

Swanwick had become a recognised face in political circles. A year earlier, she had worked with the future prime minister Ramsay Macdonald and the future Nobel laureate Norman Angell to set up the anti-war Union of Democratic Control. On her husband's retirement in 1913, she moved to London to edit the *Common Cause*, the magazine of the constitutional suffragettes – she had no time for the window-breakers and arsonists encouraged by the Pankhursts. With many male friends who supported women's suffrage, she believed in the power of reason to overcome the conviction she was still expressing in 1927, in an article for the magazine *Time and Tide*, that 'most men have not a notion how immensely better the world could be made for them, by the full co-operation of women.' She was physically attacked after pacifist meetings and sent hate mail, but regular contact with 'ordinary' people sustained her. Her housekeeper after Frederick's death, Agnes Rushton, told her: 'I can't write and speak myself, but I can set you free to.' Swanwick recalls in *I Have Been Young* how a Yorkshire woman told her after a suffragette rally: 'What you bin saying, Ah bin thinkin long enough, but Ah nivver getten t'words reet.'

Scarcely a hint of this appears in her Country Diaries, however. There is a brief reference to the joys of ordering continental roses after the armistice and a tart quip that metal for plant stakes was unavailable because the country apparently preferred to use it to make bombs. But Scott had told her on her appointment that the paper was already more than heavy enough with the news and analysis of fighting. 'Do gardening, perhaps, or anything you like about the country and its inhabitants,' he wrote. The diary was to be a breath of purer air, a reminder of places and values that would outlast the war.

For Swanwick, it was also a break from her campaigning commitments. But just as she argued her way through the logic of suffrage extension and the effects of warfare during the week, so she gave crisp planting instructions and definite rulings on flowerbed colour matches at the weekend. Of all the female Country Diarists she is the sharpest when encountering error, whether from clueless tourists at Kew Gardens or neighbours who sowed a new lawn at the wrong time of the year.

There was a long interval between her two spells of diary writing, because in 1924 she was appointed to edit the Union of Democratic Control's magazine *Foreign Affairs* in succession to ED Morel, the Labour MP who had sensationally defeated Winston Churchill in Dundee in the 1922 general election. Scott tried to persuade her to stay on, telling her in a letter, 'We shall miss your hand sadly.' But within the year she was also appointed by Ramsay Macdonald, now the country's first Labour prime minister, as an official government representative to the new League of Nations in Geneva. Needless to say, she discovered closed doors to push against there.

Women may have won the vote in the United Kingdom, partially in 1918 and fully in 1928, but at the League they were allowed to discuss only a limited range of supposedly 'appropriate' subjects, such as drug trafficking and the protection of women and children. Swanwick and her allies got this changed by 1929, when she was re-appointed by the government and played a prominent part in debates on foreign affairs, including the controversial Great Power mandates in Syria and Palestine.

The 1930s were a productive time for Swanwick, with a series of books on what she considered the folly of re-armament, a correspondence MA from Dublin and the distinction of being made a Companion of Honour. But she became sick at heart as events took a different course from the peaceful cooperation she hoped to see. Convinced that Germany had been wronged at Versailles, she gradually lost political allies to whom the realities of Nazi rule were more obvious. In the end this included the *Manchester Guardian.* As early as 1930, Scott's son and successor as editor, Ted, had opposed inviting her to write a political column, noting: 'On the League of Nations specially Mrs S would be apt to take a rather strong un-*Guardian* view.'

She nevertheless resumed the Country Diary in 1937 in retirement at Maidenhead, but within two years was completely disillusioned with the paper. She wrote to the editor, William Crozier, who had taken over in 1932 when Ted Scott was drowned in a sailing accident in Windermere: 'I suppose that it will not be long before you eliminate little extras like "Country Diaries" but before this happens I wish to say that, in any case, I will not maintain even the slightest connection with the MG and will therefore not send anything more of any kind.'

She was 75, unwell and lonely, admitting in a second letter to Crozier: 'I am old and hope soon to die.' This does not show in her diaries with their abundant curiosity, but the outbreak of war confirmed her worst fears, an experiment in taking in evacuees proved too much and in November she did not recover from a deliberate overdose of sleeping tablets. An appreciation in the *Guardian* described how 'her fearless rectitude and sense of justice seemed to burn like a searchlight in all dark places.' She also illuminated the natural world.

Christmas colours

December 1915

In the wilder garden the Christmas roses are in bloom. You can only get the flowers in perfection by putting bell-glasses or frames over them, but these are rather ugly things, and in the wild garden it is possible to have your Christmas roses fairly clean if you grow them among fern, whose dying fronds shelter them, or among ivy or St John's wort or dwarf heaths. So also the shining white blossoms look most beautiful. This is the earliest of the hellebores. All the beautiful Lenten roses are only yet in bud. The spreading tufts of many-lobed leaves, very dark green, leathery and sturdy, have stood all the heat and drought of summer and ten or more degrees of frost this winter; now, at the base of their stems, appears a mass of fat greenish buds, which will in February or March expand into lovely bell or cup-shaped flowers, many of them over a foot high, white, greenish-white, pink, lilac, purple and claret, many of them thickly spotted with red or purple and some striped with green. I can find no cyclamen flowers left, but the still very marbled leaves of *Cyclamen coum* lie in drifts all about, and here and there a few late crocuses still linger. The Siberian squill has poked its nose up, and the thread-leaved iris is several inches long already. *Iris stylosa*, set in the driest, dustiest corner against a sunny brick wall, is crowded with promising flower buds.

A female chaffinch keeps watch beside a hedgerow

Tucking in the tuppenny

January 1916

The soil in gardens is full of little earthquakes everywhere; hoeing has become impossible, and even work with the rake or hand fork has to be very cautiously done less you break off the nose of some early adventurer. The earliness or lateness of gardens in various positions is sometimes very puzzling. For instance, I know a garden where the soil is light and very well drained and enriched, the aspect sunny and sheltered, yet some plants in it come two or three weeks later than they do in gardens quite near. Just now in the afore-mentioned garden the hybrid hellebores are in full bloom; *Iris filifolia* has displayed its foolish long ribbons since November last, and the Darwin tulips are an inch up; yet these last two will not flower till May, and their behaviour is not economical. On the other hand, the snowdrops are only just piercing the soil, and the Siberian squills are a little ahead of them, while a handsome variety of the winter aconite (*Eranthis cilicica*) is not yet at its best. These freaks are very difficult to account for. This winter aconite comes out of the ground in just the same way as its common sister, tucking in its 'tuppenny' (head) and in so doing exhibiting the fine rosewood stem. Some of the roots send up as many as five or six flowers in one bunch, and when this is the case they often raise the earth in a solid plate, making it look like the lid of a box full of gold. Today on a bud a drowsy bee was perched, slowly preening her wings.

A correspondent asks why potatoes become sweet when frozen. Potatoes contain 15 to 20 percent of starch. The action of frost breaks down the starch cells, and a process of decomposition sets in, which converts the starch to sugar.

The beauty of brambles

March 1916

The brambles are breaking into leaf. These form an extremely interesting group of shrubs, and the great variety in their stems is one of the chief points of interest. Some are covered with a sort of paste, grey, bluish or pure white, and when these break into leaf, as they are doing now, the effect is very charming. *Rubus giraldianus* is a very large and stout species from China, whose stems, eight or ten feet long, spout up from the ground and curve over, looking in midwinter like a fountain of milk. Another very large and handsome species has smooth, shiny stems like Indian lacquer. Yet others, like *Rubus phoenicolasius*, which comes from Japan, have the stems covered with bristly hairs of a rich rust red. The effect these make is sometimes very curious. Looking at a handsome Chinese specimen, I was surprised at a number of what I took to be great iron rods, an inch in diameter, until I found on closer examination that these rods were the stems of the plant itself. As spring develops, the rising sap makes the reds more and more vivid, and the young leaves, emerging hairy, or spiny, or downy from their sheaths, make elegant embroidery over the stiff lines.

Souvenir gardening

September 1917

Bits of a suburban garden of my acquaintance are christened 'Cornwall', 'Dorset', 'Surrey', 'Norfolk', because of treasures brought from holidays in sundry earthly Paradises. 'Cornwall' is a delicious little spot. The mesembryanthemums have to be given as much space as the length of their name suggests, for they sprawl far and wide; but the other treasures have been kept in smaller proportions.

The one about which most pride is felt is the Burnet rose; this had to be dug for with a penknife, through hard turf, into the bowels of the earth. The tufts of minute leaves suggested an easy prey, but the wiry stem lengthened itself out underground, inch by inch, with never a sign of a fibrous root, till at last it had to be cut, with an uneasy sense of robbery. This little wilding seemed to declare that you might hack it but you couldn't transplant it. Yet every piece has rooted. As aforesaid, it grew in grass; it was transplanted to a border, where grass would have been out of place, so it was necessary to devise some other way of keeping the roots cool in sun. They were buried a few inches deep in earth, and along their length stones were placed. These are of Cornish serpentine, red and purple and lilac and green; now that autumn tints are beginning to appear among the tiny glaucous rose leaves nothing can be prettier than the emulation in colour between them and the pebbles. Near by are bits of sedums, little tracts of vernal sandwort (which even now has an occasional star), mountain thyme and thrift and bloody cranesbill.

Peace at last

November 1918

It is one of the little joys of our new peace life that we may, if we like, order those new rose trees for which we have been longing, and it is not too late for planting. People tend to be rather herd-like in their ordering, and one sees a rather monotonous planting, especially in suburban gardens, of such well-known ramblers as Lady Gay or Dorothy Perkins, and though the scentless Frau Karl Druschki and almost scentless Madame Caroline Testout are handsome and useful, it is possible to have too much of them, if they are repeated in every other garden to the exclusion of other beauties.

For small beds near the house or in very tiny gardens, one would like to see more often the very charming and free-flowering pompon polyantha roses, which are among the hardiest of the rose family and which require very little attention beyond syringing and occasional thinning and cutting off of dead blooms. Most of these have no scent, however, and for this reason one prefers the China roses, nearly as floriferous and quite as perpetual, but a little larger, both in growth and blossom.

Suffering fools

February 1919

Just in front of me in the Alpine House today there was a very positive lady, expounding all about the flowers, very much in the style of Mr Podsnap, to an unfortunate 'foreigner'. This Mrs Podsnap pointed out the fluffy buds of *Adonis amurensis* and remarked: 'In England we call it winter aconite.' Farther on she conversed lightly and confidently of the 'Sassefras', many varieties of which are now showing bud or flower in pans. The Adonis does, it is true, belong to the same family as the winter aconite, but it is not the same thing, and it must be a very superficial observer who can mistake the anemone-shaped variety from the Amur for the neat buttercup-shaped winter aconite (Eranthis) which is now starring the beds and the lawns outside.

Sassafras is a tree – my only authority for the statement is Charles Lamb – whose bark makes the foundation of a drink called 'saloop', 'the precocious herb-woman's darling': it has nothing to do with the saxifrages, Alpine plants of small stature, which so charmingly adorn the pans in House No 24 at Kew. There are some eight varieties beginning to flower, and many more to come. There are also a few crocuses of the minutest kind, some tiny primulas, a few pans of Romulea, which never shows so well as in a pan, and sundry Iberis and Ornithogalum.

Scottish malpractices

July 1920

It seems as if the grandeur of the scenery paralysed the average Scotsman in the making of Highland gardens. The Scots are notable gardeners and yet it must be confessed, as one travels in and out of the sea lochs and about the islands, that their arduous efforts at embellishment have mostly resulted in a marked uglifying of the scene. The bits of gardens look like scars upon the hillside, and one is glad to get by them. For one thing, the steep ground is too often banked with turf, which even in this moist air become very brown and which takes incessant, arduous labour to mow. Then they seem to have a mania for torturing the beautiful shrubs that would flower and grow so luxuriantly if left alone. The escallonia, which will make such gorgeous crimson hedges, is clipped to some stupid shape till barely a flower is left, and I have even seen fuchsia and cotoneaster drilled to ugliness.

The beautiful gardens are mostly kept by cottages, where you may see the flowering shrubs run riot; where osmunda fern stands well over the head of a man; where the Chilean tropaeolum* runs like a flame up the white wall to the eaves; where a group of astrantia clusters its lace-like blossoms by the gate; where the patches of grass occur only on bits of level land and are cropped by the cows going to and from the byre. All the hard rectangles and straight lines of the villa gardens are ugly irrelevances on the tender curves of the lower slopes. Rock gardens, shrub gardens, with walks and steps of the 'native' stone; flowers in beds following the contours of the hill or in no beds at all; above all no sharp line of demarcation between the cultivated plot and the natural gardens beyond, are loveliest.

Keep off the grass
June 1921

I find on a visit to Geneva for disarmament talks that I greatly under-rated the height to which the meadow-grasses will grow. I have just stood among flowering lawns that topped my head, that is, over 5ft 6in. It is curious that in soil that will grow meadow-grass with such magnificent vigour, lawns are poor and thin, and maintained with much difficulty. Everywhere it is '*Defendu de marcher sur le gazon*,' and the little children may not roll and tumble on the grass, but must content themselves with gritty, pebbly gravel, very destructive to the knees.

---

* Proper name Tropaeolum speciosum.

I picked a handful of 17 different kinds of grass flowers with the serious intention of sorting and naming them. But when I passed the little fallow deer in their dusty enclosures, they ran so wistfully to beg of me that all my specimens went.

Flowers out of place

August 1922

Plants develop very various habits under various conditions. In my garden there are several weeds that I try to keep in their proper places. Of course they refuse, in the manner of weeds, to recognise that they have any proper place at all and sow themselves where they are not wanted or expected. Then they adapt themselves so amusingly to the inappropriate conditions that one hasn't the heart to pull them up. The rosebay, for example, or willow-herb (as beautiful as its names) springing in ordinary soil, sends up a long, straight shoot five or six feet high, tipped with the rosy-lilac flower spike. It has seen fit to send its winged seeds from where it was planted to a piece of crazy pavement some distance away, and here the seedling, as it grew, developed an array of horizontal side-shoots, some 35 in number, close to the ground, like spokes in a wheel, and these shoots give the plant quite a new expression, humble, not proud like its border sister, as though, after all, it had to beg for toleration in its absurd situation. The common balm, too, in the border a lanky and inelegant but deliciously lemon-scented plant, has sprung up between the stones, and there makes flat cushions on which one can freely tread, with much satisfaction to the nose.

Holiday horrors

July 1923

The single-handed gardener who deserts his garden for some weeks at this time of year certainly pays dearly for his holiday. The cold and windy drought of June, unmitigated by artificial watering, caused most of the poor apple crop to fall; cherries, which were swelling nicely at the end of May, have remained much the same size and will be no good; loganberries have three-quarters of their crop shrivelling in a green state, while every conceivable pest seems to be enjoying itself. Some established plants have died outright. One of the surprises is the white *Oenothera speciosa*, a plant that increases very rapidly in this sandy soil, but which now makes a large tract of completely withered stalks; pulling these up, we find the roots all perfectly dead. It is a shallow-rooting plant, and doubtless this is the cause of its death. Japanese maples are badly rusted, but will put out fresh leaves. That engaging weed the willow-herb stands up handsome and proud, drawing its sustenance from a foot or two down by means of its long tap-root. I had an interesting experience with this plant. Finding it encroached too much, I pulled up a number of shoots (they come up very easily) and at once cut off the flowering spikes and put them into water. I then cut a few more spikes from the growing plants. Within ten minutes all the spikes that had been uprooted were drooping and within an hour, all their flowers and leaves were dead, while the flowers cut from the growing plant remained fresh. The message sent up by the root must be almost instantaneous.

Stars of the shrubs

May 1924

Magnolias are glorious now. The great pure white *M. conspicua* is at its best. The earlier starry magnolia has been wonderfully free in flower this year; they have greatly increased the plantations of this lovely little shrub in Kew Gardens and now it shines from afar in many quarters – in the barberry dell with the early tamarisks, near the greenhouses, and, best of all, in that garden in the grass that is beautiful at all times in the year, the Azalea garden. Here, too, the willow-leafed magnolia has flowered very well this year on bare stems. It is an extraordinarily graceful and symmetrical tree, slim, with a well-marked leader quite unlike the better-known spreading varieties. The handsome yellow-flowered *M. fraseri* has not yet unrolled the tissue paper from its buds.

Note. A misprint in last week's diary might lead people to suppose that the climate of Kew is even more wonderful than it is. Quince and cherry promise a record, not a second, flowering.

War on the wasps

June 1937

Our great event this week has been tackling a wasps' nest. Near the business end of the garden, with pit and tap, there are three lean-to cupboards against the tool-shed. In them are kept leaf soil and peat and such sundries. The youth who cuts the grass reported that wasps in numbers were settling on him, and we traced them to one of these cupboards, by the side of whose closed door they had contrived a chink large enough to admit one at a time. Opening the door cautiously I saw, partly under an upturned basin and partly overflowing on to the leaf soil below, a grey mass over which wasps were crawling and buzzing. The door shut, we consulted together. The youth wanted to cyanide the wasps. But I found he had never carried out this operation himself and I vetoed it.

An alternative method worked well. One of us stood several yards away holding a hose, which is armed with a water-gun. With a long-handled hoe in one hand and a bucket in the other, I gently opened the door, propped it open with the bucket, turned the basin over with the hoe and fled, calling the order to fire. A powerful stream of water was directed into the cupboard for a minute or two. The wasps seemed disturbed but still full of vigour, so the jet was renewed. I found then that, with the aid of that invaluable tool a 'little gripper', I was able to pick up big chunks of the grey mass (which turned out to be larvae) and drop them into a bucket of nicotine solution ready prepared. A good many wasps went in with the larvae, which were on the point of hatching out, the head, thorax and abdomen being easily discernible through the delicate tissue in which every one was wrapped. The door was left open for several days so as to discourage the surviving wasps from making the cupboard their home.

An idiot's garden

August 1937

Derek, my three-year-old neighbour with silver curls, has been told by his mother that he must not go into my garden unless he is invited; he does not yet distinguish between beds and paths. One day this week from my window I saw him slyly push open the gate and creep in. He paused and then began to explore. Suddenly he grew red, even under his curls, folded his arms tightly, clutching the elbows, gave a furtive glance right and left and slunk out again, racing away as if something were after him. I was puzzled by his behaviour.

An hour or two later, when I was in the garden, he came by and paused, eyeing me malevolently. Then slowly and emphatically he remarked: 'You're an idiot.' 'Oh, why?' was all I could find to say. 'You've got a silly garden.' 'Why?' 'It's a prickly garden.' That's true, when I come to think of it. The whole front is given up to roses, with a rampant sweetbriar hedge on the road and barberries all along the house. Poor Derek! Like the impudent boy in the German folk-song he had been told by the roses that they would tolerate no liberties.

To make amends, I invited him to visit the lily pool. He silently slipped his hand in mine (Derek is a man of few words) and was safely piloted past the prickles and through the house into the back garden. The goldfish were all up, basking in the sun, and Derek stared at them, speechless. One fish was so still and close in among the rushes that I said: 'I do believe I could catch that fellow.' Only half believing what I said, I put my hand under it and lifted it out. It lay bright and beautiful, but quite still, on my palm and I cried: 'Oh, it's dead!' We gazed at it with concern for several seconds; then with a flick of its tail, it sprang away and down into the depths. Derek paused for a moment to look and then, overcome with sudden homesickness, the little silver fish bolted also.

I hear today that Derek is to have a fish pool of his own. His adoring parents are making him one.

Bombs not tree-stakes

August 1937

Staking young trees in a windy region is a difficult task. I am now up against it. I thought I was well provided-for with an assortment of stakes, but none of those I have is quite suited to the requirements of three little eucalyptus trees that were planted in May as saplings four feet high and have shot up to a height of eight feet, with big heads of heavy leaves and stems scarcely as thick as my little finger. They offer great purchase to the west wind, which comes romping over from Wales, and they offer in resistance only the charming grace of a helpless pretty woman. They seem to throw upon their fond owner the whole responsibility for their support.

I possess stout, heavy iron stakes, tubular, six feet high, which I have used to support thorns and crabs and acacias and many kinds of maple, plums and cherry. But these are all standards with substantial stems. The eucalyptus would look preposterous tethered to a stake four times its own thickness. Besides, some 18 inches of the stake would have to be underground, so over three feet of lovely, irresponsible weaklings would be left unsupported. I decided to get some much thinner but strong iron stakes with a double foot, so as to hold well, and I gaily ordered these. But it seems we are re-arming and must have bombs instead of tree-stakes. My ironmonger says I may not get any stakes for weeks, perhaps not for months, perhaps not at all.

The kind of stakes that are most wanted are not made. Those for very slender saplings should themselves be slender, of tubular stainless steel, made like a fishing rod in four-foot lengths to fit into one another, the lowest ending in a solid point. For stouter trees the stakes should be stouter, from four to ten feet high, in shape half a tube, an inch or more in diameter; into this hollow the stem of the sapling, well packed with tow, would nestle securely. The bottom should be pointed; there should be several holes pierced to allow of tarred twine to be passed through for tying; they should be painted brown, not green.

Fairy fog

October 1937

A neighbour passed down the lane and, seeing me setting lily bulbs among the azaleas-to-be, she threw at me the exclamation 'Awful, isn't it?' Dazed, I queried: 'What's awful?' 'This fog!' was her indignant reply. There is, and has been for several days, what I would call a river mist, opalescent, gauzy, with a perceptible sun in the heavens. At night this mist, which does not attain the zenith, distributes the rays of the full moon and makes the woods and meadows fabulous. No one who had ever really appreciated a London or Manchester fog could possibly call this fairy thing by the same name.

We have had three weeks of absolute drought, but the mist condensing on blades of grass and leaves of many colours enhances their brilliance. The garden is drenched but still warm. On a little mound in one corner are three balsam poplars, tall and very loose, a tender yellow in colour. In front of them, to the left, is a low-spreading shrub of the most gorgeous scarlet imaginable: *Pyrus arbutifolia*.* To the right *Buddleia alternifolia* sends its long dark green wands spouting up ten feet with drooping tips like a fountain. In front of these, and following the curve of the bed, is a dwarf shrub, which would be even more acceptable than it is were it not quite such a 'good doer'. It has an appalling name, too, and as if to emphasise their crime, the botanists who at first called it *Plumbago larpentae*, subsequently went five syllables worse and renamed it (take a deep breath) *Ceratostigma plumbaginoides*. To visitors it is called 'Plum'; not a bad name, for in the mass, at a distance, it looks plum colour. This result is achieved by the combination of deep-red leaves and masses of ultramarine flowers. *Crocus speciosus* thrusts up through the purple mat; *Fuchsia riccartoni* pushes forward with its troupes of dancing girls spreading their skirts; a few red-hot pokers blaze away in the farther corner.

Chrome, scarlet, dark green, plum, lilac-blue, crimson and purple, flame. It sounds gaudy but it is not. There is a considerable background.

---

* Now known as *Aronia arbutifolia*.

The bullying robin

December 1937

We are being shamefully bullied by a robin, and we don't know what to do about it. This is a very fresh-air house, but one can't leave a window open without the little wretch coming in and making half-a-dozen messes in no time. If bread or even bread-and-butter is put for him on his special window-sill and he happens to be in the mood for pine kernels he flings the despised food all over the place with contemptuous wings and then scolds heartily. He will perch on a shoulder and beat the cheek with his wings. One long window-sill is decorated with a row of ferns in pots and he must know that these are a treasure of the inhabitant of that room, for when he feels particularly naughty he gets among the pots and makes havoc with the soil and the fronds. He has no pretty ways. He comes when he pleases, not when he is called, and he has never sung for us, though he utters impatient chinking for food and angry screams should another robin come near the place. He is a bonnie fighter and no other has a chance with him. A closed window excites his wrath and he flies up to the panes in obstinate endeavours to get in. But really, when he gets in, the mess he makes on books and papers and needlework and polished furniture! People who write about the 'dear little birds' never seem to mention these drawbacks.

The mysterious fisher

December 1937

A neighbour came round to inquire about my goldfish. He has a much larger pond than mine, and in it some handsome goldfish as well as four other fish, some three times as large, which he calls orfs. In one night all four of his orfs disappeared. My 13 goldfish could still be counted. He suspected herons. We do have herons flying over us from one reach of the river across country to another, but I have never seen one alight in any of these gardens, and they are shy of houses. Two years ago a redshank perched on the roof of my garden house and called for hours on end most plaintively, but he never came down.

I am inclined to think that – unless the thief was a two-footed fisherman who came with crumbs and a net – the most likely creature to have stolen the fish is a cat. A neighbouring cat used to lie on her side by my pool and, hanging far out over the water, attempted to scoop up the fish with one paw. She was shooed away repeatedly, but always returned, till one day by good luck I was able to deal her a sharp blow on the back with a willow wand, since when she has not come back.

The robin invasion – part two

December 1937

We have had some frost most nights since November 9, when we had one of six degrees, but they have so far yielded to sunshine; not enough, however, to melt all the ice that we rake from the fish pool and which lies about untidily on the grass. They do say that fish will endure being frozen in, and even frozen through, but I don't care to risk that. On December 6 there was a rather unusually timed fluctuation of temperature. When I set the minimum thermometer at 4pm it recorded 40deg, and by 10pm it had dropped to 22deg. I anticipated a very cold night and covered the window plants with newspaper, but by midnight it had become sensibly warmer, and by 9am on December 7 it had risen to 40deg again.

A correspondent writes: 'If you want to get rid of the robins, why don't you keep a cat?' Quite so. But the trouble is that, like so many of my fellow-creatures, I want to have it all ways. I like the robins to come in, but I would also like them to behave as perfect gentlemen, and that they are not. In one room where a window is never shut, a robin now perches on the inhabitant's lap or on her plate at dinner, and yesterday he roosted among the ferns on the window-sill. Has anyone ever explained why a bird stands on one leg to sleep? And does he change legs at intervals so as to rest each in turn?

Spud peeler gardening

January 1938

Some of the most useful little tools I have were never made for the garden. One is a potato-knife with a sharp point. I have made a wash-leather sheath for this, and it goes all round the garden with me. It scrapes those obstinate bittercress and nettle seedlings from between the knees of the iris rhizomes; it makes just the right sort of holes for pricking out one's own seedlings; it cuts the slug neatly in halves; it cleans the hoe when that clogs in damp soil and frees the rake from weeds and leaves.

The ordinary spud is very useful for weeding in the borders, but it makes too wide a hole in the grass. So I chose a carpenter's gouge, the narrowest made, and got my ironmonger to set it in a light stick, five feet long; the gouge cuts down to the roots of plantain or thistle and dandelion and scarcely marks the turf. Of course it is kept sharpened and oiled.

A third invaluable tool is a packing needle. There is an interplait fence with roses which have to be trained along it, and at first it was a bothersome job to coax the tarred twine between the slats. Now I thread the twine through the needle and pass it easily along. This autumn I handed over the task to a jobbing gardener. When I went round to inspect, I found that every single knot he had tied was a granny.

In bed with a wasp

January 1938

Sleepless, I was vexed by a buzzing that I could not locate. I wondered drowsily whether it was merely one of those obsessions that haunt the long watches when, in between catnaps of a minute or so, one confuses sounds with dreams. Then in the early morning hours at last it revealed itself unmistakeably; I had a wasp in bed with me, and she was just emerging, very cross from her long struggle, from between the blankets under my chin. I had thought we had finished with the last just before Christmas. We have had an unusual number this year hibernating in the loft and have killed as many as 56 in a day.

A pleasanter reminder of summer are the seed catalogues now pouring in. Shall I never learn to order what I can profitably use and no more? In and out of early flowering dwarf shrubs there is room for a fair number of annuals, which are gay in the dull midsummer months. So here goes for an assortment of Dimorphothecas, running about nine inches high and very striking, with daisylike flowers, white or buff, ringed with purple or green or blue. The heraldic-looking Bartonia, some 15 inches high, is another favourite, shining buttercup-yellow. Half-hardies I either sow in boxes and prick out in May or sometimes under glass caps in the open; of these I must have that other graceful two-foot daisy *Arctotis grandis*, the blue undersides of whose rays give a moonlit effect. Pimpernels and Portulacas will sprawl about at the edge with jewelled stars. The number of self-sown annuals in this light soil is always great. I never need to buy snapdragons or love-in-a-mist, linarias, phacelias, eschscholtzias, or that delicious little fair-weather friend the Kingfisher daisy, *Felicia bergeriana*; they are up all over the place now.

Work for the dole

January 1938

My friend 'C' fell out of work just before Christmas, a cruel fate to befall a man. He is a mason and an excellent workman, but the house he was engaged on was finished and there were no more orders, so he was paid off without a single day's notice. It seems a shame that a man can be treated so. He made my lily pool and sundry cement paths, and he is a great favourite in the lane, having made several more pools since he made mine. The time had come when my two garden refuse pits needed turning over, so I dropped him a card to ask him to do the job if he were still free and was delighted when he replied that he couldn't come till Saturday afternoon, for that meant he was in work again. True, the work is eight miles away but he makes nothing of that on his bicycle. He tells me it is work he likes: 'Scaffling'. Very skilled and responsible, but very well paid. Workmen about here do many different sorts of skilled work; my friend is just as good at setting bricks and making drains.

So the two pits have been completely emptied and the black rotted refuse of the earlier summer ('Grand stuff!' he said) has been put on top of the comparatively green refuse and well trodden down so as to be ready for distribution in March.

The adventures of Mitzi

July 1938

The chaffinch has deserted her nest in the honeysuckle and her chicks are dead. We had faithfully kept her secret, and no newspaper boy or milkman coming to the door had suspected the existence of the little family. But last week the young gardener remarked: 'Do you know there's a nest by your front door?' Two days later the chicks were calling all day in a weak little chirp, and we said: 'They'll soon be flying now.' But the silence on the following day was so marked that for the first time I parted the leaves and looked close. They would chirp no more.

In this lane there are two small Englishwomen round about three years old. Mitzi's parents are Austrian, but she was born here and is therefore English, though bilingual. She has a garden of some two acres in which to disport herself and a sandpit and every imaginable toy. But this small Eve has only one craving: to get out of paradise and join curly-pated Clementina some 50 yards down the lane. This she cannot do because there is a gate to paradise, and she cannot unbolt it. But she can stand on it, an exquisite brown figure, mother-naked and calling like a bird. Clementina, with a French mother and a Dutch father, is also English and of an exceedingly venturesome disposition. To her little garden there is no gate, so she could run along the lane to the gate of paradise and throw her bucket and spade over the gate, which, about five feet high, is solid as to the lower half and barred as to the upper. Clem found she could just grasp the top bar with her hands, and she pulled herself up till she could wriggle her feet between the bars; then with the adroitness of a young chimp she put one leg over the top, turned round, and dropped down on the other side. The two young monkeys, shrieking with glee, ran off to the sandpit. Presently I heard Clem's mother call 'Clem! Clem! Clementina!' and Clementina ran home along the lane, having shed her last garment with Mitzi in paradise. The young gardener came in with a sad and angry face, saying: 'What do you think that lady said to that little curly-headed girl? She told her to go and put on her clothes. Didn't she see there was a Man?'

An island in the flood

February 1939

This cottage has been an island for a week and the meadow at the back is a lake with scores of seagulls swooping and alighting. It has not been as bad a flood as the one we had six years ago, when some of the bungalows in this lane had water inside and it lapped up to the fourth of my five doorsteps. But the path from the front door to the gate has been covered by about a foot of water and we have had to walk on planks. We retrieve the goldfish from the lawn and put them back in their pool, which has become unrecognisable to them. Scores of earthworms lie drowned and prove tantalising to the blackbirds and thrushes, which waddle around the fringes of the flood where the rising lawn emerges. They make tentative inroads on the water, but don't get far, and the gulls won't come inside the paling. In a day or two they will have a fine feast. The disgusted expression of my neighbour's old cat and the beauty of the moonlight on the water diversify our marooned existence. But to be honest, we would give all these diversions for the use of the drains and a hot bath. How painfully urbanised one has become.

CHAPTER

Two

Watcher in the Forest

Janet Case was a friend and political colleague of Helena Swanwick's but could hardly have been less like her in character. In this largely diffident and modest group of writers, she was the least self-confident and most anxious about her weekly 300-odd words. After finally agreeing to Swanwick's urgings that she take over the Wednesday slot in 1924, after Helena's appointment as editor of *Foreign Affairs*, she had cold feet and sent a nervous note to her friend. 'I wonder if I was too hasty,' she worried, adding that she thought it might be wiser to back out.

No-nonsense Swanwick predictably replied: 'Nonsense' and gave her the necessary backbone to take the job, at 10/6d a week (£21.50 today) which helped Case's modest household at her retirement cottage, Hewer's Orchard, in Minstead near Lyndhurst. She rallied and for the next 12 years recorded the beautiful part of the New Forest where she lived with her sister, Emma, but her nagging doubts never went away. After Case's death in 1937, Emma wrote to the *Guardian*'s editor, William

Crozier: 'She was always very doubtful about the merits of her writings though I often differed from her.'

Diffidence is a useful guard against complacency, and this had proved to be so in Case's earlier career as an exceptional teacher of Greek. She had many pupils who later became famous, none more so than Virginia Stephen, the young daughter of the publisher and editor of the *Dictionary of National Biography*, and better known to us today as Virginia Woolf. Woolf was a predictably challenging student, whose best-known exchange with her teacher was her revelation that she was being sexually abused by her stepbrother George Duckworth. Woolf recorded in a letter to her sister many years later: 'When I came to the bedroom scenes, she dropped her lace and gaped like a gudgeon. By bedtime she was feeling quite sick.'

Woolf enjoyed teasing Case, particularly with a teenage girl's curiosity about sexual matters. She raised a suggestive piece in Aeschylus that compared a woman's maidenhead to a piece of ripe fruit in an orchard, only to get the reply: 'Yes, the use of the instrumental genitive in the third line is extremely rare.' But Woolf was devotedly loyal to Case; indeed the figure clad in greenery whose visit to the dying diarist is recorded below, may well be Woolf, who like Swanwick was often at Hewer's Orchard in Case's last days.

Both were attracted by their friend's self-effacing humour. She was genuinely modest but not in a dull or pious way. In a pencilled note to Woolf written just a few days before she died, she recalled how another pupil, Lady Diana Cooper, 'used to come to her lesson like a nymph scarcely dry from her bath in a gauze wrap, and used to say "My good woman" in an expostulatory tone when I objected to an adjective not agreeing with its noun or some such trifle'. Then, Woolf reflected, Case would have had a friendly chat with the young socialite about the previous night's party, frocks and gossip ' ... until even she could stretch her one hour no farther but must cycle off, with her little bag of textbooks, to teach another pupil, perhaps in Islington, perhaps in Mayfair'.

Case had herself been an outstanding student, first at the experimental co-ed school run by her parents at their home in Hampstead, whose pupils included the future Tory grandee Austen Chamberlain and other notables. When she arrived in 1881 at Girton College, Cambridge, where she later met Swanwick, she was admired for her ability to throw a ball and play tennis as well as a boy. Tall and striking, she was a keen actress and in 1883 played Athene in the university's triennial Greek play, traditionally an all-male affair (and one that had the *Times* critic enthusing about the 'exceedingly beautiful' Rupert Brooke in a female role). No other woman was to join the cast until 1950, when the future Baroness Brigstocke broke the tradition, this time for good.

Case won a first-class degree and was praised in 1905 for a translation of Aeschylus' *Prometheus Unbound*, which the *Manchester Guardian* called 'a charming little edition ... no more delightful volume could be desired by those who have still some Greek but are conscious that it is getting rusty'. But the social mores of the time demanded that she live at home to look after her ailing mother, cycling out to her Greek pupils in between times to help meet household expenses. Word of mouth had spread the news of her skill, the humour she brought to lessons and, in the case of the artist Henry Holliday who signed up for a course at the same time as members of the family of the prime minister, Herbert Asquith, other qualities. He had agreed to learn Greek only if a teacher could be found who looked like Athena or Electra and, he told friends, 'was much surprised to find that such a one lived on the Heath, close by'.

Case had also been a suffragette from the first, a moderate, 'constitutional' one like Swanwick, with whom she campaigned, although unlike Swanwick she retained faith that the Liberal government would eventually come round. Her uncle Sir James Stansfield had been a notable Liberal reformer, a friend of Mazzini and Garibaldi, and her parents were Unitarians from a similar Liberal background as CP Scott of the *Guardian*, with the same faith in practical good works. She plunged into political work when she could find time.

Her obituary in the *Guardian* made an interesting comment about this political work, which included standing for the council in 1915 – a local newspaper headline said, with an almost audible sigh, 'Another Woman Candidate for Hampstead'. The *Guardian* noted that putting herself forward like this was untypical and must have required someone like Swanwick to give her a shove, because her speciality was doing 'much drudgery for the Liberal party as well as for the Women's Co-operative Guild'. Pondering the distinctive virtues of female Country Diarists, this is another I would suggest: a willingness, even eagerness, to work for good causes as a footsoldier rather than (as men might mostly prefer) leader. The view from footsoldier level is often more interesting than that from on high, especially when dealing with minutiae, as the diaries tend to do.

Also in 1915, alas, Case suffered a severe breakdown in health, which made her effectively an invalid for the rest of her life. Her doctors forbad her outdoor work and after her mother's death she moved with Emma to the New Forest. Here the sisters gardened and went for walks, often with local farm or forestry staff who appreciated Janet's unassuming ways. Her constant and constantly frustrated search for buzzards in company with one of these neighbours forms a theme of her contributions.

She was not allowed to roam far and so her records were small-scale. I have talked to several present-day diarists who worry if they can't get about in the car, and Case's example should reassure them. Her small scope sharpened her observations and intensified her interest; and this is another quality that female diarists can justly claim to exercise more skillfully than men. Exactly 30 years after Case's death, Enid Wilson began a Lake District Country Diary by recalling a fairy story in which a girl travelled far and wide in search of happiness, only to find it on her own doorstep. Through illness, Enid said, she had 'forsaken the fells for the confines of my own garden and have learnt much as a result'.

So it was with Case, as she described her small but beautiful world to *Manchester Guardian* readers. On a visit to Hewer's Orchard, Woolf regretted that her old teacher had given up her classes. Were there really no other girls who could benefit from Case's signal system of 'learning Greek without grammar', a focus on the essentials that also served her well in her Country Diaries? Woolf was appeased when Case explained that she was too busy; there was always a bird to watch, a flower to plant and – in a very striking phrase – 'the Forest itself; how could one bear to leave it unseen?'

Woolf was with Janet Case in her final weeks as cancer completed its relentless work and shortly afterwards she paid her old teacher a fine tribute in the *Times*. 'To sit by her side when she knew that death was near was to be taught once more a last lesson, in gaiety, courage and love.'

Felling the hedges

March 1925

The hedge-cutters are busy now, and I see with a pang of regret that the great hedges by the stream at the Forest's edge are down. They had been allowed to run on for years untouched, a shelter for cattle, 15 to 20 feet high. Birches and sallows, hazels, oaks, hollies, thorns and cherries grew side by side. And now the long branches are lying like a swathe all the field's length at the foot of the hedge, purple and bronze and brown, with here and there a green holly. Some hedgers will leave a holly or an oak while they cut and lay the rest for the quicker-growing trees to overtake again; others will pare all down, leaving only the stubs, so that the holding looks like a featureless country intersected by dykes. These hedges have at least escaped the last indignity, but, docked and dwarfed and cut to one dead level as they are, their glory is gone. The withies and the hazels will soon be up again, but there will be no cherry blossom in the spring, and no oaks and hollies for longer than I care to think.

The secret orchid

June 1925

In the cool of the evening, we went to look for the butterfly orchid. Our way took us through one of the oldest beech woods of the Forest, giant trees, some looking still in their prime, others getting thin and showing naked boughs. In the nobbly holes of one gaunt, bare trunk, the jackdaws build. From another an owl took his silent flight. Beyond the wood is a wide stretch of heather with bracken growing thick around it, and there our search began. The slender stalks with their pyramid of delicate greeny-white flowers (not looking in the least like butterflies) hide shyly by twos and threes under the bracken, hard to see till the eyes grow accustomed to the search, and then one by one they seemed to raise their heads where there had been none before.

They are honey-sweet, and we had rather hoped to be guided to them by their scent, which is stronger in the evening. But in the fragrant twilight it was just a part of the scented whole, indistinguishable till one bent close over them. They are capricious in their choice of growing place, but happily the Forest holds many of their secret haunts.

Between green walls

March 1926

As you bicycle down the long slope of the Manor drive between two walls of rhododendrons 20 feet or more in height, you get few glimpses of the woodland stretching at their backs; just the tree tops rise above the hedge of sombre green, broken now by crimson blossoms, and helping to close you in, and that is all. And then the green walls end abruptly and you get a sudden vision, as I did yesterday, of the sunlit floor of the wood, starred thick with white anemones, one stretch and then another and another. When primroses carpet a copse they make a sheet of clear pale yellow; bluebells are a sea of blue. But wood anemones, like daffodils, make a crowd and not a mass. The white stars lifted above their green crinoline of deep-cut leaf keep their individuality like stars in the sky, their frail petals never emerging in a blurred and indistinguishable whole.

The colours of winter

December 1926

A flurry of wind and the air is darkened for the moment by the blown leaves tossed all ways by the gust. They are falling quickly now, and the trees are showing the soberer colours, as beautiful in their way as their autumn glory, of the bare trunks and branches.

To an ex-Londoner used to the monotone of a smoke-grimed bark, the richness and variety of the winter colouring comes as a fresh revelation every year, even after more than a dozen years of country life. And what with the plough-lands and green fields, the emerald green of rain-soaked grass, and the darker green of ivy, the greys and purples of the distant wood, the snatches of bright colour still left upon the trees, and purple hedges where the old man's beard lies like a trail of smoke, there is colour enough and to spare in spite of the absence this year of the usual harvest berries.

Bogbean and buzzards

August 1927

The buzzards are making me feel humiliated. As luck will have it, I have never yet seen or heard them here – 'the master birds of the Forest', as the old keeper calls them. In the early year he said: 'If you were just to sit with your book on the hillside it would not be a matter of five-and-twenty minutes before you heard her cry. Pi-ou, she says. Like that.' But I did not feel exactly disposed to sit with my book on the wet grass of that bleak hillside in the biting spring wind, though I have been there often enough since – but still, to his concern, in vain. So the other day he took me in hand himself and promised a sight of their nest and almost promised a sight of the birds as well. And here was more humiliation waiting for me. I found we were covering the same ground as I did that day in June when I found the bogbean. I must actually have passed under their nesting tree – a tall, straight beech with a crown of green atop – at the very time when the young birds were in the nest. I remember glancing up and down for a likely hole for a woodpecker, but I didn't tilt my head back far enough to see the great structure of twigs up aloft – enormous, some four feet by two.

Then we sat down in the likeliest spot, with an open view and a clear sky, to watch for the birds. But no birds came.

The woodpeckers' drum

May 1928

From the edge of the wood came the loud, snorting drum of a woodpecker, an amazing volume of sound. Now was my chance. I longed to watch the drumming. I crept in under the high beeches with the dead leaves crackling like pistol shots underfoot and stalked it to its tree – an oak. But no bird was visible. I have watched them flying to and fro from their special trees, and twice I have identified the rolling drummer as the male great spotted woodpecker as he came into sight a moment after, upright and gently tapping on a branch, but actually drumming – never. Once it was a short hoarse roll repeated from the oak, Tr-r-r-um, and answered at last by the long rolling drum from another tree. For minutes on end the two calls alternated. Was it the female calling to the male? I call the two notes F and M but I have not yet identified the female. F's drum does not change in tone. M's alters with a change of position. Sometimes you only hear them tapping. Once it may be F gives a short roll from the oak, and getting no answer flies silently away. Or M repeats his long drumming, and if no answer comes will fly off with a wailing note, something between a sigh and a creak. He flies straight through the trees, undulating in the open, and all around wood wrens call and shiver in the silvery coolness of the young beech leaves, wood pigeons blunder through the branches, and a squirrel scampers over the rustling leaves and skims up a towering stem to swing from branch to branch in the high tree tops.

A green and purple world

September 1929

It is a pleasant thing to get down among the heather on one of these hot days when the sun is getting low and its rays are level with the heather-bells. Every one is lighted up until it twinkles. All around about you the air is full of honey and the humming of the honeybees that crowd about. Every hummock casts a long shadow. The tall flowers of the grasses are like shining spearheads in the sun, and the blades of grass below are the tenderest, translucent green. The yellow points of the dwarf furze break into the green and purpleness. A butterfly dances by and settles on a patch of white gravel, folds its wings, and is at once indistinguishable from the little stones and their shadows. Here is another. The two circle about each other for a moment on their cool, greyish mottled wings; then go their ways. Where the heather ends at the top of the lane wood betony takes up its colour, with here and there blue harebells and jasmine.

Fearless finches

September 1930

It is a week since I walked on the Forest knee-deep in the honey-sweet, sun-drenched ling. At the bottom by the stream there is purple-headed scabious, and thorns and other bushes break up the colour; and among them a small very blue-green seedling fir – one of a race accursed in the open forest but singularly beautiful set in that sea of frothy pink. It will be sodden now and tarnished by the heavy floods of rain; and one is kept busy tying and staking and retying and restaking Michaelmas daisies and heleniums blown anyhow by the gale. Apples lie pell-mell on the grass beneath the trees – the biggest and best too; the windfalls are running the crop close. Under the trees the cut grass saves us from hide-and-seek in their basketing; but the rest is uncut still and is the goldfinches' – as it is our – delight. As the 'charm' grows bigger, they grow more fearless. They come within a few feet of the windows now. They do not mind the rain. They are there through pelting showers, restless, inquisitive, dipping and rising with the hawkbit's springboard stalks or manoeuvring to reach the bent stalk's seeded end with exquisite balance and infinitesimal steps. Starlings alighting will send them flying, but they don't care a toss for the blackbirds on the lawn, preoccupied with worms.

Hunting buzzards again

April 1932

We set off early, old 'S' and I, to look for the buzzard. 'They'm building now,' he said. 'We'll be sure to hear her if we don't see her. We won't come back till we do.' But that savoured of rashness, and I suggested a time limit. 'It's a proper day for her,' he would say at intervals, 'not a breath of wind. We'd hear her now if she was over that far ridge.' But the sky remained empty and silent. He had seen her a week ago. His son had seen them that very week, three of them together. He showed me the badger's earth and the two straightest beeches in the Forest –

boles of 50 feet before the first branch starts. He told tales of the old adder-killer, no longer living. He showed me where bricks had been made in the forest once for the building of a great lady's house, all gone back to forest now, not one brick left upon another. He was distressed that bents and heather were encroaching on the rides so that they no longer offered a check to forest fires, and he lamented the new plantation of Douglas fir as alien to the forest. He knew the name of every clump of trees for miles around. Good talk; but of those buzzards we had gone out to see, neither sight nor sound that day.

Spring has sprung

March 1933

Go to town if you want flowers. The streets and shops in London's Surrey suburbs are full of them, and the parks are gay with crocuses, purple constellations in the grass under the trees.

Occasionally, less happily, I must confess, you find a mass of white and yellow, like poached eggs in an oval dish. The sparrows seem to have left the yellow crocuses alone; I saw no traces of their ravages. And London's almond trees are out. In gardens colour grows apace. Such a clump of mauve hepaticas is under my eyes. But beyond the gardens, flowers are still few and far between. A celandine, a dandelion and a barren strawberry were all I saw in a short walk; these and a brimstone butterfly upon the wing.

The thorn hedges are covered with bright dots of tiny rose and lemon buds. Some are almost breaking into green. The catkins on the sallows have turned to yellow puffs, a primrose cloud in the brown copse. And there are grey poplar catkins, hanging like hairy caterpillars, dun and grey with the glow of lurking red and black and yellow underneath, but mostly red, the subtle colouring and texture of a silky Persian rug.

Dry as dust

July 1933

It was a satisfaction to see on waking glistening raindrops dripping from the thatch and to smell the damp air. It had rained all night. Most of the hay hereabouts is carried. Only yesterday in despair – or was it in hope? – we had puddled the dry dust and planted out the rest of the waiting seedlings. Gardens have all the look of late summer; even dahlias are out; and in the Forest what with blighted beeches, prematurely brown, and a plantation of firs scorched and charred in a forest fire, not to speak of rowan berries turning red, there is already almost a look of autumn. Bees hummed and boomed on different notes among the bracken and heather, but birds were hushed – except for the endless little piping question and answer of a pair of linnets on a furze bush. But I noticed, not for the first time, that as other birds' songs fall off, the song of the goldfinch seems to gain in power and liveliness. There are bursts of singing from the trees, though we see little of the birds in the garden till we let the flowers go to seed.

When primroses carpet a copse they make a sheet of clear pale yellow

An uncommon common

July 1934

I spent some days last week on the edge of a Berkshire common, where I fell asleep to the churring of nightjars, and I hoped to wake to the voice of a corncrake which had been heard morning after morning; but to my regret while I was there to listen he was silent. It is many years since I heard that sound, once so familiar. One evening last spring I stalked a voice I hoped was his, but only to realise on a nearer approach that it was no corncrake but a frog. Quite lately I heard of one doomed by a keeper to be shot (but happily saved by the intercession of a bird-lover) 'because it made so much noise'.

On the common, the willow-herb was making drifts of pink among the bracken and the furze, where a linnet sang his sweetest. I saw two things that struck me as rather odd. I watched a pair of chaffinches walking up the straight bole of a pear tree, for one. And, for the other, among a crowd of seedling birches, which were bare of leaves but had not been quite destroyed by a fire evidently of very recent date, were some with only a single tuft of leaves, but these grown to abnormal size. They were as big as poplar leaves. And even on the birches whose foliage was unimpaired, the leaves showed astonishing diversity of size. They varied from the normal to the same grotesque proportions as on the single tufts.

The bluetits' long day

May 1935

No one wants a wet Bank Holiday; but, barring that, we do want rain. We watch expectantly the clouds that gather – but they disperse again unshed. The drought and the dry, cold wind, alternating with hot sun, are being very hard on the seedlings and all things newly planted out. Already some of the plants show a tendency to droop and wilt.

'H's' persistence had its reward. On a second pilgrimage to look for the bogbean the elusive spot disclosed itself, and there they were, all a-growing and a-blowing, one of spring's loveliest flowers. Our bluetits must be getting ready to fly. There has been no leisurely watching these last chilly days, but the pace is fast. When we draw the curtains, say at half-past eight, the devoted parents are still at it, bringing titbits to their rapacious young; and in the morning I can vouch for their having started work before 5.30 – how much before I cannot say – but at the lowest reckoning that is a 15-hour day. They deserve a rest, but the time for that is not just yet. They feed the fledglings even after they have fled the nest.

Great balls of fire

September 1935

Waking round about two o'clock the other night I was puzzled to see – not darkness, but a queer dim yellowish half-light in which the garden shapes were plain to see. Moonlight? But there was no moon, and not a star was visible. The fag-end of sunset? Impossible. Too late. The first glow of sunrise? Far too early. I went to sleep again with the problem unsolved. From another side of the house a watcher had seen a great ball of fire, and had imagined the flames and belching smoke to be a burning rick. In the morning we learned that a neighbouring house some three-quarters of a mile away had been burnt out.

The September flowering of the roses, which promised so well a week ago, has had a rude setback from the ruthless slashing of the rain. In one garden, I hear, the roses lay strewn upon the ground as if cut by a sharp knife.

View from a window

October 1935

With one's outlook on the country strictly circumscribed, delimited in fact by the window-frame, I count myself lucky to see as much as I do. The sky alone has provided a gala programme. There was the day of ceaseless wind, driving torrential rain before it. Through the streaming window-panes it was a fascination to see grey veils of misty rain blown slantwise to the whole at times and disappear like puffs of smoke. There have been evenings, too, when filmy wisps of cloud caught fire from the sunset and flamed a while and then went out, leaving the sky more ashen than before; and night skies riddled with stars and a full moon making unnatural brightness and unfamiliar shadows in the garden; and Venus in the early morning, incredibly brilliant till it pales, shrinks, and disappears in a rose and saffron sunrise. The outlook is still mainly green, though the night frosts have overlaid it with a wash of russet. The snowy mespilus is aflame with cherry-red and orange. A wren, looking curiously yellow in the sunlight, runs mouse-like up and down the thatch that frames the window. It is a contenting thought that all the bulbs except the tulips – which I am in no hurry to plant – were in the ground a week ago.

Flood, drought, frost and wind

April 1936

An east wind that cuts like a knife is buffeting the daffodils that dapple the orchard field with light. It holds back the buds on the drifts of *Narcissus poeticus ornatus* which, outstripping the Pheasant's Eye by several weeks, flowers before the grass has grown too high.

The ground is too wet for seed-sowing. It is too cold to prune the roses. These things must wait. But the buds are breaking on the apple trees – the crabs are in leaf – and there is a film of green, which grows more visible every day, on the hedges where the blackthorn buds are showing white. The first cluster of wild violets caught my eye the other day upon the hedge bank – such an exquisite mauve.

After several blind years the Crown Imperials, to our delight and – shall I add? – to our surprise are crowned with buds; and I am as far as ever from mastering the secret of their caprice. In the last 12 months they have had floods and drought, unseasonable frosts and bitter winds. What do they want?

A tree full of rooks

November 1936

The rooks were busy in the big oak this morning. These night frosts have put the oaks a stage farther on their way. They are a glowing mass of tawny orange now, against which the rooks shone crisply black. Arriving in a little company, they were quickly lost to sight among the leaves. Then rising sharply again in company and for a moment sharply defined, they would settle again with no sign visible beyond the tugging at the acorned twigs.

The garden has begun to wear its winter look. 'P' has cleared off the old herbaceous growths, put in new tulips, and done a little scratching to the surface. More than that he won't attempt. 'It's all too full of stuff,' he says, for anything else short of a fundamental upheaval, for which this is not the appointed year. But already it has assumed the forward-view look, which may or may not be followed by fulfilment.

We had a dish of raspberries this week. But there was no merit in that – and mighty little flavour!

The whispering wren

May 1937

Spring flowers are here, spring warmth comes and goes, but still the migrants linger. Not till April 22 did the little willow wren pour out his little whispering song in the garden, though very likely he was earlier elsewhere. And this morning for the first time I heard a note I had been waiting for – the first disjointed purring of the turtle-dove before he gets into his stride: Curr … currr … currr. The cuckoo, on the other hand, has already changed his note and is saying cuck-cuck-oo, before I have once heard the female's blustering reply.

With the coming of May the orchard is tricking itself out in white and crimson and pink – *Pyrus malus floribunda* has for days been a delicious spectacle of rosy buds and blossoms; and a scarlet apple of indifferent merit – so dull that I forget its name – is wreathed in crimson bloom. There is every prospect at the moment of a good quince crop; but it often belies its promise. Sometimes it is wind and weather that defeats us. Last year we think it was the badgers that ate the fallen fruit.

Daffodils are passing or past and tufts of white narcissus take their place. A garden warbler is singing away this morning..

Little white birds

June 1937

For some days now it has been my lot to lie where I can stare for hours on end into the heart of a glorious beech tree – watching the shifting interplay of light and shade among the leaves, and with greater curiosity watching for the return of two aerial visitors in shining white, which I did not hesitate to call 'the little white birds'. But when I said 'Have you seen the little white birds?' I felt rather than saw looks of kindly incredulity – so judged it better to keep silence even though a lovely trilling note came from the tree, which dominated the chorus of chaffinches and blackbirds and the quiet little pip-pip-pip of the anxious mother blackbirds on the lawn. But more cogent than any look of incredulity came the thought that there was no little British bird to fit the case – so there was nothing for it but to wait.

And when the days of hot sun began again my ethereal visitants returned in numbers – not birds but butterflies – out of the green leaves and back into the leaves again. Looking of more than normal size and of more than normal whiteness, they came dancing, fluttering, wavering, weaving fantastic patterns of light upon the green as they zigzagged in and out of the picture, sometimes singly, sometimes linked together – an endless joy to watch. Now I say, with unassailable assurance, 'Have you seen the big white butterflies?'

The cuckoo falls silent

June 1937

And has he really left us for good – our vociferous cuckoo? For two days I have listened for him in vain. Hardly had the clock struck four when he would break the silence (not first from the nearest group of trees, but drawing nearer bit by bit) and accompanied or unaccompanied he would continue his monotonous call till silence fell again some time after five. Sometimes a chaffinch would join in, occasionally a blackbird or a thrush – not till later in the morning do the turtle-dove, the garden warbler and the wren join the chorus of song. Yesterday there was no sound except the tiny cheeping that came, I imagine, from the gaping mouths of nestlings in the creeper on the wall. How strange the silence seems after the wearisome iteration of his call, and how odd to think that a note we hail so gladly in the spring should end by nearly maddening us with its monotony. Is there any other bird in parallel case? I think the chaffinch is of their number; he ends by wearying us with his vain repetition after gladdening our hearts with his first song, a sure and certain sign that spring is upon us. Though the cuckoo wearied me, I rather miss him now he is gone.

Her final entry

June 1937

Someone came into the room positively enveloped in green, like the 'Jack-in-the-green' of our childhood days. Such a picture she made; one arm clutching an armful of the lovely crinodendron making with its waxen roseate bells a delightful splash of colour, the other grasped an armful of a creeper covered with four-rayed stars – white stars set close in the green and very free – something after the manner of an outsize Clematis montana. I am not sure of the identity, nor was the donor. Is it American dogwood?*

---

* The American dogwood (*Cornus florida*) is a small tree not a creeper although it does have "white four-rayed stars" which are, in fact, the bracts that surround its inconspicuous flowers.

An Understudy Makes Good

Katherine Arnold Foster was the third in line of the *Guardian*'s female Country Diarists. Her husband was the official author but when he was too busy to do it, he asked her to step in. It was all very matter-of-fact. A busy, bustling civil servant and disarmament campaigner, Will Arnold Foster wrote to the paper's editor, CP Scott, in December 1928 saying that he had been hectic but 'my wife has been doing the notes for me'. In a second letter the following year, shortly after moving to London, he suggested carrying on in the capital 'by visiting Kew etc with my wife's help'.

There are not many entries by Katherine Arnold Foster but they are better, to my mind, than those of her husband, who was perpetually on the go. He was the specialist in scribbling skeletal diaries on trains, one with seven sections as he chuffs down from Inverness to Cornwall. None are terribly informative except about the weather outside the carriage windows. But he was a genuine expert on plants and created a sensational garden at Eagle's Nest, the home on the cliffs above Zennor that he shared with Katherine and their small son, Mark, later a distinguished *Guardian* journalist in his turn.

It was Eagle's Nest that came to Helena Swanwick's mind in her role as the Country Diary's recruiting sergeant. Hearing that the paper was looking for someone south of Oxfordshire, where Basil de Selincourt was based, she wrote to CP Scott in December 1924: 'I suppose you hadn't thought of Will Arnold-Foster? He lives near the Land's End and is the keenest gardener and painter. An astonishing person because he is also an expert in foreign affairs and in the technique of Blockade! He is the owner and chief gardener of a most uncommon garden of boulders and Himalayan shrubs.'

Will's long tenure of Eagle's Nest saw the garden become increasingly famous, until on his death in 1953 it was bought by the artist Patrick Heron, who had visited the Arnold Fosters as a boy. On taking possession, Heron exulted to his friend and fellow artist Herbert Read about the Mediterranean brilliance of the place, alternating with hot, steamy summer mists that turned the carefully placed Cornish granite menhirs into grey Chinese silhouettes.

Will's wife was also exotic. She is better known as Ka Cox, a boyishly attractive undergraduate who took Cambridge University by storm before the first world war. Dressed in Peter Pan collars and modishly decorating her rooms in Newnham College with plain brown paper, she fell in love with the famously beautiful Rupert Brooke and is thought to have had a child, sadly stillborn, with him. They were fellow members of a coterie who called themselves the Neo-Pagans, skinny-dipping in the Cam between artistic and literary discussions.

Affected in the harmless way of students, they were all very well-connected and part of what contemporary social commentators called the 'upper ten', the 10,000 people in Britain who called the shots. When Brooke enlisted for the war that was to make his celebrated poem *The Soldier* come true, with his death in Greece en route to Gallipoli, he wrote to Cox about the dreadful mud at his training camp in Dorset. He would write to their mutual friend Winston Churchill, he said, to get it cleaned up.

Brooke's last note to Cox, when he knew that he would not recover, called her 'the best thing I found in my life', and she had sterling qualities behind the flip undergraduate facade. She was from a privileged background, the daughter of a wealthy London stockbroker, but in 1915 she sailed to Corsica to run a camp for Serb refugees and on her return took a job as a civil servant organising protection for Allied shipping. Through this work, she met Will, who combined a strong sense of public duty (his father had been a Conservative cabinet minister) with reforming ideals developed during three years' studying at the Slade school of art in London.

Marriage meant settling down, at Will's newly discovered paradise in Eagle's Nest, where Ka was content to start a family and serve as lieutenant to her husband's landscape plans. Tall and striking, she was nicknamed Big Stick by the locals while the petite and dapper Will was Little Stick. Her former Neo-Pagan friends were snooty about the change, however; the writer Gwen Raverat wrote to Virginia Woolf about 'Ka so pathetic and lost in Cornwall' and Woolf, even more sharply, noted in her diary after a visit to the couple in 1923 that Ka's figure was like 'a sack of the commoner garden vegetables'.

In practice, the move to Cornwall lost Ka none of the enthusiasm, curiosity and fun that had endeared her to fellow students at Cambridge. It shows in her Country Diaries, with their staunch defence of the landscape along Britain's new A-roads, whose ability to speed her round the country with Will (when he wasn't on a train) was so useful. It was during the early 1930s, when Will was working for the Privy Council office and briefly had to abandon writing for the *Guardian* altogether as a condition of employment, that she was most called upon. While her husband wrote to the paper's offices in Manchester to say that he had been 'muzzled', she got out and about, inspecting cottage gardens and teasing orderly *Guardian* readers with her liking for that tenacious pest of the borders, bindweed.

The poet Frances Cornford (confusingly married to the poet Francis Cornford) made a telling observation about Ka's character that is relevant to her skills as a recorder of nature, and those of most of the other women in this book. 'To be with her was like sitting in an open field of clover,' she said. 'She accepted everybody, as she did the weather, and then gave out, not knowing how much she was giving.' Such unselfconsciousness, almost self-abnegation, is much rarer in men.

But it was not the same as passivity. Ka also got stuck in to the local community and public service, as she had in her first world war days. She supported Will's campaigns for the League of Nations and a limit on new battleships, and tried unsuccessfully to break the Tory and Liberal hold on north Cornwall by standing as a Labour council candidate. She became a magistrate, and with an interest in young people fired by her own family (the 'M' in her diary about cats is her son, Mark), she specialised in juvenile cases and young people at risk.

It was this that led to her extraordinary end, aged only 51, when she came to know a seriously disturbed young woman living in a lonely cottage nearby. It appeared that the girl had been drawn into group sex and naked rituals on the moors behind Eagle's Nest by the self-declared Satanist and 'Great Beast', Aleister Crowley. Not only were Ka's magistrate's instincts aroused, but she had an interest in the mental conditions that can be created by belief in the supernatural. She and Will had reluctantly accepted a ouija board session at Eagle's Nest with Ruth Mallory, the widow of the climber George, shortly after he disappeared high on Everest in June 1924. The glass moved and Ruth was convinced that she and George had enjoyed a reunion.

With this in mind, and not least because any Satanist ritual would have threatened one of her favourite badger setts, Katherine marched up to the cottage where the orgies were said to happen, intent on removing the girl and taking her to a safe haven. She confronted someone, who may have been Crowley or one of his acolytes or, according to the many theorists who delight in this subject, a manifestation of the Devil. Whichever it was, the stress gave Katherine a seizure and she died after being stretchered off the moor at two o'clock in the morning.

She was mourned in the *West Briton* and the *Cornish Guardian* as a woman who had enjoyed 'universal popularity', and Will, who as usual was travelling, this time on a ship to Canada for talks on how to prevent the increasing likelihood of war, was devastated. But he resolved to commemorate Ka's enthusiasm for nature and gardening with fresh efforts of his own, and these had lasting results. As well as the continuing development of Eagle's Nest, Will wrote a standard account of Shrubs for the Milder Counties, published in 1948 by *Country Life*, and this in turn helped to inspire another outstanding woman to create a memorable garden. The sculptor Barbara Hepworth contacted Will soon after moving to Cornwall with her husband, Ben Nicholson, and their triplets, in August 1939, 15 months after Ka's death.

The advice he gave her led to the creation of the beautifully planted sub-tropical oasis at Trewyn Studios in St Ives, now the Barbara Hepworth Sculpture Garden. It is a place where you can understand the vision she shared with women like Ka and this book's other diarists. To put it in her own words, in an article in Herbert Read's modish magazine *Unit One* in 1934: 'In the contemplation of Nature we are perpetually renewed and our sense of mystery and our imagination is kept alive.'

Roadside delights

July 1931

The roadsides have put on their second set of yellow trimmings. The celandines and the buttercups came first, and now down in the west every stone 'hedge' is covered with the most brilliant shining hawksweed, mixed to perfection with blue jasmine. Through Somerset the low stone walls have often a coping of yellow stone crop, and below in the rough grass between wall and road there are patches of blue purple cranesbill ('thunderflower', it is called in Wiltshire),* which makes another yellow and blue highway decoration.

Even along these maligned 'unpreserved' main roads of England there are many good sights. Nearly every cottage garden just now has great clumps of Madonna lilies, which might be envied by any millionaire. I suppose they flourish so because they are seldom, if ever, disturbed in those small plots, but in the country now it looks as if the lilies put forth their best for those who toil and spin. And in these gardens, too, there is often a high bush of mock orange against mellow stone or warm brick.

So the moment's fashion seems to be white for the gardens and yellow for the hedges, but there is a fine sprinkling of other colours flouting the conventions. Sweet William is in the gardens and poppies by the road.

The beauty of bindweed

August 1931

Have any notes ever been made on the sentimental as well as the botanical history of the convolvulus? Its real flowering time, I think, must have been in Victorian times, when it smothered the garden arbours and opened its lovely fluted flowers, warmed by the artless admiration of crinolines and ringlets. So clinging yet so strong, so beautiful and so short-lived, the convolvulus

---

* It is the wood cranesbill (*Geranium sylvaticum*) that is also known as "thunderflower", and not just in Wiltshire.

The North Cornish coast where Katherine Arnold Foster lived with her husband and son

could suggest all the proper reactions to those of true 'sensibility'. The convolvulus strays, too, over the engraved title-pages, or decorates the albums of that period; it must have been without doubt its best 'day'.

I confess to a great weakness even for bindweed at this season of the year, when it runs along any sun-parched cart track or dry hedgerow with its multitude of small flowers – their shading carried out in just the right two shades of pink. A great green hanging let down over a hedge or fence, starred all over with the white bells of the common convolvulus, is a noble sight (as lovely as any tropical creeper). And 'Morning Glories' always seem to be one of a summer day's best miracles.

Purple and gold

August 1931

The sky has been heavy with thunderstorms as we drove west today. When we climbed Glastonbury Tor at midday all the distance was blurred, but the pattern of roads and dikes and line of elms pricked out over the plain was clear enough.

Yellow ragwort is a despised flower, witness as it is of rank, poor soil, but all the steep slopes of the tor were showy with its rather sullen yellow mixed with quantities of the large purple thistle. Just at this time of the year there are always several of these rather handsome companioned colours. Poppies and charlock in the fields, autumn gorse and purple heather on the moors, and this show of ragwort and thistle in the waste places. None of them are colours one would choose to mix in an herbaceous border, but fine and effective under autumn skies and set among its yellowing fields and dusty greens of path and hedgerow.

Glastonbury Tor, with its gold and purple weeds, was a royal sight under those heavy, towering clouds.

Leopard's den

August 1931

Because cats easily adapt themselves to town life and are happier in a housebound existence than dogs, one perhaps does not so often think of them out of doors. Here, where 'M's' great orange-tawny cat plays on the rocks and is to be found sunning himself under his favourite tuft of heather, cats are as common a garden sight as I suppose leopards may be at Whipsnade. In a small valley garden near here, as we stood talking of this plant and that flower, this wet summer and last cold winter, a lovely cream Persian cat came through the long grass. Then another and yet another, and then we saw two more curled up in the sun and yet another playing with a fern. Beautiful in colour and movement, a troupe of country-bred Persians seem the proper inhabitants for a wild garden. Town cats have bad garden manners it is said, but these creatures seem to do no harm to the garden and are as fine and handsome an addition to the flora and fauna as any bevy of peacocks.

Badgers at dusk

July 1932

Supper was late, and I got up to look at the last sight of shine on the sea. There were the two great cats playing on the lawn; but their movements seemed strange, their shapes in the failing light had a curious slope of the shoulders – a rake forward. The two young badgers came near – just pleasantly cruising over the lawn on an early evening stroll. As I slipped out of the house they slipped under a patch of veronica bushes. But I saw them a few minutes later moving over the rocks at the back of the house, the white stripes on their masks enabling one to pick them out easily – dark-grey badgers on dark-grey granite, outlined against the lighter greys of sea and western sky.

It was a still, windless night, and in a few seconds I heard their rustling passage through the high bracken and heather below the pile of rocks. They were making their way down the moor to the old sett of many openings, which must have been the home to countless generations of badgers.

Pink in the rocks

July 1932

The silver-pink mesembryanthemums are out on the walls and in the cracks high up at the top of the Giant's Snuff Box – cracks so exposed and dry that it would seem impossible for anything to root there; but year after year the cool pink flowers froth along the granite ledges. Most of the rock plants are over, but there are clumps of a vivid pink dianthus, which give a sharp accent to the garden. Some of the flowering grasses mix very happily with rock pinks; they supply a waving background of shaded browns, going on to pink and dull purples. In the fields of rough pasture the numberless grasses are at their best now. Yesterday, as I brushed along a small bunny trace through grass plumes heavy with dew, the subtlety and variety of their colour seemed like a choice example of what could be done with a carefully selected and restricted palette. The brightest of the early field flowers are over, except the poppies by the roads, which are flaming always. Most of the purple and yellow fashions of late summer have hardly got going, so the grasses wisely time their ripening for the between season.

Keep your eyes on the road

July 1932

Driving through some of the roads of England, between high hedges, overarching, shaded, green, one almost recaptures the delight of those bracken passages, secret, warm and fragrant, whose complicated system of communications was unknown to the grown-ups who went by on the bypass paths. The rate of progress, too, is slowed down, happily enough, if not to the tummy-crawl of bracken tunnels, at least to a contemplative pace.

There are times, however, when one feels that with these low cars much of the pride and glory of travelling has gone. A high dogcart was the real thing to give the driver a proper conceit of himself. Passing between the hedges one gazed out over their tops, free of the countryside and with a fine feeling of command over all one surveyed. But I suppose the toll of the road would be even heavier if we were free to regard the landscape to right and left, and did not drive with bodies low, necks rigid. We've narrowed our travelling vision the better to pursue our conquest of time and space.

And I hate to hear even the main roads of England despised for their looks. There are, indeed, distressing outbreaks of petrol-pumps and bungalows, but what can rival some of their views? And crossing a burnt Surrey heath the London road cut through a level flood of bright pink willow-herb, stretching as far as one could see; no Persian garden could have shown a richer and more lavish spread.

Cottage colours

August 1932

The general mix up of flowers in cottage gardens, together with the feeling that another plant or seedling can always be shoved in somewhere, another scrap of colour added, gives one a fine feeling of lavishness and riotous living. But this week I saw a cottage garden just big enough to stand a planned treatment but without losing any of the proper spontaneous cottage look. First, there was almost the best group of *Lilium regale* I have ever seen. And they were planted on a bank a little above the brick path, so that you looked up at them high and fragrant against a far landscape of heavy elms, the downs and grey clouded sky. Then there were roses planted all together – a dozen plants of the same rose, in such a garden, are worth two dozen 'assorted'. There were, of course, lots of other ingredients, but the whole had been planned with an eye to one or two bits of colour in the right place, which give character and flavour to the whole garden.

And this garden had not failed to include the rose 'Mermaid', without which no cottage is quite complete.

Out with the deer

August 1932

Since horses have nearly vanished from the countryside there is little left to see of the beauty of swift movement. Cows, like women, to transpose the saying, should never run, and it is only occasionally on the downs that one can see a string of racehorses really 'moving'. So watching some fallow deer, which were so near the house that you could see them early and late and shadowed under the trees at noonday, I felt as if I were rediscovering the excitement of four-legged creatures. The carriage of their heads, the does almost equally with the bucks, as they slide off into their springing, easy canter suggests a rhythm and balance from the low bonnets of the latest sporting models! Suddenly, too, one of the does breaks into that absurd and delicious high-stepping prance, with its young trotting behind. Their movements have such a natural ease and yet a stylised heraldic look that one feels if they could be translated into music only some Scarlatti air with a syncopated rhythm might fit their prancings.

They harbour, as seals do (creatures as different as the elements they move in) the warring instincts of shyness and curiosity; they will dash off in a panicky crowd, then pause and, if you remain still, come quietly back sniffing the air suspiciously but ever edging nearer.

Wide open spaces

August 1932

A southerner has the feeling that she must stretch her eyes among these wide Northumberland hills so as to miss nothing of the sweep of road or moor or great fields running up to the sky. And even the side roads are so often quite straight for a mile or two, hedgeless and delightfully switchbacked, so that ones gets an intoxicating exhilaration of space and movement if motoring. The heather just now looks as if a soft pink purple mixture had been poured over the hills, so smoothly and evenly it is spread, hardly broken sometimes at all by bracken or rock.

Then one can turn down to a stream, one's eyes no longer 'stretched', and play with the water, flooding some tributary with a carefully devised dam, watching the way the alders always take the right shape and how the rocks and moss arrange their decorations; this is occupation enough for the whole day.

But I must turn south again with some unsatisfied desire. I have smelt bog myrtle, played in streams, and return refreshed by the sight of this wide, large-scale country, but this time I've found no Grass of Parnassus – and for that alone I would come the 300 miles up through England.

CHAPTER

Four

A Chirrupy Sort of Person

Gwen McBryde marks a complete change in the character of
the *Guardian*'s female Country Diarists, as you can see from her
first recorded appearance in public life. She was a secret weapon
of her father, Frederick Grotrian, a Conservative politician who
in 1892 briefly stormed and captured the East Hull constituency,
a Victorian Liberal stronghold. The exuberantly partisan
magazine *Yorkshire Leaders* described 'Mr Grotrian's extremely
sympathetic and ideal wife and daughters. Their kindness,
philanthropy and ministering visits in Hull are welcomed and
dearly prized.'

Gwendolen Grotrian was 14 at the time and so probably
more of an ornament than an effective philanthropist, but the
electioneering showed a lasting side to her character. She liked
to get stuck in. At home in Ingmanthorpe Hall she made
gunpowder with her brothers for a home-made cannon, built
tree houses and came in for dinner coated in mud after dipping
for newts or waterweed in nearby streams.

Her Country Diaries frequently refer to a golden childhood;

golden literally in the case of her curly fair hair. This and her sweet expression as a little girl earned her pocket money as a ten-year-old model for the American artist Anna Lea Merritt, a friend of her parents, whose sentimental and at the time immensely popular studies include young Gwen depicting Love in a large allegorical oil, now in the Tate Gallery collection. But she was happier fighting her brothers or making miniature theatres out of shoeboxes, lined with the Turkey Red fabric beloved of the Victorians, or playing with two exquisite dolls sent by a contact of her father in St Petersburg. They had tiny shawls of genuine Shetland wool and pale blue trunks for travelling. Gwen called them Arnia and Gonlia.

This has mild echoes of the Bronte sisters and their miniature books about the imaginary realm of Gondal, and Gwen showed an early enthusiasm for making up stories and illustrating them. This was to remain with her, although her hopes of writing a successful novel were never realised. Anyone who has tried will feel a pang of sympathy with the kindly letter she received in 1952 from the editor of the *Guardian*, AP Wadsworth, to whom she had sent a proposed book called *The Adventures of a Kitten*, a rollicking affair that also involves hummingbirds and flying fish in the West Indies. He replied: 'The pictures are charming but I am not sure that you tell the story simply enough and that the "plot" so to speak is really clear.'

Clarity comes second to cheerful vigour in McBryde's Country Diaries, which often leap between topics and have the air of rapid work, scribbled down before a passing thought was lost. But she knew enough about literature and art to hold her own when she was invited to make up a party for the May Ball in 1902 at King's College, Cambridge. In the course of the idyllic evening, she danced frequently with a young undergraduate from a farming family in Shropshire, James McBryde. The young pair's developing love affair was watched with benevolent interest by a distinguished patron of James McBryde's, Montagu James, the future provost of King's, and later Eton, who already had a name as MR James, master of chilling ghost stories.

It was Montagu James rather than James McBryde who was to become important in Gwen's life, for although the couple were married in 1904 and the bride was happily pregnant within months, the fairy tale ended in less than a year. James McBryde died of appendicitis on the threshold of what might have been a promising artistic career. He had gone from Cambridge to the Slade school of art in London and had already contributed appropriately sinister illustrations to an MR James story.

The reticent bachelor academic agreed somewhat fearfully to become legal guardian to Gwen and James's daughter, Jane, and maintained a regular and witty correspondence with the girl and her mother until his death in 1936. McBryde was the only woman in his voluminous correspondence whom he did not address formally, although it took him 20 years to relax enough to drop 'Dear Mrs McBryde' for 'Dear Gwen'. He greatly enjoyed teasing Jane in a donnish way, and also encouraged McBryde with her writing about nature and the English countryside. He died four years before she wrote her first Country Diary for the *Guardian*, but she was contributing pieces to *Country Life* and other magazines from the early 1930s and James sought out anecdotes that might stimulate her imagination.

'Four pails of black beetles have been removed from the house kitchen,' he reported in one letter that revealed an unusual side of Eton school life. Another described how he had returned to his study after dinner one evening to find a toad crawling ponderously across the carpet. 'What,' he asked with a touch of his ghost story omens, 'does it portend?'

The McBrydes served another purpose for James, who liked escaping his solitary quarters and also had business as a mediaeval historian with many of the country's ancient churches. After the first world war, Gwen and Jane moved to Herefordshire, eventually settling in a beautiful old farmhouse called Dippersmoor Manor on the edge of the hamlet of Kilpeck. The village is a bit of a muddle these days, with 20th-century infill almost outnumbering the older houses, but the church is an outstanding example of Norman architecture. The McBrydes revered it but also had endless fun giving nicknames to the extraordinary collection of gargoyle corbels, especially the cartoon-like dog and hare (which exactly resemble characters from Wallace and Gromit).

James greatly enjoyed visiting Dippersmoor, and the nearby farm of Woodlands where the McBrydes first lived. Both were close to a supposed track of ley lines, invisible highways of the supernatural, and the numinous atmosphere of the quiet hills and valleys was borrowed for many of his tales. He adapted the view from his favourite walk through bluebell woods without amendment for the story *A View from a Hill* in his ominously entitled collection *A Warning to the Curious*. 'Across a broad level plain they looked upon ranges of great hills, whose uplands – some green, some furred with woods – caught the light of a sun, westering but not yet low. And all the plain was fertile, though the river which traversed it was nowhere seen. There were copses, green wheat, hedges, and plentiful pasture-land.'

This was the setting for Gwen McBryde's weekly diary, which is full of acute observation of animal and plant behaviour that *Guardian* readers grew to love during her 18-year stint. She was chosen for inclusion in the first of the annual *Bedside Guardian* compilations in 1952 and for two later volumes. Fitting the weekly note in between the endless demands of farming – 'It swallows everything, time and money alike,' she wrote to Wadsworth – she made a precise record of her small patch. Observing flycatchers, she speculates correctly that a pair whose nest was on a stove stopped sitting when the temperature rose above 72 degrees; like the maleo birds of Indonesia that bury their eggs in warm volcanic earth, they sensed that incubation no longer needed their help. She records the first arrival of grey squirrels in Herefordshire in 1946 and realises that the reds will be doomed. She often strays to her cats, dogs and neighbours who frequently take precedence over their backdrop, however lovely the landscape, weather or flowers.

This prompted occasional, delicate reprimands from the three *Guardian* editors under whom she served – William Crozier, Wadsworth and Alistair Hetherington – all of whom took a personal interest in the Country Diary rather than leaving it to the section editor, as happens today. In July 1941, for instance, Crozier complimented her on 'four very lively and interesting paragraphs' but warned: 'You mentioned "Jennie the Witch", apparently about some living person. As a general rule never mention living persons in any sort of disparaging manner. It is not safe.' This did not deter McBryde for long.

I have faced one problem with her diaries. Some of the best concern Dippersmoor's seesawing fortunes during the war, when young evacuees were so charmed by its atmosphere that they refused to return to London with their parents. Italian prisoners of war dug trenches and picked fruit crops, alternately driving McBryde mad with their terrible time-keeping and charming her by singing arias in the summer sun. Land girls careered around on tractors while McBryde drove an assortment of dog-infested jalopies until the Land Rover was first marketed in 1948 and she never drove anything else. But these adventures are recounted at length in *Wartime Country Diaries*, one of the companion volumes to this book. Regretfully, I felt that it would be wrong simply to repeat them, and so the ones here are all new and unpublished since they first appeared. *Wartime Country Diaries*, however, is an excellent buy.

McBryde carried on writing until her death in 1958. Her last diary, neatly typed on a portable that she had only recently learned to use after 17 years of using handwriting, appeared in the *Guardian* on the morning she died. She was much missed, but her legacy remains in her beautiful old farm, now a rose-entangled B&B. Dippersmoor was left to Jane, who enjoyed a successful career as a horse-breeder and farmer but did not marry and had no children. In her turn, she bequeathed it to Raoul Millais, a painter specialising in equestrian studies, who had encouraged McBryde's efforts to publish her stories and drawings through contacts at Puffin Books and *Country Life* magazine. He was the grandson of the celebrated Victorian artist Sir John Everett Millais, the creator of 'Bubbles', the 1886 Pears Soap advertisement. Bubbles shows a little boy in velvet, but with his small pink face and curly fair hair, he could just as easily be that other child who was to sit for Anna Lea Merritt two years later.

A sweet life

May 1940

I am told that stone fruit has been spoilt by frost, but up here I cannot see that it is damaged. I have lost my strawberry crop – some late blooms may open but the advanced fruit is blackened. Below in the valley oaks look singed and shrivelled and early potatoes are cut down. I suppose there will be some more apple blossom but the trees look brown now.

The scarcity of plover nowadays is a serious matter. They were great scavengers of wireworm. People collecting the eggs for sale have left us with hardly a plover. Wireworm seems to come to the surface when the sun has warmed the ground and to go down again if it is cold or wet. In the middle of the day when it is sunny I have seen rooks digging for them.

Old days on farms used to be very pleasant, with workers personally interested in the stock and proud of their teams. There is nothing to be proud of about tractors, even when they do consent to work. I sometimes think of an admirable cowman who said his father had 'a sweet life as he had never been beyond Hereford and Leominster'.

The dippers' waterfall

February 1941

There is a waterfall at the bottom of Dippers Wood. It is well worth a visit at this time of year. It flows over large blocks of stone, a ten-foot drop. Today it thunders down, brown and foaming, bringing along branches and stones and leaves. Usually it is a tranquil stream, with clear pools between slabs of rock and you can find your way over to the opposite steep bank, where there is a flight of rough stone steps up to the oak roots that grip the top of the slope.

If you hunt under the stones in the stream you will find crayfish. They are like little lobsters, black, and I think with something of the repulsiveness of spiders. I was once persuaded to have some crayfish boiled; they turned a beautiful scarlet, but here at any rate they do not grow big enough to be worth cooking. When I was having a dam made the men came on some crayfish; they declared them to be a sort of scorpion and could not be persuaded to handle them.

Today, as I had hoped, I saw a dipper. His white breast made him very conspicuous as he stood for a moment on a slab of rock flicking his tail. He flew off downstream calling 'Chit, chit'. I had not the good fortune to see him go under water.

Glories of spring

April 1941

In less strenuous times I made a collection of varieties of cowslips and primroses, partly because their names have always

Dippersmoor Manor, the 12th–17th century farm of Gwen McBryde

fascinated me – 'curled cowslips' or 'Jack-in-the-Green', 'Galligaskins', 'the frantic cowslip'. I love the charming double primroses, but they are delicate. I found a dark-red cowslip wild when I was a child and an old woman gave me a red 'hose in hose' for my garden. There are plenty of wild oxlips here, though once I was told that they cannot be the genuine thing, as they grow only in Suffolk and Norfolk, but I think it unlikely that all these wild ones are merely a cross between polyanthus and primrose. I once found a lemon-coloured kingcup (marsh marigold). I did not trouble to cultivate it because, after all, the deep gold of the kingcup is its glory.

Wild daffodils have a way of fading out quite suddenly, but primroses can be relied on to go on blooming to the end of May, hidden from sight by the vigorous growth of bracken and grass.

Frost in May

May 1942

The effect of drying east wind on the soil is to turn it into cast iron – not a hopeful condition. I only trust the cherry and pear blossom has not been damaged. Ground frost has not done much harm yet, I think. My old pensioner, Powell, remarks, 'There'll be as many frosts in May as there be in April.' He is, as ever, against anything being done in a hurry, and will certainly endure his many waistcoats, including the leather one that reaches almost to his knees, until well into June.

The cuckoo at last is hard at it, and Powell remarked, 'I heard un a week ago, but I didn't run.' It seems that when you first hear the cuckoo you should run or you will be lazy all the year.

I saw a swallow on Easter Day and have never seen one since. The only really energetic singer except the lark is a starling who sits on a gable end and gives a good impression of a blackbird. There is no doubt that birds dislike an east wind as much as human beings.

Eat brown bread

August 1944

In the early morning I went by a woodland path to see if the water ram was working; we have waited for a new tap for three weeks. It was dry and rustly in the wood. Nuthatches and squirrels have strewn the ground with nutshells. Little runnels of sunlight ran down the ash stems and the twisted honeysuckle.

An old woodman used to cut walking-sticks from nut or ash that had honeysuckle twined round and grown right into the bark.

We threshed a field of rye for a neighbour. It is a useful crop on high ground, affording as it does good grazing. In Holland one gets many interesting sorts of rye bread; here it is used for proprietary foods. In England there is a prejudice against dark-coloured bread. For my part I would eat any form of brown rather than white bread.

Our barley is threshed and sold for malting, and we are cutting a hilly field of wheat with the Caterpillar tractor. Two years ago this field was said to be the worst bit of land in the neighbourhood. It grew reeds and wiry grass, but last year it yielded good beans and the wheat crop is excellent.

The life of bees

August 1945

I hope next summer to be able to take some hives of bees to the heather on the Black Mountains. Here the honey flow stops all too early. After the fruit has blossomed there is no certainty of a good honey flow; even if the weather is right and there is apparently plenty of white clover, it may be dry and hold no nectar.

The life of a bee does not seem to me to be a satisfactorily arranged affair. Worker bees are born with a fixed amount of energy, charged up rather like a dry battery; and they neither slumber nor sleep. By day they forage and all night they work in the home. (Rather reminiscent of a farmer's wife!)

There is the work of moving the honey from cell to cell, attendance on the young, circulating air by wing fanning, repairs and building. The only thing they seem to be spared is mechanisation, so they may have a chance of surviving us. They share with us the hazards of weather and are even more dependent on its caprices. They have to be on the lookout too for robbers – wasps are not strong enough this season to be dangerous.

No rest for the farmer

May 1946

A determined effort recently on the part of the tractor drivers has completed the planting of the lower meadow. The dry weather makes the soil a light pink colour and the surface is smooth as a lawn. Holidays do not come to farmer owners, but for my part I do not mind. Not having been away for five years, I am inclined to agree with the man who said 'Life would be tolerable but for its pleasures.' I do not wish, like the sturdy Welshman, to go to the races. He told me when inquiring about them yesterday that he would be a rich man but for the racing, but he had enjoyed every minute of his life. He is 70 and started coal-mining at 12, and gave up recently owing to not agreeing with the present way of running it.

I find it very pleasant in the kitchen garden with the strong scent of apple blossom coming on the breeze and the cuckoo sailing around with its spring call softly modulated; and I like to see the stir of the tits flicking about in the trees and perhaps a tree creeper. Beetles have kindly buried the mice I trapped near the peas.

Midges and ducklings

June 1946

Heavy rain does not seem to quench the exuberance of midges. It is a mystery to me why they are experts at biting humans when the opportunity to do so can only come rarely to one in many generations of midges and can hardly be regarded as necessary. It appears to be really bad luck to start and end all of your life's span on one of these wet summer days, but possibly it is all one to the midges, and they may even like it.

A string of wild ducklings crossed the road in front of my car. I hope they have survived in spite of the heavy rains. What is considered to be good for ducks is not good for fluffy ducklings, as they drown easily. If they try to get up a steep bank beside a pond they are likely to fall on their backs and drown. I was told of a very young boy who 'made it rough' for some ducklings who were swimming on a little tank, with the result that the ducklings were all drowned.

While I was discussing hay crops with a farmer he said we were mowing at this time last year and that we are three weeks behindhand, which I can well believe.

Tewkesbury underwater

December 1946

A trip that took me through Tewkesbury impressed on me that there are worse spots than my home farm. There was quite a seaside appearance as waves broke over the floods and up to the road; the Abbey alone in the distance stood out beyond the waste.

Between storms we have managed to get some red beet pulled. It is mild and very exhausting dragging your feet out of the clogging ground. Almost worse than the weather are the struggles with worn-out machinery and the difficulties over the chops and changes of animal feeding-stuffs. It is pathetic to see some old farmer presenting what he imagines may get him some food for his calves and being told that somehow it represents something to do with seed clover he grew. There is very little autumn colour except for the yellow ochre of the oak trees and already the stems of the golden willow are conspicuous in a grey landscape.

Primroses and violets like the wet; I had a narrow border of phlox and pink primroses; the rain has spoilt the phlox. There are some fine *Primula japonica* in bloom and lots of wallflowers.

The stream is in spate and the volume of water bringing branches and mud stops the dam from working. There are nasty scratchy little footprints on the mud; rats are around.

When I motor down an old coaching lane I can count on seeing the golden coat and white waistcoat of a fine stoat; he is brought up sharply in his hunt. Or I see a dark streak – a small weasel going all out to get across to the opposite verge.

Tired of the mud

January 1947

There is still a lot of clearing up to be done, and hedging and draining are always with us, but all crops except the red beet are harvested. The factories could not take it earlier. It is not a popular crop to get; Germans are much better on a straightforward job like draining and odd labour takes so much motoring to and fro. Young men seem indignant at being roused at 10am, not but that their fathers are out and about long before. Everyone is tired out with the mud.

How eagerly we turn now to the hope of spring and the lighter days! This morning I was in a cottage; the small children showed no interest in the toys and relics of Christmas but took me out to the trampled garden; a three-year-old said: 'Look at my garden.' She bent double and put her finger on a little green knob that had pushed up above the ground, a hyacinth. The other said, 'It's spring and the bulbs are coming up.' The usual winter birds are about; they have not suffered yet from hard weather. White frosts are frequent, but every few days there is a gale and rain. I have just seen a tree creeper, a bullfinch, a green woodpecker, wrens, tits, robins and a mistle-thrush and of course magpies. I make my usual resolve to have their fine roofed nest removed from the orchard; five young magpies made their debut from it last summer, and so it goes on.

I was confronted by a large and very angry stoat in the barn; the ratcatchers had left a trap under the barley and the stoat had got into it; rather hard luck if he was after rats, but, as it is said, 'he is noways perticler.'

The vicar's owl

December 1947

It has been a wonderfully good autumn for farm work; we are well-advanced and ready for spring planting. Planning food for stock and laying pullets is a great anxiety; everything to an ounce has to be calculated for next year.

The vicar's wife told me a little owl fell down her chimney, and that he was as black as a sweep; she picked him up and he fainted. She fetched brandy and gave him some in a spoon and he revived. She put him out of doors and his mother flew down and collected him. I once picked up a tawny owl after a gale; he was apparently dead, but he came round after some time spent on hot pipes. It is surprising what warmth will do. I have revived many a cold, stiff lamb on the Aga lid, wrapped up in a blanket.

I do not know what to do about Flossie, the sheep dog, now that I am going away again; they tell me she made herself very 'arkard' once before, refusing to eat or speak to anyone. She was very put out at losing the car; they say she rushed out when any motor approached, and when it proved a disappointment, she made it felt.

This and that

May 1948

A strong west wind is forcing a dark cloud steadily in this direction. Field beans already in flower ripple in lines of silver as the wind lifts and exposes the pale under-side of the leaves.

Everything seems restless and uncomfortable, but we need the rain.

A profusion of the delicate lady's smock and cowslips incline one to ignore the lesser stars, though I often think that there is nothing more trim and delightfully fresh than tiny massed daisies on a lawn. What are described as 'lush' meadows of buttercups and hemlock never appealed to me, partly perhaps because it means bad farming.

My Jerseys have produced 13 bull calves; I am not consoled by being told by a lady that she knows a man who had 40 bull calves running; in fact it is alarming.

I have been kept from my desk for two days while books were being cleaned. I cannot but admire the nerve of a lady whose daughter-in-law has just unearthed a case containing over 100 unopened letters – and this before the days of 'forms'.

Students and Poles

September 1949

A tawny tint is spread over grass and stubble – the drought has drained away all colour. Leaves here and there are falling, shrivelled and thin as burnt paper. It is still hot when the almost imperceptible white rippling clouds are not spread over the sun. Clun sheep efface themselves on a shady bankside, and the golden cows lie quiet until they move off slowly to the milking shed.

All the week the Poles have been knocking down fruit, and students from the camp seemed to enjoy picking up and bagging it. A six-ton lorry went off with the load; the ground is so hard it was able to drive around the orchards.

There are virtually no butterflies, but then there are very few flowers and no white clover left. Two very fine Red Admirals visited the sweet split pears; there are usually lots of moths and butterflies on these. Tiny cyclamen have struggled into bloom a month late, and the beautiful soft-glowing Mexican fuchsia has bloomed itself out to the topmost buds.

Snake in the grass

August 1950

I came upon a beautifully marked silvery grass snake; it was three feet long. As it did not slip away, I looked at it carefully and concluded that some foolish person had attempted to kill it. It was damaged just behind its head. I picked it up and decided reluctantly to finish it off, as it would have slowly died. Grass snakes do a lot of good because they live on grubs and insects. It is a pity people are afraid of them, as they are perfectly harmless.

Two young cuckoos were sitting on the telegraph wires, possibly preparing to leave the country. One might easily have taken them for hawks with their speckled plumage. I believe many young cuckoos are shot in mistake for hawks.

I have been taking in honey. The hives are jammed up with it. I am never quite clear about the way bee scouts direct a queen to a residence chosen by them for a swarm. I suppose they close round her and all go along together. Perhaps the method of dancing on the combs is used, which is done when a find of honey has been made and information of its whereabouts is conveyed by the finder to the other bees.

A bounty on squirrels

October 1951

I often see the white owl in the early morning mist, skimming over the grass in search of mice. I fear the big barn is too busy a place for her now, and there are so many good ratting cats.

Grey squirrels are another matter, and seem to have no enemies. I hear that the damage they are doing to young trees in some places is serious. The agricultural committee is offering three cartridges for every squirrel tail, but lack of time is the trouble; farmers have none to spend watching for squirrels and certainly none to traffic in tails. The harmless red squirrel has gone from here; it never seems to survive once the grey one is established.

Bumble bees, at any rate the smaller ones, seem to have a longer working season than honeybees. Possibly the English wild bee is hardier than the Italian bee. A most interesting insect is the bumble bee moth; its appearance mimics that of a bumble bee. It has no sting. Birds seem to know that a bumble bee is to be avoided and they would have to be very clever to distinguish the difference between this moth and a bumble bee. It is possible that seen upside down the rings on a peacock butterfly represent eyes, on a face that would frighten away a bird; there is a moth (foreign) that represents faithfully the eyes and face and colouring of an owl.

Men from the ministry

October 1951

Cider manufacturers are getting anxious now about non-delivery of fruit. It has not been possible to get anyone to pick it up, and more important crops have occupied men who would have had to knock the fruit down. The sacks sent out are full of holes and would have to be mended, and haulage and labour makes it all hardly worthwhile.

Rain holds us up today again but there is plenty of office work. I have just opened 30 communications. Here and there one may get hints from Whitehall, if the Ministry of Agriculture is in the mood, such as a paper composed by two women, which modesty forbids me to read. It is suggestions for 'the control of wild oats'. Another paper remarks that 'in the light of investigation there is no scientific justification either for national measures aimed at reducing appreciably the rook population or for encouraging its increase.' This accords with what is understood to be the Ministry's present attitude to the rook.

The honeybee, I gather, is unlikely to come under control since we are merely informed that 'Honey is the sweet product manufactured by bees which they abstract from the blossoms of many trees and plants.' Control is not suggested so we must grope our way on. The kitten is all for a bit of office work, and is showing great promise; she has just fished out most of the papers I had just put in a big envelope and sorted them on the floor.

Lambs by the stove

March 1952

Snow is now deep. I have read of it being elsewhere for some days before it finally got going here; it arrived on the east wind, which has been blowing for three days. Daffodils have the appearance of poached eggs, and tulips are snowed under; not that this matters, but it is very bad for lambs and they are still arriving. There will be heavy inroads on feeding stuffs.

The shepherd's dog has come in tonight and smiles ingratiatingly from Flossie's basket, so that provision for Floss must be made in the kitchen. Teepy, the kitten, has her usual armchair in the library and some barn cats have inserted themselves in the scullery. In the office is a tray of emergency feeding arrangements for new-born lambs and a box placed in readiness by the stove. The weekend is always difficult for stockmen; someone is always away 'off' and special work has to be replaced in spite of some extra men being got in.

I think a lot of this sheepdog worrying trouble is caused by people not feeding their dogs enough. I know how much cooking of oatmeal and buying of bones and offal is necessary nowadays to keep a working dog and the barn cats. It should be compulsory for dogs to have a collar with the owner's name; a dog that has killed lambs and sheep in this country has now been tracked and shot, but it is not known who owned it.

The character of sheep

March 1953

Sheep are just now the main concern and anyone who looks on them as all alike and just a flock is in a state of comfortable delusion. They are as individual as, and as difficult as, a rest house of old ladies. It is etiquette to keep with the flock, but each ewe has her personal friend – aunt, grandmother or sister – and she does not mix with the rest; each little group holds together. Then there is the nursing stage. One very small ewe lamb with a large brother was about starved out in the sense of the North Country 'starved' which denotes cold as well as hunger, and one foggy, frosty morning I brought her in and revived her with warmth and gave her glucose and brandy and hot water in a teaspoon. She remained for a night by the fire, but unlike most lambs she loathes a bottle. She seems to survive with her mother now. Triplets are doing all right and they, too, fight against any extra help. Then another one of triplets has to manage with a restless, dissatisfied foster-mother ewe. To start with, the ewe had perforce to be tethered in the courtyard grass plot, and when put in the field with others, we had to keep the rope on her for a bit. The tiny lamb ran in and fed the moment it saw one of us put a foot on the rope that kept the ewe stationary – pretty clever for an infant, but there is nothing 'silly' about sheep. They know the time of day and when to come down to be ready to go into the lambing orchard. In the winter an ancient 'ewe' who is still called 'Lamie', (she was once a 'bottle lamb') leads the flock up each afternoon, when she thinks fit, to the hay racks.

Above the floods

December 1954

To live on high ground is something to be thankful for. I looked down from above Four Hopes yesterday from a lane called the Witch's Pitch; it was not a favourite with motorists as there were slabs of rock in steps across it, but one undoubtedly gets a fine view of the river and valley. At present floods have spread over the meadows for miles and give the appearance of a lake. Today it is less stormy and there is even a little watery sunshine now and again. For a week, drying room and kitchen have been loaded with sodden, dripping clothes, as journeys to visit stock meant beating uphill against a north-westerly gale and torrential rain. It is remarkable how the sheep are keeping their good condition.

When there is a batch of lambs in the same field as some older sheep they always keep in a party to themselves. If you wish to find a particular ewe she will not be far from her own near relatives – mothers, aunts or daughters. All are so tame that one ram expects to have his breakfast in bed and does not get up from among the ewes, nor do they move even if you go through their ranks with a torch.

The cats crowd into a huge market basket to sleep when the nights are wet; of course Teepy or Katy or Whitey have their own particular resorts and never feed or mix with the rest. Teepy has always gone to bed on a chest in my room before I arrive up there, Katy remains on a stool in the library and Whitey has the window-sill in the office.

The green of summer

May 1955

We are imperceptibly slipping into the green of summer without having really had a blossom time. I was talking to one of the men who had done everything possible to get a field ready to sow. He said with the admirable patience of the countryman, 'There hasn't been all that rain; just bothersome.' We went on concreting the floor of the wainhouse, having removed the beaten-down soil and used it to fill up ruts in gateways. The mixer grinds on until dark and lorries that have arrived with loads are always having to be towed off by the tractor.

Clun sheep are being got off to the Oxford Show – with all the paraphernalia, including the rams' white linen travelling coats. Indoors there is a constant procession of people; the favourite track is through the library. Katy considers it uninhabitable and has gone off to sleep in a cardboard box, which has a convenient layer of shredded packing paper in it. Teepy has hers in the potting shed half full of sphagnum moss. She had a busy time; I was sticking rows of peas. She hurried to help, holding every stick and indicating little holes and rolling small clods of earth out or into the way. Before I had quite finished one row she evidently thought I ought to have got the idea and could carry on while she had her neglected breakfast and did a bit to her face and hands.

Cider time

November 1956

Milder weather has given a rather belated impetus to the picking up of cider fruit, and some dry leaves have been collected to store apples in. It is lovely in the evening in the fields by the woods; golden cattle move slowly, grazing; dull gold oaks match them in colour and the big grey willow trees seem to melt into the mist as darkness falls. Meg and Betty are out to bring in parties of sheep, and lie watching in corners of a big field. They quiver with excitement, each intent on her job, awaiting a signal to move on her bunch to the wainhouse now dimly lit, where food and shelter await the sheep. Gates are closed on the sheep and the dogs are ready to escort their own suppers from the house to the loose boxes and enjoy a well-earned rest. The barn still has rather the appearance of Noah's Ark; the wooden structure is completed. A visitor who came to lunch had an active time groping and climbing about in the house roof, as his hobby seemed to be the crock trusses – namely a roof truss of two curved pieces of timber or cruck blades, convex side outward and joined at the top to support the ridge piece. There is a good example of this on the north side of this house. I believe the term is akin to 'crutch' or 'crook'. Alas, there are no longer these arches in the big barn. The interior looked like Gothic arches in a church.

It must be a 'mart'

January 1957

There are some animals so rare and shy that few people ever see them and indeed it is often pure luck that eventually brings a glimpse of them. Pine martens are such creatures. I saw them here in the days when they were more plentiful than they are now, and I saw one again in December 1951, but lately my only rewards have been a line of pawmarks, or even one solitary pawmark on a muddy crag below some crags or deep in a fir wood. Sometimes there are droppings on the ledges of the crags or other small signs. Two years ago, one was seen in full daylight on a stone ledge above one of the lakes, and now not far from the place a number of puzzling happenings are being attributed – rightly or wrongly – to a pine marten.

The hens at the farm are shut up in a barn at night, some fields and a beck away from the main buildings, and one morning recently three were found dead and partly eaten inside their barn. The hens went through a trap door which closed behind and left no egress except for a creature very much smaller and more 'lish'* than a hen. So the hunt was fetched and a very small fox was caught – 't'laal varmint' was gone and all would be well – but next morning a large number of hens were dead and the rest terrified. No decent-sized fox, otter or badger could have got at the hens, and local opinion is adamant: it must be a 'mart.'

Enid Wilson

---

* Lish is a Cumbrian dialect word meaning fit or agile.

Planting for the future

November 1958

It is not with the idea of getting any pleasure in my time from them that I have planted a line of young oak trees in the gap left by the uprooting of the enormous elms in a gale. These oaks have outgrown the position they chose to grow in; they are about 20 years old but oaks are never lanky or ugly when young. They seem to merge into their surroundings, unlike evergreens and Wellingtonias, which were named after the Duke of Wellington. Larches are better and have quite nice colouring in autumn and spring.

The young ram Poppet is now called Pop, as he is a married man with many wives. At the moment he is shut in a strip at the back of the sheep pen with some other rams, and he is not in the best of tempers, as they have to be jammed into a cubicle with bales between them, so that they cannot attack each other. If there is enough space to enable them to run at each other, there will be broken necks; they will settle down soon and go out again. The wholesale poisoning of the red-beaked finches* that were devastating corn crops has relieved the danger for the present, but there is some danger in attacking nature; maybe a weed that was kept under by the birds will now take the upper hand. In England our spraying of wheat has recently killed a lot of cows. Poisons and explosions, I feel, may not win the day, and possibly in the end insects will inherit the earth.

---

* McBryde may have been confused here. There is no species called red-beaked finch nor are there any finches in the UK (in the wild) with red beaks although the goldfinch does have a bright red face.

CHAPTER

Five

The Soft Thump of the Iron

Enid Wilson was even more diffident than Janet Case, were that possible. For her first ten years as a Country Diary writer for the *Guardian*, she insisted on having the column's already modest byline of plain initials jumbled so that she appeared as WEJ. Yet she was responsible, when the world eventually beat a path to her Lake District farm in the form of a TV documentary crew, for one of those occasional pieces of deception that even virtuous newspapers such as the *Guardian* accept. For the sake of the programme, a completely fake editorial conference was organised in London, presided over by the then editor, Peter Preston.

As the cameras rolled, Tim Radford, the deputy features editor who was responsible for the 'facing page', the plum spot opposite the leaders and letters where the Country Diary resided, held court in what he hoped the viewers of Border Television would imagine was the style of a senior London journalist. No copy from Washington yet, he said, and the writer of the big political feature still had a few hundred words to sort out. 'But at least we can be sure of Enid Wilson and her Country

Diary; even if she's probably up to her waist in stinging nettles as we speak.'

His performance was convincing enough to take in the *Daily Telegraph's* TV reviewer, who compared the smart and worldly young Londoners with their wholesome Lake District colleague. The programme was a great success. But Wilson typically only took part with great reluctance, and after being persuaded that doing so would be good for the *Guardian* and the Lakes. When the crew assembled at her home between Keswick and Blencathra in April 1986, the weather was filthy, bitterly cold with even colder showers, and an attack of arthritis had stopped her from getting very far to find material for the diary in the previous few weeks. She was bucked up when a letter from Preston arrived, recounting the success of the filming in London. 'They were a nice lot from Border,' he wrote, 'and it was a great pleasure to think that they were pursuing such a worthy subject. I was also pretty touched, when they went round asking questions, to find how many of the individual journalists here are keen followers of your diaries. There were many moving speeches and I felt generally much cheered up.'

Preston referred privately to Wilson as 'the greatest living Englishwoman', and he was not the only admirer of her writing at a senior level in the national media. From the earliest days in 1950, her contributions had been followed with pleasure by her fellow Cumbrian Melvyn Bragg, now Lord Bragg, and by the 1980s a panjandrum in London arts circles. He was the man who persuaded Hodder & Stoughton to publish a selection of Wilson's diaries covering nearly 40 years in 1988, clinching the deal by offering to write the introduction.

This allowed the sceptical publishers to put his famous name on the cover in type only slightly smaller than Wilson's almost unknown one. Within a few months, Wilson's surprised editor at Hodder, Ion Trewin, the former literary editor of the *Times* and today administrator of the Booker prize, found himself preparing for an awards ceremony to honour his demure new author. Recalling how the book won the Lakeland Book of the Year prize in 1989, he struggles to describe her: 'She was, well, just how I expected. She was ... um ... she was an "Enid".'

By which he meant an old-fashioned, polite and quiet woman, surprisingly not a spinster but otherwise resembling a nice elderly aunt. It was an impression that misled many. Fittingly, Enid was not an 'Enid' but an 'Ennid', the Welsh pronunciation that she and those who knew her always used and that points to a far from conventional background.

She was the granddaughter of a Royal Academy artist and the daughter of the celebrated Keswick photographer and rock-climber George Abraham who took her bird-nesting on Sunday mornings when, as she put it, 'everyone else was being proper'. He didn't mind when she ran away from school repeatedly, not because she was unhappy but simply to roam free in the beautiful landscape around the town. Abraham was also a freelance tester of new cars for motor companies such as Morris and Ford, and took Enid and her sister on perilous roads such as the Honister and Wrynose passes before they were in their teens. Their job was partly to be ballast and partly to leap out with a rug to slide under the wheels when George and his co-driver Sandy Irvine, who later disappeared on Everest with Katherine Arnold Foster's friend George Mallory, skidded on the gradients.

Wilson's mother had a BSc from Girton College, Cambridge – Helena Swanwick and Janet Case's *alma mater* – and was a skilled field botanist. Father and mother were a lucky mixture for Wilson, who also adopted Dorothy Wordsworth as a third 'parent' when she discovered her writings at school. As things turned out, she soon became a parent herself, marrying locally and happily not long after leaving school, and devoted herself to bringing up children and looking after their home. Her change of direction only came in 1950 when she was 44, and her children had left home. Over the breakfast table one morning her husband noticed a vacancy among the *Guardian*'s Northern Country Diarists.

'Why don't you do that?' he asked. 'I couldn't do that,' she replied. 'I've never done anything serious in my life.' Mr Wilson said: 'Go on, try.' So off went a couple of trial paragraphs to AP Wadsworth, the *Guardian*'s then editor. 'He replied saying: "Yes, you can have a go," and he put me on probation,' she told Bragg as they worked on her book 37 years later. 'I hope I'm out of probation now, but I don't really know.'

Wilson had always been a *Manchester Guardian* reader. It chimed with her Northern background, and she also had a radical streak from personal experience of the way that 'gentry climbers' in the Lakes cold-shouldered her father and his brother, Ashley. Running a photography business in Keswick meant that they were in trade and also tainted, through several successful illustrated climbing books, with 'exploiting' the manly hobby of conquering crags. Neither was accepted into the Alpine Club although George was finally given honorary membership when social attitudes relaxed before his death in 1969 at the age of 96.

Wilson approached the diary with an ingenuity that she had honed during challenges set by her father, designed to teach his children that they had to work hard to win rewards. His favourite was placing half-a-crown on top of a difficult scramble and then telling Enid that it was there. It took her a long time to learn the useful lesson that ' … no Abraham was going to put that sort of money on top of a rock if there was any danger of anyone getting it easily.' She sought out hidden places and spotted clues – animal tracks, the effect of wind direction on moss – that almost any other passerby would miss. Profiling her in the *Guardian*, which typically failed to review her book because of a muddle during a change of literary editors, her colleague David Bean said: 'Like many of the creatures she writes about, she is not often spotted, tending to move around early in the morning or late at night. Four-thirty am is a good time to catch her – if you know where to look.'

She was also a master of the diary set in a small world. After an illness that led her to miss publication for one of only two times (the other being on the death of her husband), she was confined for a while to her own garden. Initially frustrated, she was soon writing this: 'Once upon a time a girl in a fairy story travelled far in search of happiness, and came home to find it on her own doorstep. The same sort of thing has happened here for, because of a temporary incapacity, I have forsaken the fells for the confines of my own garden and I have learnt much ...' She was very pleased when one of the succession of Country Diary editors during her 38 years, Chris Maclean, showed the same talents. En route to the Lakes, he stopped by a stream, did some dipping and found the carapace of a freshwater shrimp, which he presented to Enid on his arrival.

Wilson's might be considered an uneventful life compared with the vigorous campaigning of Helena Swanwick or Katherine Arnold Foster, or the cheerful bustling-about of Gwen McBryde. But when you read her diaries, you appreciate just how active she was. She wanders everywhere, in all weathers. Time and again, she introduces the column with a gentle sketch of a Lakeland farm, usually at the end of the day, its occupants weary round the kitchen fire, the soft thump of the iron on the shirts and the murmur of TV next door where the children sprawl after finishing homework. In comes the diffident diarist, always welcome, ready to listen quietly and absorb extraordinary amounts of local gossip and lore. Like Jane Austen, sitting demurely in the margins but missing nothing, Wilson has left a small but marvellously detailed picture of a particular society over three decades. Harry Griffin liked to say, in his usual robust fashion, that he marched round the mountain tops while Enid Wilson was responsible for valley life. The eagle and the mouse. But this mouse had sharp eyes.

Evening at the farm

December 1959

Hospitality has always been part of the North, where it springs almost wholly from goodness of heart and owes only a very little to the interest a visitor can bring to a lonely hill farm. I went yesterday unheralded and with nothing to offer to a farm on the slope of Skiddaw. Dusk was thickening and the white ducks half-asleep outside the kitchen door glimmered, more than life-size, and lights shone dimly in the byre. The sons of the farm were already milking but the daughters, on their way to their outside tasks, and the father and mother now almost retired from work, were having a last mug of tea. The oil-lamp was lit in the kitchen and though it left mysterious shadows in the rafters, where bunches of dried herbs and two hams hung just above head height, it glowed on a clutter of farm tackle on the dresser and on the pictures of farm horses on the walls. Almost by magic, it seemed, there was a white cloth on the scrubbed table, and there was home-made bread and tea-cakes thickly spread with farm butter. There were jam and plum cake, shortbread and cherry cake, and a huge apple plate-cake – all homemade too. The tea was hot and sweet – all part of a warm little world shut in from the dark outside.

And what did we talk about? We talked of our children, the absent ones, of parish affairs, of the sleepy adders curled for winter in the peat stacks, and of the boldness of the foxes who bark at night on the fell and try a staring match with the farmer in daylight. I had gone to the farm to buy eggs but who in such a situation could not mix business with pleasure?

Crack by the fire

October 1960

The darkness seems to come down suddenly and very solidly in these late October days; there has been low cloud and mist on the hills and in the valleys for several days. Heavy showers of rain drown the daylight early. Everything was very quiet at the farm this evening after the lamps were lit: the dogs were silent in the barn, wearied no doubt by a long day on the fell collecting sheep; the terrier on the hearth-rug before the fire barely stirred in her sleep and even the fire burned quietly with no wind in the chimney to draw it into life. This silence gave a comfortable air to the conversation, an idle 'crack' full of ruminative pauses and digressions about people and places, but especially about people, for here – where so many are related by blood or marriage, or both – there is plenty to talk about. How would you describe a woman who can never stop talking? Here she is a 'three-ha'penny rattle', a 'bletherskite', or even a 'chitterwallit', but does not really deserve criticism. Criticism is reserved for one who is a 'hard-faced un', 'a proper boilin' bit' (remembering knuckle-ends of ham) whose face 'wad spoil a pick'. How much happier to be labelled 'that nice old-fashint folk', or to be like the man who lives on the other side of Skiddaw. He is dumpy, shiny-apple-cheeked, and smiling and is said to be 'a cheerful laal beggar, he shines like a closet door on a frosty morning.'

*The summit of Haystacks, one of the finest
smaller fells in the Lake District*

Dancing in the barn

June 1961

The floor is being renewed in the big barn. It is quite rotten with age and worn, indeed some of it collapsed in the winter under the hay. This morning each board that came up – broad, long boards, which look as if they had been there for hundreds of years – sent dust flying in the sunlight up to the cobwebbed ceiling and down into the cow-byres and the stalls below. There are small calves in the stalls, seemingly unconcerned with the noise and the new daylight. Their mangers and hayracks and the green slate divisions between them look, too, as if they were very, very old. Often the travelling craftsmen who built these places left their own marks, an initial or a date or both, on their work, but who can explain VIIII for this part of the barn? It has seen lively times as well as workaday ones: 50 years and more ago it was used for dancing: people came from far and near, including two fiddlers. Home-cured hams had been boiled in the sett-pot, supper was laid on the farm kitchen, and coats left upstairs. Calico had been stretched round the lower parts of the barn walls to protect the girls' dresses and everyone was very merry. Indeed, some 'merry' in their own particular way found the little steps down into the haymew very convenient – it was a short, soft tumble down them to sleep it off in the hay.

Hunter in the gloaming

August 1962

Bat-light, owl-light, moth-light – what should one call the first onset of darkness when the fells are no longer visible across the lake and the smell of white jasmine and night-scented stock begins to flow across the garden? Here it is cat-light, too, for it is then that the kitten changes from his daylight self and his real nature comes to the surface.

I did not intend to have a cat, there are too many birds in my garden, but this kitten, an orphan whose owner was forced to part with him and had nowhere else to send him, is fast becoming part of the place. He is still very young, only a few months old. He plays a lot and sleeps a lot, too, as young things must; but at twilight he settles on a boulder outside the door, immobile but alert, paws under chest, surveying his small world. Let a moth or even a daddy-long-legs go by and he is off in a series of stalks, leaps and pounces. He can twist in a jump in mid-air, his body and over-long tail a flying curve, his paws separate and widely spread. When the quarry is caught it is carried back to the boulder or to the step and eaten noisily and with evident relish – indeed one almost expects him to rustle when picked up so full of wings must he be. There are other hunters, too, in the twilight: the bats come early from the eaves, the spiders – one of which is huge, grey, and almost iridescent – wait in their webs in the jasmine and all the time the brown owl hoots softly in the trees below the garden.

Ice and the otters

January 1963

There is no doubt that the otters enjoy snow and ice. It is possible to find slides they have used to play on the river banks where the slope is steep enough to take them down-bank towards the water, but I have never seen them in action. My young cat treats the snow in much the same way and is otter-like in looks – short, sleek coat and over-long tail. He has a variety of snow games. He follows a thrown snowball, which skims the surface of the frozen lawn, at a fast gallop that often ends in a four-pawed skid or on his side sweeping the ice clear of its snow-covering.

The otters have snug homes in the river bank and the cat his fireside but the hares who live on these upland meadows can find little comfort in this bitter weather. I met one last night near midnight in the moonlight and deep snow near the Castle Rigg stone circle. It was searching for food and it looked thin and seemed much slower than hares usually do until it found an opening in the wall where a beck runs out of the field and then it was off over the hill. It looked very big and dark, however, against the moon-shining snow and its shadow ran with it as it went. The ground inside and round the stone circle is criss-crossed with hare tracks and the moonlight showed, too, where the snow was plastered against the stones and cast long blue shadows on the hard ground. It touched the flanks of the encircling hills, Saddleback, Helvellyn and the Derwentwater fells and, far to the east, the long line of the Pennines, as substantial as a silver cloud.

Cubs and cops

September 1964

The farm kitchen is very unlike itself these warm September evenings with the household god of the kitchen fire unlit in the grate. It takes a long time for everyone to come in; the young swallows have stopped twittering under the eaves and the bats are swooping against the red sunset before the farmer settles himself in his corner, shedding his clogs and wriggling his stockinged toes peacefully. It has, he says, been a good year for grass – enough rain, enough sun – but the 'early' taties were a feckless lot. The ground was too cold then. Some young fox cubs (would they, I wonder, be the ones seen learning to hunt by the lake shore a month ago?) have been in one of the hen houses, killing 13 hens and leaving the rest silly with fear. This is the typical senseless killing of cubs learning their job and is bad to bide.

It seems a far cry from fox cubs to village policemen, but evening talk is like that, many-sided. Policemen come and go too much these days and never become part of the valley as old Tom did. Everyone here remembers him – a huge, red-faced man who would surge slowly into the pub at closing time on a Saturday night and say, 'You young lads get off t'dance now,' and, when they had gone, 'You old beggars can stop on a bit.' He would tell the girls after the dance to get their bicycles (lightless) down the road 'before I come out', and such was his standing that even the day his own bike frame collapsed under him, just outside the reading room, no one laughed on the spot – but they still remember, with joy.

A secret stone

June 1965

It is obvious that the good old days were not good for everyone; but there was a sort of contentment in the countryside, which still lingers, and with it a wealth of stories about people and places which, unless someone records them soon, will have gone for ever. The road from Keswick to Grasmere is lined with history, not the sort that left the problematical grave of King Dunmail on the Raise or even the stone on which Wordsworth and his friends scratched their initials, but the everyday, ordinary sort. Now that this road is being widened, the highway authority has several small problems on its hands. They are going to move the Four Mile Stone, which marks the limit of a dissenting minister's approach to Keswick during the time of religious schism, to a new site; but there is another stone quite near it that is almost as interesting and almost unknown. This is the Echo Stone, part of the roadside wall between Yew Crag and Shoulthwaite Moss, where stage coaches and later ordinary coaches used to draw up so that drivers with coach horns could astound their passengers with repetitions of the echo bouncing across the valley. It was all part of the trip. I went there lately on a lovely midsummer morning with a ring ousel calling up beyond Yew Crag. It was useless shouting, the cars shot past with unnerving regularity, but a sharp handclap went back and forth beautifully, scaring a buzzard out of the crag.

Lonely outpost

April 1967

Mosses and mires are not so much part of this district as they are of, say, the Border or the Pennine hills, and today the big moss that lies along the foot of the Skiddaw range looked desolate and colourless in spite of a flash of umber for spring on its birch thickets. There is no white cotton-grass yet to add an ephemeral lightness to the bog, and only the pools, left where peat has been dug, give back the changing colours of the sky. The cold northerly wind has blown for weeks now, inhibiting growth. The wind slices icily round the farm at the edge of the bog, filters in through doors and windows, and creeps across the stone-flagged kitchen floor. Even the big fire of ash logs barely conquers the chill, but at mid-afternoon, with the eggs collected, the hens not yet ready to shut in for the night, and the men out milking in the byres, there is time to talk. 'It is nice,' says the farmer's wife, 'to have someone to crack with.'

The men are 'terribly quiet', and with the telly on in the evening, even the lass home from school must hush. We talked of the bog, poor land and 'sicvey' (rushy) and the home of foxes, two of which lately visited the pullets, doing a lot of damage until the foot-pack came early one morning and picked up the scent by the hen houses. One fox, after a fast run, was bowled over on the fell breast; the second doubled back on its tracks to the bog and lay under the lee of a wall as the dogs, unknowingly, jumped over it – a ruse that might have succeeded had a man not seen it and given a halloo. Hunting is not an end one would wish even a fox, but with those defenceless-looking lambs out on the bog, who would care to say what else could be done?

Old faithfuls

January 1969

Does it surprise anyone that there is only one working horse now living between the Westmorland border of Dunmail Raise and Keswick – and that one, Sandy, works in the Thirlmere forests on 'banks' too steep for tractors? It surprises me. Horses in Cumberland were numerous in proportion to other livestock in the Middle Ages, for tenants were required to keep horses capable of carrying a man (often in armour) to fight the Scots and therefore horses were used on the land here rather than oxen. Some of the farm horses were characters as well as their masters – like the horse who always brought his sleeping master safely home from market. It had, however, learned to stop at all the pubs on the way, much to the chagrin of its other users. Sandy, too, is one of a long succession – Old Tib (who could turn a cart in its own length), Bob and Royal, and Charlie and Billy – but life was hard in the steep woods and on the hilly roads and one should not regret their passing but, rather, pause to read the small stone in the wall on Dunmail Raise. It is dated 1843 and reads: 'Fallen from his fellows' side the steed below is lying, in harness here he died – his only fault was dying.'

A cure for boils

May 1970

There will be no gooseberry or young-rook pies for Whit this year, although both were once peculiar to Whitsuntide here – it is quite an early Whit and a late spring. The gooseberries, well-visited by honey bees, are still only small, and the young rooks are (mostly) just fledged. One wonders how much longer some of the old traditional recipes and cures will survive, but it is astonishing how many do – in a quiet way. An old woman told me when my son was small that he would be difficult to rear; he had an ivy mark (a little blue vein on the bridge of his nose) and she was quite right. She added that it would be wise to bury a jar of cream in the garden ready to dig up and lay on his vaccination mark if it gave trouble. I did not do so, but not so long ago a local doctor said he had come across the same practice in Borrowdale of all places – a sophisticated valley now, if ever there was one. Country children still pick and eat young hawthorn leaves, calling them 'bread and cheese', and an old Westmorland farmer says that there is nothing like young hawthorn leaves and elder shoots as a cure for boils. He, however, calls elder 'bull tree' and it is sometimes 'bour tree', too. It seems that, as a small boy, he was plagued with boils until his schoolmaster told him to gather elder and hawthorn on the way home, get his mother to seethe them and stand them all night, and drink the liquid in the morning. It cured his boils and now, in old age, he is very lively, and he and his brother know a variety of simple cures – comfrey for bruises, figwort to draw 'spells' (thorns), and at this time of the year they make and eat herb pudding – as I do, but because it is delicious as well as 'cleansing'.

Deer in the moss

April 1971

I went up the fell, alone, early one morning this week while the lower spruce wood was still in shadow but the sun was already warm in the higher beech wood, where the thin, grey beech trunks and the warm brown of the fallen beech leaves make a perfect foil for the red deer – but there are no deer to be seen. There were round, flattened beds in the leaves where they had lately lain and deep slots where their hooves had sunk into the leafmould. It was very quiet and there was a sense of being watched. The character of the wood changes as it rises: spruce, alder, beech and high-level stunted larch, but nothing marks the change more than do the mosses and lichens. Liver-worts are in flower near the roadside, polytrichum and tamarisk moss make green cushions in the deciduous woods and higher up the beck (in the black shade of the spruce) alone, three-cornered triads of *Fontinalis antipyretica* hang over the wet boulders. It seems strange to find this moss, usually associated with the deep streams, in such a place – *Fontinalis antipyretica* (as its name implies) was used in Scandinavia (and maybe still is) to fireproof between stone chimneys and wooden roofs and perhaps, too, it was used at Hawkshead in Westmorland. A bill there, among old papers, is 'for re-mossing roof'. The deer had been nibbling the newest juniper shoots near the top of the fell and knocking the grey, woolly hair moss off the scree, but they were still invisible and it was dusk, and another day before I saw them – four hinds, alert and very watchful.

Combing the country

December 1972

One of the books being given this Christmas is about beach-combing and how to identify what you find – but what about country-combing? I have done this for much of my life and though, understandably, time has taken many of my treasures, some remain. They are mostly local, simple, and of little value to anyone except me but they serve as reminders of a time, a place or even, maybe, a person. Their time-span covers hundreds of years. I have, for instance, a large flake of volcanic rock discarded on the south scree at Great Langdale when Neolithic men were roughing out stone axes in that place. I have, too, a grainy piece of pottery from the Roman fort on Hardknott Pass and an undated stone, smooth and palm-fitting, which now serves (on a string) as a door weight. There is a handful of grey and stone-like hazel nuts dredged up by a spring storm from the sunken forest off the south Cumberland coast on a wild day, when the sound of the sea and crying of the nesting gulls wove into the wind's cry. A mixture of discarded birds' feathers – nightjars, short-eared owls, falcons and a varied lot of ducks and small birds' feathers – comes from fells, lakes and sea-marshes. A shed roe-deer tine reminds me of a summer's day in a green yew thicket on the Westmorland limestone but one of the (to me) most treasured things is an ancient jawbone of a badger from a pile of earth outside a local sett – a place where, over a stretch of ten years, I learned almost all I know of the ways of badgers and their cubs.

Leaning on the gate

July 1973

It is seldom that anyone who lives in the country and gardens, or keeps bees, or picks and preserves their own fruit, gets any leisure at this time of the year to stand and stare – to take time, even on the longest day, to be plainly idle. The summer days here are usually over-full and yet, today, for reasons quite beyond my control, there was almost a whole day to watch the hours go by and to see what they had in them. I have, sadly, no hive bees now but there was time to watch other people's bees busy on the white clover on the lawn and on the more ordinary garden flowers (modern roses have no nectar worth speaking about and little pollen). The bumble bees who work so much harder had been out since early light and, in the noonday hours, they were joined by hoverflies and a wandering dragonfly who darted and hovered in the hot sun. There was time, too, to watch the wren feeding her now noisy young in their nest in the dark corner above the side door – she is fearless, singing with loud confidence, and seeing far more of me than I of her. The late afternoon, too, was leisurely and there was time to lean on a gate (a country-dweller's traditional but seldom-used prerogative) and let the smells and sounds of summer soak into a quiet mind. A lonely strip of meadow, deep in grass and flowers, part-marsh and willow-edged, stretches from the gate to a far wood and there was just enough air stirring to bow the grasses but not the willows and to spread the unforgettable scents of ripening grass and burgeoning meadowsweet and alien – and yet not – the tang of a distant sheep dip.

Gaustering chitterwallits

November 1974

Farmers are sometimes taken as pessimists, complainers, a label most Cumbrians (including me) would reject – especially in the Lake District. After all, sheep-farming on the high fells is the staple here and mountain weather and sheep make a man a philosopher – or nothing. However, this year gives real cause for complaint. Seldom have the fells been more sodden, grass so poor, and prices and prospects are grim, too. Sheep at Troutbeck sales that last year fetched about the £12 mark are, this year, barely above £3, and a long and chancy winter lies ahead. But all is not gloom, cheerfulness breaks in, even 'on a dull November day like this with mist and cloud low on Helvellyn and the moor – seen from the farm kitchen window – made sombre brown and purple with rain and dusk. The wood fire crackles and flames in the grate, there is a warm smell of ironing in the air and the soft thump of the iron (even if 12 sheets await a better washing day) makes a descant to the voices. Apples, unlike grass and hay, are plentiful this year and must be stored outdoors in a hog (a clamp) lined with straw. Recipes for sweet pies made with mutton, fruit and brandy – robust forerunners to the present-day mince pies – are discussed but, as so often, the talk turns to families and friends. These are not always one and the same. Some are remembered with wry amusement like the farm wife who is a 'chitterwallit' (an aimless talker) or another who goes gaustering on (laughing needlessly) or with affection, like kindly Mary who always means well but who, however, does not always 'flee when she flaps her wings'.

The badgers build

March 1975

One of the most cheerful sights in early March is the liveliness in and around the badger setts. The badgers are hard at it now – cleaning out, re-digging, and in some places dragging clean grass bedding. There will be cubs soon but no one will see them until, say, mid-April. The setts I visited this morning are sheltered from the easterly wind and the sun lights them quite early, so as I went down the muddy track I could see the outline of huge heaps of new earth against the misty blue fells and the bright sky. This is steep and shaly ground but old oaks hold the banking steady and the badgers make use of the roots. There must be many unseen, underground roots for roofs and supports and two of the holes have stout oak porches and lintels. One even has a stone- and oak-slabbed side. The warm, pleasant smell of badger hung about the place but, naturally, there was not an animal to be seen. It was easy to see, however, where the night had sent them – digging out a grub-riddled stump, working on a new hole and bulldozering through the blackthorns. The badger latrines are up the fell in the edge of a spinney and one row is set almost communally on a tree root – reminiscent of a row of wooden-seated earth-closets that once adorned an outhouse at Seathwaite in Borrowdale, only perhaps the badgers' ones are neater. There were splodgy fooprints on the path down the fell, both inward and homeward bound. The outward looked leisurely but the homeward had hurried, perhaps run, pushing pad and paw marks deep into the mire.

Rhubarb and eggshells

November 1976

A wild-goose chase often has rewards quite unrelated to its original goal. This happened lately when a rare flower was reported near Penrith, and even though the message sounded improbable it seemed as well to go and look. It was a damp afternoon with cloud low on the ridges of Blencathra, and shot through with stray sunlight, which turned the wet rocks to silver and the dead bracken to fire. The plant (as expected) was a comparatively common garden one but the rest of the afternoon made the cause well worthwhile. There was a remnant of warmth in the sun and more than a remnant of colour left in the village gardens in spite of rain and gale, and there was time, too, to lean up on a low wall on the way home and admire the thicket of sprouts, the ranks of leeks and their edgings of marigolds. My sprouts this year have suffered with cabbage fly, so the owner of the garden told me to stick lengths of rhubarb below each small sprout next year on planting. Her friend said his potatoes had been riddled with small black slugs – the sort you seldom see except in potatoes – so I offered my time-tried habit of crushed eggshells, thickly strewn under the potato seed. There was a lot else to talk about too. It seems that a woman down the village is plagued with arthritis and though she may not have a cure at least she has an alleviation – willow (salix) leaves. She gathers them before they get too tough, dries and crumbles them to eat, year long, sandwiched between bread and butter. And what do they taste of? 'Nowt,' I was told, 'except if they speak back – then they taste of kippers.' Well, if they help arthritis, and kippers stay the price they are, a lot of us will be heading for the willow groves and, after all, willows and aspirin have the same chemical in common – salicylic acid.

Exploring a bridge

September 1977

The lately controversial bridge that carries the A66 over the gorge of the river Greta, east of Keswick, is not noticeable if you drive across it. It is better to walk over, for it gives a clear view of the western fells. Better still, try walking under it. The bridge has its own stark beauty, seen from below, with its rather flat, springing arches carried on tall slightly fluted columns, which play games with light and shade. It is new-looking at present but time, of course, will alter that just as it has altered this narrow valley. It is quiet now but once it must have been a bustling place and while one must salute the men who built the bridge, one should never forget the men who, about 1567, drove the still-existent tunnel through the solid rock beyond and almost below the bridge on the south side of the river. It was done the hard way to carry the water for the furnace bellows and stamp-houses at Brigham where the ore (mined in Newlands beyond Derwentwater and ferried across the lake) was smelted. The industry went on until the civil war, when it was destroyed but even then the water was used at The Forge for a variety of small mills, forges and works until a few years ago. All the sounds were soothing, down by the river, this evening – the rush of water over the rocks, the near-constant sound of traffic overhead, and the whistle and splash of a pair of mallard settling for the night in a backwater. The water is gathered to the tunnel by a long curved weir whose timber top is still securely bolted to its stone base even though runs of water fall through it over curtains of green moss to nourish a wealth of rosebay willow herb, orange and yellow mimulus, and tall reeds. The sluice for the tunnel is permanently closed now but water gets through – deep and dark it lies almost up to the tunnel roof – and I wished as I walked along the green path alongside its hidden length that it could be drained – just once – to see what it is really like inside and how the old men who made it and who still seem to haunt the place had gone about their work so long ago.

Tracks and trods

February 1979

January was the sunniest month since September, and there have been many clear, sunny days in February, but very cold ones, so it will be a long time before the snowdrifts go from the higher land where they have been driven against walls and into gullies and hollows by the wind. The tops look Himalayan rather than Cumbrian. The moor and the rocks are clear of snow, dun-coloured in the sharp light, but the drifts point up all sorts of shapes and oddities, almost unnoticed in greener months. If you look, for instance, across the valley from the A66 to the wide expanse of land that girdles the end of the Helvellyn range – Wanthwaite End and Wolf Crag – you see a multiplicity of patterns, white on brown. Sheepfolds are circles of white; one big enclosure edged with green rushes in summer is easier to see now, and the old road over to Matterdale glitters icily in the sun. Tracks and sheep-trods lead up to them from the valley. But it is in moonlight that the mountains and high land come into their own. The moon was up tonight before the sunset was gone – silver in the east, gold in the west with ice-blue clarity above Scafell. The light died quickly from the ridge of Castle Rigg stone circle and though a dense bank of cloud shut off the Pennines it never rose to the face of the moon, which sailed serenely up with a star beside. The stones were starkly black against the grass and the blown snow – there may be theories as to what this place was, but now is its time, with not a bird or a beast stirring, only the Valkyrie whistle of the east wind through the thorn and the wire fences – and all one's clothes.

A fan of bats

June 1980

A weaving pattern of bats has been flying here against a clear, sunset sky. I wish I knew more about their ways, but a nationwide bat survey is going on – so there is hope. There have been bats over this garden for at least 30 years in fairly consistent numbers (except, perhaps, after hard winters) but, sadly, none in my roof. They used to come and go from the gabled end of the next house and then, for no obvious reason, moved to another house. One of their first landlords disliked them and called the pest officer, who firmly said they were a protected species, but the second one accepts them happily – after all, he once walked ankle-deep and shoeless in dried bat dung in a deserted Indian mosque, and did not find that objectionable. We usually see them first in April or early May, hunting zealously even on cold nights, and then they disappear for at least a month. This April there were pipistrelles as usual and one much larger, which kept apart –was it a Daubenton's bat? Now, as last June, there are between eight and a dozen; are these new families? A city cat spent last summer here and he and the bats seemed to have a mutual fascination. He was a dark tabby, but when he sat on the lawn in the dusk the bats swooped down and round his head so that he flicked it up to show his shining white bib. Did it attract them as pale moths do? My sister and I, as little girls, were told that bats came to white things, so we waited in the dusk in white pinafores and self-induced shivers, for it was also said that if a bat tangled in your hair, you became blind. They nearly touched our heads, but never quite. There seem to have been fewer moths these last years but last night, in a damp and misty half-dark, the air under the trees was alive with their soft flight – good for the bats – and good to see so many again.

No good for plovers

April 1981

There are some farms it is impossible to go past without stopping for a crack – and who would want to? The farmer had just given extra feed to his lambing ewes as I went past the field gate this chill, sunny morning. The lambs have come quickly this last week and they and their mothers look in good fettle. One ewe, with twins born during the night, was easy in a small stone hut where the warm sun shone in; but the orchard corner opposite had a more unusual sight, a rough-faced ewe with four very small lambs a few days old. They are still tottery but 'furnishing' (filling out) and unless cold rain comes should do well. The damson blossom, which overhung them, is still in bloom, things are late on the fell-end. But I had really come with a piece of horse furniture that has been on a high shelf for years. It is a stout, buckled strap of thick leather with a brass plate flanked by a heart and a shield. The farmer says he thinks it's a bit long for a 'martin', 'martindale' to him, a martingale to others. It is more like a 'yam': this is a hame, part of a draught horse's collar with hooks to take chains for dragging timber, a harrow or whatever is needed. We both belong to a generation for whom draught horses were part of life and, as we talked, a tractor took a roller over the growing grass in the next field. No good for plovers, he said, remembering the horses who gave man time to shift nests or young to the field side. He had one bit of good news to add – last year, and this, there were and are many more curlew nesting on the marshy lands below the farm well out of harm's way.

Mysterious terraces

October 1982

It gets more difficult as the years go by to see what the face of the land, of the lower fells, was like in times past. Land goes into different use and farm buildings fall, leaving only some slight indication of their existence – say, columbines on an empty moor or a morello cherry tree in a wall corner on Helvellyn's side. I sat this morning on a slab of Skiddaw slate high up in one of its ghylls, with the bracken turning to bronze and the sun drawing the mist up from the fields. Thirty years ago this place showed from the valley as a series of deeply terraced fields in a green oblong below the heather. The terraces have always been a puzzle. It is said that they were brought into cultivation in the corn shortage of the Napoleonic wars. Certainly, 'tatie haver' – many-headed oats used for haver bread – was grown at much the same height on Whinlatter Pass across the valley. The outline of the farm is still here – piles of Skiddaw stone from its walls, Borrowdale slates from its roof, and a fine Borrowdale gatepost lie in the rushes and nettles. The terraces are being swallowed by the bracken, but what turf remains is some of the finest on the fell, starred in summer with heartsease and now with the frilled faces of eyebright. A month ago there were mushrooms too. Two tall elms stand above the gatepost and, at the foot of one, an owl's feather stirs gently. So the place is not wholly deserted.

Nightwalking

July 1983

It seems foolish these nights to waste time by coming home to bed – so many lost and unreturning hours while the summer half-light and the moonlight, together, fade towards dawn. The day's heat often draws moisture from the land and, after sunset, it lies along the high narrow valley and its beck, softening every contour and filling every hollow. The white May blossom on the isolated fellside thorns floats like snow above the mist and the muted green of the fields. There were, last night, few sounds by the beck – only the run of the water, the crying of a curlew disturbed at its nest and the champ and snort of grazing cattle. They walk out into midstream to eat the water dropwort, a plant highly poisonous to man. There is probably a new badger home on the sloping river bank, half-hidden in nettles; for nettles mark badger occupation just as surely as they do old human use. The sett is, however, as well-guarded as any royal residence, not by the police, nor the military nor even a menacing landowner but by a large herd of inquisitive and gieversome (playful) cows. They are only too happy to join in whatever is going on but while I like cows (who does not, within reason?) they are no help at all in badger-watching. So that sett is written off. The next valley on the way home, edged with pale elderflowers and wild roses, seemed more promising, it had no mist and no cows – not even sheep – and only trout, jumping clear of the small pools to fall back with a gentle plop, broke the silence.

A drowsy day

August 1984

A sprained ankle is of little use to a Country Diarist – down off the fells, not driving a car, but at least it is a good time to be idle with soft fruit over, apples unripe and time to look at things that might normally get overlooked. There is a feeling of autumn in the air and a freshness lost since early summer. Many days begin with silent mist blotting out all but the nearest trees. The early sun is only a silver orb in the mist, its light catches in the dewed cobwebs in the grass and it was on such a morning lately that a fox-coloured, white-patterned spider drifted her line from the yellow clematis to a column of cypresses across the path. The outline of the web was finished and now she was working from the hub outwards making her perfect cobweb pattern. Her feet are slightly oily so she moved neatly, attaching each thread to its line with a dab from her rear before reaching for the next. It was mid-morning before the web was complete and by mid-afternoon all but the frame of it was gone and the spider quiescent on the cypress. So I moved with the sun to a baulk of timber between golden rod and buddleia, between hoverflies and butterflies. The female butterflies, slightly darker and stockier than the males, fed assiduously on the golden flowers unruffled by the males who paused abruptly in rapid flight and mated with no time wasted. Theirs seemed the only action in this hot and scented garden, where even the butterflies drowsed.

The lost domain

May 1985

It is possible to live in these fells for a lifetime thinking that you know every hill and fold of land, each barn and farm, even in ruins, and be proved wrong. I came on a small, ruinous house on a shining May morning. It was tacked on to, and concealed by a newer, sounder barn whose three doors stood open showing cobbled, stone floors and ancient muck. The roof and the first floor were mainly fallen, but to judge by what remains this was no ordinary house. Its four, small south-facing windows are eyeless now but have good stone mullions, and there is nothing to stop shafts of sunlight falling into what was once the kitchen and picking out the dark cavity of a bread oven heated with wood or peat before the baking could begin. Its round back juts out from the outer wall. A cramped dairy pantry faces north and has stumps of beams – which have held shelves – above a cooling slab whose stone pillars remain. A massive stone staircase spirals up nearby, rounded into the north wall leading now only into space and its stone steps lean drunkenly. No one will climb it again. Some places even in age and ruin keep their feeling of past peace and contentment, as this one does. Swallows are back in its eaves, sheep and lambs rest in its garth under old ash trees. Its spring still runs green under cresses.

The face of time

June 1987

Someone said to me recently, talking of a long-dead friend, 'She always had time,' meaning time for other people, for their joys and sorrows. I thought of her lately on a rare, sunny July morning when I went slowly down the valley of the river Derwent enjoying the tall spotted orchids, the red ragged robin and the blue field geranium along a side road, when I met a small procession. First, well ahead came a watchful sheepdog, then a fine black and white cow grazing along with a wobbly-legged calf at its side, and last of all, the farmer, barely moving. They were taking their time and I had come to look at another face of time in the hollow where the church of Isel sleeps in its now green and flowery graveyard. The sun was hot on its south wall, picking out each patch of lichen – grey-white, yellow and orange – and sharpening up the lines of the three sandstone faces of 'mass tiles' (sundials) grouped beside a window about eight feet from the present ground level. All are old and weathered, the sandstone set on slate, and each has a centre hole from which the lines for the hours radiate. Only one has 24 (and a north indicator), the next marks the hours from 9am to 3pm while a third has only four lines. They were set here in 1876 but are of pre-clock time and are still called mass tiles locally because a bent twig, stuck in the centre hole, could tell, simply, the hour of the next mass. That day the grasshoppers sang, too, to tell the sunny hours.

Six

Roaming the North

Veronica Heath is the doyenne of today's female writers of the Country Diary and the only person in the column's history to have inherited the job. She roams the hills and coast of Northumberland in the footsteps of her father, Harry Tegner, a Newcastle upon Tyne businessman who became one of the best-known naturalists in north-east England and an international authority on deer. He wrote more than 40 books, although just one of them makes a useful summary: *Beasts of the North Country: from Whales to Shrews.*

Veronica works in Harry's former study at Seven Stars cottage in Whalton village, a line of mellow stone buildings off the road from Newcastle to Jedburgh, with a pub at one end and a manor house adapted by Edwin Lutyens at the other. The cottage is more the size of a rectory and was once Whalton's second pub; apart from its name, a last trace is an enamel Guinness Is Good for You sign blocking a pothole in the drive. The view sweeps up towards the Cheviots at the front and the coastal plain to the back. 'Good hunting country,' says Heath over tea and home-made cake beneath portraits of her and her brother as wide-eyed country kids. 'You don't mind me saying that, do you? You being from the *Guardian*?'

Hunting and the knowledge of nature that its followers acquire does have a place in the Country Diary's history, almost as venerable as that of the protesting 'antis'. In the 1920s, the great otter expert and fly fisherman George Muller saw off a concerted campaign to dismiss him from the Country Diary by readers opposed to blood sports. But he lost a separate column solely about hunting and with it a guinea a week, as he never ceased to remind Quaker friends whose national society had lobbied CP Scott to sack him.

The strong feelings work both ways, and Heath sometimes opts for tactful vagueness when she is out gathering material and hunting friends ask her where her work will be published. Luckily she also has a choice of answers. Over 80 now, she remains a regular contributor to the *Northumbrian, Countryside Matters* and other journals. She walks, reads, watches and (for her *Northumbrian* column) cooks a new Geordie speciality every month to keep up this freelance portfolio.

She first showed the necessary initiative and energy seven decades ago when – after watching her father typing away at the study table – she wrote an article on How to Catch Your Pony and sent it to the *Field*. It earned her two guineas, useful at the age of 15, and launched the pseudonym that she still uses, instead of her married name of Blackett. Tegner was a byline already familiar in countryside magazines from pieces by her father, who suggested she adopt her first two names. Thus was born Veronica Heath.

She was never short of material. When you meet her striding round Whalton, often in her trademark cherry pink, it is easy to picture a childhood constantly out-of-doors with her father as an expert guide. 'We spent every single holiday stalking deer,' she remembers enthusiastically, 'or getting up with Dad very early in the morning to go cubbing. Have you ever been cubbing?' She is a writer who wants to share the excitement she gets from the grand Northumberland landscape and the life – from whales to shrews but taking in plants and people as well – that flourishes within it.

She was able to do that with her own family – four children, two horses and plenty of dogs. They grew up in an atmosphere familiar to anyone raised on the spate of books after the second world war that despatched jolly children into the countryside with an assortment of knowledgeable uncles. Perhaps the books seem rather innocent today, but they banished entirely the exclusion of women that had dogged so many earlier generations. Ethel Walter's *Yours Adventurously*, published in 1956, sees a boy called John accompanied on his rambles by his sister Betty, 'with her long fair plaits streaming behind'. *The Young Bird Watchers*, an extremely informative book couched as 'a rattling good story for young people' in 1948, has 12-year-old Michael initially sulky that his convalescence in the country was to be joined by a girl. But she turns out to be a tomboy called Chips, an ace bird-spotter, who gets into 'frequent trouble over torn frocks and the tousled state of a very unruly mop of golden curls'.

Most influential of all were John, Janet and Pat Thomson, who are taken for two walks a month by Uncle Merry in Enid

Blyton's 1944 *Nature Lover's Book,* and the 'two happy children' Richard and Susan Rennie in the companion *Animal Lover's Book* published eight years later. Both are lasting arguments against the teenage lament that there is nothing to do in the country. They also set a high cultural standard. The Rennies read Edward Thomas' atmospheric poem *Out in the Dark*:

And I and star and wind and deer
Are in the dark together, – near,
Yet far, – and fear
Drums on my ear …

This was relevant reading in the household at Whalton, where Heath published her first books when the children were young, using her daughters to illustrate guides to riding, training gundogs and keeping ponies. She had to get up at 5am to fit in two hours of writing before the non-stop demands of a house full of children began. It was useful training for the day in 1977 when Harry Tegner decided that he could no longer range about enough to keep his Country Diaries going.

'He was worried that he was failing and he asked me how I felt about having a try,' says Heath. 'Then he wrote to Peter Preston [the then editor] and asked: could my daughter take over? He got a letter back saying: get her to send one in. I did and heard not a word, but I have carried on ever since.'

Such dynastic exchanges had been commonplace in society both generally and specifically at the *Manchester Guardian*, where the editors had all come from one extended family from the newspaper's foundation in 1821 to the death of Ted Scott when his yacht capsized on Windermere in 1932. Very soon after Heath's succession, almost all appointments to the paper were to become openly competitive. Her unique status is safe, probably for ever.

But the seamless handover was valued by readers, because Northumberland is such a magnificent county and both Tegner and Heath have covered it so comprehensively. Their diaries range from pit ponies caught like ghosts in car headlights at night as they cross the road between mineshafts, to strange fish washed ashore (the coast with its castles and golden sand was a favourite walk of father and daughter), the white cattle of Chillingham and the Roman wall. 'I love my county and like to feel it under my feet,' says Heath who, like Tegner, enjoys testing London subeditors with phrases such as 'checking the rabbit smoots and hogg holes in the dykes' (deliberate gaps for sheep, rabbits and hares in Northumbrian drystone walls). 'Turning into my parent may seem alarming but in my case it has been more or less unavoidable.'

Her children, one a journalist, another a factor (Scottish land agent), are regular visitors who help to keep her up to date with natural history. So do her 13 grandchildren and the school in Whalton village, which recently lost its shop but is still a thriving community. In the summer, you may spot an outing of under-tens marching along Hadrian's Wall in Roman costume. Staunchly wearing her own, adult legionnaire's helmet, Heath joins such parties. She goes to the WI, the Mothers' Union and the beautiful old parish church. Seven Stars has hosted the village fete. It is a joined-up, country world and its characters duly appear in the diary.

This gets posted by hand, always by Heath in person, religiously every Monday at the nearest post office, three miles away in Belsay, extra payment for next-day delivery. 'I've tried with a computer but it doesn't work for me,' she says (although she is up to giving website references in the occasional diary). 'I think in longhand and then for the *Guardian* I type it out.' A Harry Griffin, whose 53 years on the diary set a probably unbeatable record, always did the same, down to his last entry, published on the day of his death in 2003, aged 93. He felt that the process was closer than email to the pace of country life.

Invading bats

July 1989

We are looking at the remains of a long-eared bat's supper in the stables at Belsay Hall: a discarded heap of moths' wings below a rafter, an astonishing amount it is, too, for one small mammal's meal. This species of bat prefers to catch its supper and take it to a feeding perch to consume, unlike the noctule and pipistrelle bats, which catch and eat insects on the wing. As dusk falls we walk down to the lake below the hall through the lovely gardens now being restored to former glory by English Heritage. Ash trees line the old cart track and provide roosting sites for a noctule bat colony. These literally fight for position here, in open conflict with the greater spotted woodpeckers, apparently the latter most often seem to win. Rose bay willowherb, hemlock and cow parsley shroud the path to shoulder height. Cries of excitement as a single bat swoops overhead and disdainfully disappears again. This lake offers perfect feeding for the resident bat colonies but, like most wildlife, when a sortie is organised to watch them, they fail to oblige and are conspicuous by absence. Back to bed, and at dawn a phone call from our new neighbour, the canon in the rectory over our garden wall. 'Can you tell us anyone who could advise on invading bats?' Apparently, not content with roosting under the eaves of the house, one bat had had the temerity to slumber on the pillow in the bedroom. Several have become so partial to entering the room that when the window is closed they beat on the window panes. 'It sounds rather like Dracula,' remarked the canon's wife stoically. Delegates from the county bat group have visited and report a nursery wing for 200 pipistrelle bats. These will disappear and hibernate elsewhere but are likely to return. It seems boxes put up on buildings do not tempt bats at all but they will use boxes when they are constructed on trees.

Tidying the Tyne

January 1990

The north-east has always been renowned for its landscape gardeners and the lovely walled and woodland vistas that they created. Standing on the 200-acre site of the National Garden Festival at Gateshead, you can see a new dawn rising among the skeletal Dunston coal staithes built in 1890 and the scars left by the decline of our great ship-building and mining industries. 'The region is going back to its roots,' remarked a redundant colliery employee. Tidying up the Tyne has already resulted in recreational parks, meadows for cattle to graze on and salmon spawning again in the upper reaches of the river, but I was unprepared for the transformation taking place in the Team valley on the recently derelict site of redundant gas, tar and coke works. The Northumberland Wildlife Trust are showing how an opencast coal site can be made into a wildflower meadow complete with pond and wildlife on a half-acre site at the festival, and the habitat looked well established. More than 1,000 bluebells and native wildflowers have been planted and a fen area already hosts lady's smock, ragged robin and wet meadow plants. 'Tussock sedge usually takes many years to establish,' said Francis Rowe from the NWT. 'But it has established here and seems happy among the flotsam we brought from Druridge Bay.' Contorted tree trunks, branches and stumps black with hundreds of years of salt sea washing, have been plonked among the sedges. A pond with a central island is already stocked with dragonflies, fish and amphibians. Ducks will be brought in to join the pair of mallard that have already nested on the site. A surfeit of water voles at Slimbridge has released a pair for this conservation corner at the festival. 'We have a place ready in Newcastle where they can acclimatise,' said Francis. 'They should take easily to this habitat and we hope they will breed.' Next door I could see mature alder, oak and birch trees on the blossoming British Trust for Conservation site and heard that these trees had all been transplanted successfully from doomed sites. 'Come to see us when the Festival opens in May,' said their spokesman. 'Then you can learn how to cleave an ash pole, bodge a chair leg or try your hand at willow piling.' I shall look forward to doing so.

The wild, romantic Cheviot hills in Northumberland

Silver darlings

July 1991

The aroma of smouldering oak chips hangs heavily over the cove of Craster and a queue of connoisseurs is forming outside the fish shop. It is kipper time. Only the choicest herring are brought for this delicacy, locally recognised as the miners' high tea. The fishwives were busy, hanging the fish on tenterhooks after they had been gutted and soaked in a tank of brine to cure. The smoking shed bustles with activity and a woman in a long rubber apron carries a cran of golden kippers into the shop. 'I reek when I gan home,' she said cheerfully. Even in midsummer the supply of fish is controlled by the weather and with generations of experience behind them fishermen on this coast take no chances. When the fleet brings in a shoal of 'silver darlings' the yard will be at work 24 hours a day. Frozen fish are not suitable for kippering, they must be fresh or the oil content is destroyed and the fish shrivel up in the shed. The flesh of a good kipper should lift off cleanly without any bones adhering to it, and then you will know if it has been cooked correctly. Baked in the oven, or grilled, never fried. The succulent taste of a Craster kipper is an annual treat, and according to the woman who served us, the kippers have health-giving properties too. After a picnic in the shadow of Dunstanburgh Castle, with the tide out we walked the rock-strewn beach line dodging sanderlings, rock-pipits, oystercatchers and a turnstone. Both kittiwake and fulmar frequent this stretch of the coast for breeding but these oceanic species spend the rest of the year out at sea. The fulmar is not a gull, but a tubenose or petrel. An intriguing pelagic bird that must be one of the world's natural gliding experts.

Edge of empire

October 1992

Belting my coat up and pulling my hat down, I followed my grandson around the remains of the Roman fort at Housesteads. The stones tend to be sunk in the ground so it is easy to miss some of them but he went from one heap to another reading that one enclosure was the west gate, another the north gate and so on. He had arrived to stay with one of the National Trust's Living in the Past children's books. This one was Julius Lupus and the Raiders. James is pre-school age, but the book with colourful illustrations and a short text had caught his imagination. It told the story of a Roman soldier in Housesteads Fort and how he helped to guard his empire at the edge of the world. When we were children the wall seemed boring, but the National Trust has brought the stones alive for a new generation. We spent the next hour scrambling along the crest of the cliffs and crags, sometimes looking down sheer 100-feet drops on the northern face. We could see the crags and tree-covered ridges of the Whin Sill stretching invitingly ahead, flowing up and down, onwards into the distance. We slithered down a series of steep steps, locally called the Cat Stairs. The howling wind dropped and the sun came out: typical Northumberland weather. At the end of an exhilarating day we had tea in a pub that was once a popular overnight stop for carriers carting goods between Newcastle and Carlisle.

Jumps in the snow

December 1993

A week shrouded in snow has been such a joy. The dogs have had to walk to heel, so that they do not obliterate the tracks of wild birds and beasts. I have been surprised at how many foxes we still have around the village. When a fox walks, his tracks in snow show that the hind feet cover the forefeet imprints. I could clearly see the trail left by Charlie's brush too, as he tracked hedgerows and followed the sheep trods. When foxes are mating you can see the tracks of the dog fox and vixen running side by side. A dog fox may fight for a vixen and the signs of a struggle are quite clear in the snow. Stoats and weasels, with long bodies and short legs, always jump in snow so the trail shows pairs of footprints almost side by side. A stoat's jump is longer than a weasel and one I measured was more than 30 inches. Squirrels also jump, the forefeet tracks being side by side, the toes pointing inwards. In Codlaw wood I found evidence of squirrels, tracks in the snow and the remains of fir cones lying under the trees. The reds don't seem to like acorns, although the greys do. I sat very still and watched two squirrels feeding on hawthorn berries and could clearly hear them tutting and cracking stones. Pheasants are great wanderers. Game birds seem to walk and run whereas our garden birds run or hop. Songbirds mostly hop, but I see thrush and blackbirds moving on our lawn in short runs. The coots on Bolam lake's frozen surface provided a pantomime. Some children were throwing them scraps, the birds hurried towards the food but found that walking on ice is more difficult than swimming in water. First one foot shot out sideways, then the other or both feet shot out at the same time and the coots – there were ducks in on this cabaret too – landed on their stomachs. When they did reach the food and stretched beaks to snap it up, it shot away across the ice. Persevering, they slithered in pursuit. It was rather like an avian game of ice hockey, with the contestants intercepting one another trying to gain the prize for themselves.

The squirrel's warning

March 1997

Over the years, we have occasionally seen twin fawns with a roe doe in woodland around here. Many does do conceive and actually bear twins but natural wastage means that usually one dies, or is taken by a predator immediately after birth. A local forester saw triplet fawns this month in a wood two miles from this village. Born last spring, they would now be ten months old, three little bucks and all survivors, a phenomenon undoubtedly due to increased rich feeding on rape and winter wheat, which roe deer poach.

Binoculars around our necks, stick in hand and labradors at heel, we set out for the wood after tea (leaving the dachshund in the kitchen). In April, a doe will drive off her yearling buck prior to dropping new offspring – they must establish territory for themselves – so we were not optimistic of a sighting. Deer never consort with stock in winter months; they tend to gang up in small family groups and in hard weather trespass on seeds and root crops. Hidden in the wood, hoping for a sighting of the deer, there were other delights to enjoy. A red squirrel, with bushy orange tail and tufts from his ears, took a startled leap, with limbs flung out horizontally, on to an adjacent branch, where he sat uneasily at a safe distance, scolding and tutting.

Watching the squirrel, I became aware of a white rump patch moving in bracken. We each put a hand on the dogs, hardly daring to breath, and then a roe doe walked right out below us, undisturbed by the squirrel's warning and oblivious of our presence. And behind her, still together, were the triplets, skipping, head-butting and jousting with one another. By now, it was almost dark. Having slept in undergrowth all day, they had just roused for an evening's browse. Having watched wild deer since childhood, that was a thrill I know that I will not see again.

Lore of the flies

September 1999

Dead flies on our window ledges are harbingers of warm days. Our pasture adjoining the garden is rich in cow dung and edged with cow parsley. A quality cowpat is a thing of beauty to flies and bluebottles, dungflies lay eggs in them – a fly's social life revolves around manure. Male flies hang around cowpats, which is where many of them do their courting, their frantic, fidgety hovering and dodging tell the observant fly-watcher that they are on the lookout for a mate. When a female materialises, the cowpat is soon covered by tumbling knots of ecstatic, buzzing flies. Fortunately, most of the maggots laid are gobbled up by other, more attractive field residents or we should be knee-deep in them. Cow parsley is popular with danceflies. The name comes from the distinctive aerial manoeuvres employed to attract a mate: swarms of males zig-zag in hedgerows, over wildflowers and particularly slimy ponds.

One evening I watched a vixen in our field performing what appeared to be a tribal dance – she crouched and pounced and leapt into the air. She was hunting and eating crane flies, which were hatching from leather-jackets, and nosing out other juicy insects like grubs and beetles, breeding under the cowpats and horse dung. A fly's wings are without scales and generally hairless: the buzzing sound is produced by rapid vibration of the wings in flight, up to 600 beats a second. The feet have minute sucker-like hairs with which they can walk upside down. A farmer told me common flies dislike blue light and the application of a blued limewash to cowsheds used to be a means of discouraging them, although it did not actually keep a building fly-free. Horse flies give painful stings; we use a paste of sodium bicarbonate and a little water to alleviate itching. Our grandson came to us after a holiday in Scotland. He found 217 midge bites so I made up a solution of boracic acid powder and doused the itchy extremities. Next day he was whacking cricket balls into my herbaceous border so it seemed to have done the trick.

The monster leeks

September 2000

The Romans introduced the leek to the north-east, where soldiers patrolling Hadrian's Wall must have been glad of the vegetables' sustenance during harsh winters. Leeks provided vitamin C, which prevented scurvy. Today, doctors, teachers, redundant miners, butchers and the retired, succumb to *allium proam* 'exhibition', which means growing pot leeks to gargantuan proportion. In early January the monsters start and they reach the show bench in September. 'A show leek increases its weight nine times within a nine-month period,' said a man who is the doyen of our local leek club. 'Leeks need warmth, water, fertilisers, fungicides and pesticides in varying amounts at critical times.'

The idea is to have them in peak condition on show day. The champs must be edible, no hard woody centres run to seed are permitted. An ideal leek should be 14 in (35cm) long, with no bulbing, and white for two-thirds of its length, with dark green foliage. Success can come from a chance seedling showing size and quality whose progeny will emulate it, more often it is a process of years of reselection to obtain the exhibitor's desired qualities. The leek has provided an important pastime here from the time of the industrial revolution. Depressed wages and long working hours under harsh conditions, especially in the pits, created their own problems and gardening provided an escape. Nurturing flowers and vegetables helped give purpose to life in colliery villages, providing both solitude and a measure of companionship. Money-raising events are held during the months leading up to the show in order to swell the purse and a feature is that every entrant receives a prize corresponding to his leek's position in the show, so the total prize money available is important for everyone. Feelings run high: theft and vandalism may not be as endemic as leek viruses, but overnight decapitation is not unknown. 'We'll swap ideas and drop hints on the right strain of seedlings,' said my friend. 'But on show day it is every man for himself. I never take a holiday in the summer now, I can't leave my leeks.'

Coal from the sea

December 2000

High seas and strong winds mean rich pickings for fuel gatherers on our beaches. After a stormy week I went to Lynemouth to join the few sea-coal men who still forage on the shore here. They are gleaners, gathering the leftovers from an industry that once extended seven miles out under the North Sea. My friend was knee-deep in water, swathed in yellow oilskins and rubber thigh boots, raking the sea bed and the shingle with a wire net. Known as coalies, the men use flat carts hitched to ponies to carry their bags, because sand and salt water spell disaster to motorised vehicles. Sea coal is packed into sacks, sells at £1 a bag and gives off a wonderful heat for those, like us, who still have an open fire.

With collieries and pits almost all closed now, this minor industry has suffered. But there are still men scratching a living from what the tide leaves behind. I admired my friend's piebald pony. He ran his hand down the strong equine limbs and lifted a hoof to prod the inside with his thumb. 'Hard as nails,' he remarked. The ponies' work entails being constantly in salt water, which is beneficial to limbs and hooves. They graze the dune grass at Lynemouth, Druridge and Cresswell, tethered on long ropes to neck straps. The best time for coaling is one hour after the tide has turned. 'You look at the ground and you can tell from the horse's hoofprints when there is coal underneath,' said my friend. The families take care of their ponies and, in hard weather, feed quality oats. 'It's hay that's the problem,' sighed my friend. 'A few farmers still make it but it's a ridiculous price.'

Scourge of the farms

April 2001

Having avoided writing about the dread foot-and-mouth disease, now there is no escaping it. As I sit at my desk, I can see smoke drifting from three funeral pyres to the south, and there are two others six miles north of the village. Sometimes it is difficult to know whether it is the disease or the response that is getting out of control. The knock-on effect for the rural business community has been catastrophic. This crisis is currently costing millions in the agricultural sector and more is haemorrhaging from tourism. Perhaps one positive aspect is that town-dwellers will better appreciate that Mother Nature is not just a great rural theme park. Our local blacksmith's business is virtually on hold. No equines are going anywhere. In this parish alone, there are riding stables as well as three racing yards. My garden fence is collapsing so I called in the village fencer. He came with alacrity. 'I shall have it righted today,' he promised. 'I have had to lay off my two apprentices because business is virtually at a standstill.' Holiday and bed-and-breakfast businesses, which have been built up with capital, hard work and expertise are suffering numerous cancellations. The new farmers' markets have been thriving during the past 18 months. Now they are cancelled for the foreseeable future. Several farms in this area diversified into welcoming schools and families to their premises, especially at lambing time; one farm at Hartburn last year received 50,000 visitors. Sadly, this week they have been devastated by the disease. The government have come in for a lot of stick over their handling of this sorry affair. Let us hope that lessons have been learned.

A hi-tech shepherd

February 2002

A full-time shepherd has started his own internet company, writing walks for visitors to Northumberland. Jon Monks looks after 1,500 blackface sheep on 12,000 acres at Greenleighton near Rothbury. In summer, Jon uses a quad bike to go on the moor but shepherding in winter is all on foot. He has four border collies to support him. So these walks are written from a shepherd's perspective, rather than just giving directions and telling people which stile to cross, and there is information on the history of an area and the agricultural methods followed, present and future. The shortest walks are two miles and the longest 16. 'I have always been a keen walker,' Jon told me, 'and I have two young children. So my walks are aimed at every level of walker – I know how to keep the bairns interested.'

I took my children on one of the walks at Hartburn, an interesting woodland trail following the Hart burn for a short distance. They loved it. My next venture is going to be Shaftoe Crags, a beauty spot near Bolam lake, a six-mile hike with a walking time of three hours. It may take me longer because I live near and I know many of the locals on the farms. There are also town walks, in Hexham and Rothbury Town, both of which suit children of all ages. It was during our countryside crisis last year that Jon was inspired to bring out a 'foot-and-mouth walks' booklet. He was supported by Defra. Log on to www.shepherdswalks.co.uk and you can take a look around, with pictures and descriptions of all walks and places to stay.

War on the moles

March 2002

A fisherman once told me he had found a small mole in a 1.3kg trout he had caught on the river Coquet, and I must be one of few people who have seen a mole swimming. As a child, I remember watching one swim across the north Tyne river. It rolled as it swam, owing to the action of heavy front feet, snout held high and the eyes plainly visible.

This spring, brown humps have erupted along my field wall, which borders the churchyard, and the graves on God's acre are decorated with molehills. The local molecatcher told me that he uses 3kg of worms every week to bait his traps and has people collecting fresh ones for him. 'I began clearing gardens which had moles,' he told me. 'Now I am on call for the local council, the golf course, English Heritage properties and even Roman sites. Moles are persistent beggars and return to old haunts so they keep me in business!' He reckons to cover 2,000 acres in a season. He baits the traps and a week later removes the dead bodies. An eruption of molehills can look as if an army of pests is in residence but the damage is likely to be caused by only two or three of these mammals. The molecatcher is not classed as a pest officer because moles are not vermin. 'A young moley is a bonny creature,' said the molecatcher sadly, although he spends much of his waking hours in pursuit of them. A mole's territory is a system of tunnels centred on a nest under a mound of earth. The beastie is beautifully equipped for a life of tunnelling, with cylindrical body, huge hands, strong snout, powerful arm and neck muscles, small ears and tiny eyes.

The lost netty

November 2002

The Guy Fawkes bonfire is always built in our field, as it backs on to the village hall where a party is held, and the bairns can watch the flames and fireworks in safety from behind the hall. This year, our neighbour felled an old plum tree so that it could be added to the conflagration, and in doing so revealed a small brick building. This was originally a netty, a dark, damp toilet for the householders. There is no window in it, and it is a one-holer. I was once shown a particularly fine netty, in Simonburn, a three-holer, so that father, mother and child could sit in a row to relieve themselves. A hole in the side wall of the netty is blocked by a stone, and this would have been removed when the place needed to be cleaned out. A horse and cart would then have been driven alongside, and an unfortunate farm labourer would have had to clean it out. The cart was then driven to a stubble field and the stuff spread on the land as fertiliser.

One old man remembers using the netty as a lad. 'There was no toilet paper,' he told me. 'So Mother pulled moss for us to use. It was pitch dark in the hut, and you could hear rats scuttling away when you got sat down. My sister said it was spooky and wouldn't go in alone.' One time a terrier went in, presumably after the rats, climbed on the bench and fell into the hole. The dog could not get out so was temporarily trapped. 'Next one in got a fright when he sat down and the dog shot out,' chuckled my friend. 'He was out that door in a hurry, still with his trousers down!'

Catching a bat

July 2003

I woke to the rattle of fingers playing with things on my dressing table; oh dear, a swallow had flown in. It was 5.30am. I heard the thing shuffle across the carpet. Flop, flop, flop it went, as if it had on a pair of loose-fitting slippers, while making a shrill, squeaking noise. Taking care where I put my feet, I got up and drew back the curtain, and suddenly something struck the wall above my bed. I saw at once it was a bat. I slipped downstairs to collect an old landing net with which to capture the intruder. I soon had my bat enmeshed, although I had difficulty disengaging it from the net because bats have a pronounced claw on the wing joint. They are great scratchers, using their clawlike thumb to comb the fur. I put him out of the window in the direction of our church tower, where I suspect he came from.

All bats are nocturnal and the object of their irregular, jerky flight is to catch moths and insects. There are chiefly two species of vespertilionid in this county, the little pipistrelle, which was my visitor, and the long-eared bat, which prefers wooded terrain. Pipistrelles like caves, old byres and church porches; they are not blind but use sophisticated echo-location systems to fly and feed in the dark. I once spent a magical summer evening prowling around the precincts of Brinkburn Priory, studying the only known roost of Daubenton's bats at the time in Northumberland. During the 1950s, before bats were protected, I saw bats being smoked out of a house at Simonburn: the poor little gasping creatures came tumbling out of the eaves until the lawn was littered with tiny panting pipistrelle bodies. It was not an edifying sight.

The moles are back

January 2004

Molehills appear in due season along the length of the drystone wall enclosing our village churchyard. The tunnels are likely to be as old as the wall itself and will have been used by generations of industrious moles. These small black beasts begin their breeding season in April: the only time these solitary creatures come together without fighting. There are still a few molecatchers in this county because farmers do not want too many black heaps along their dykes and hedgerows – the soil thrown up can get mixed with grass and can make cattle and sheep ill if they eat it. But churchyards are peaceful places, and they are not disturbed here. I have never seen a mole above ground, and so I was astonished a few weeks ago, in midwinter, to see a tiny black figure shuffling behind a gravestone. I felt sure that this was an omen. My mother was a Highlander and believed strongly in old wives' tales. Indeed, parishioners soon learned that our vicar was seriously ill and must retire immediately. His ministry is a demanding one, with five country parishes under his care.

We have been fortunate over the past years to have had committed, caring rectors, which is vital not just for everyone's spiritual needs but as the protective linchpin in a scattered rural community. The Church of England apparently has a transfer list and those vicars wishing for a change of scene are lined up against parishes in need, so we could get hot gospel music and tambourines, or we might not have a resident vicar at all. Given the choice, I would go for the first option because it might encourage younger members of the community to join us in the pews.

Deer in a ring

December 2004

A local gamekeeper contacted me because he had found a circle of trampled grass about 2.5m in diameter in a wooded glade only a few miles from here. 'The ring has a small silver birch tree in the centre – could it be roe deer?' he asked. I went to look and this was a well-worn permanent roe ring and, as I suspected, it had been used only a month ago for a false rutting period, which does occasionally occur in winter months. This is not just a revival of pleasant memories from late summer, but a second rut.

A roe doe will come alone to a ring when in season, leaving her fawn concealed nearby, although I have once seen a male fawn persist in accompanying mother until the mature buck drove the little fellow roughly away, using his horns as though against a rival. This late rut may be nature's way of enabling yearling does to breed, as they would then be about 15 to 18 months old and mature. One naturalist told me that herbage in, or near, a ring is a feature but, in fact, when roe deer are using their rings, feeding is an incidental act. It is not unusual to find couches or lying places in the grass where deer have lain up near a ring after their exertions. My father was a naturalist who was very knowledgeable about roe deer and told me that in some Highland forests he had found unmistakable markings of these roe deer playgrounds, which were of differing shapes and sizes, usually circular or oval, but occasionally in the figure of eight. There is a suggestion that the presence of a fungus called ergot in grasses found within these temporary rings might explain the attraction of these sites for roe deer, but this theory has not been substantiated.

Friendly ferrets

March 2006

Ferrets, domesticated polecats, have always been popular with Geordies. This is Roman Wall country and it is the Romans who are believed to have introduced ferrets to northern England, to hunt out rabbits to supplement rations for their troops: Genghis Khan in 1221, and Emperor Frederick II of Germany in 1245 were recorded ferret users. Ferreting is part of spring up here, because rabbits can do serious damage to crops and, as the populations of these coneys increase, so the burrows are extended. When a ferret is put into a burrow, rabbits may bolt within minutes. When I was a child I remember our gardener taking my brother 'drummering' – using his ferrets to 'drum out' the rabbits invading the kitchen garden.

Recently, I saw a ferret being taken out for a walk on a long lead by one of the villagers; he told me that ferrets can become friendly and tractable, if you spend time with them. They can even be trained to be clean. Then I visited a boy who had a ferret as a pet. He brought it into the house to see me, and it slid along the carpet on its belly, ferreting around the skirting boards in the kitchen in search of anything edible. The lad even cuddled it, but admitted that it had not yet come up with rabbit for a pie. Unfortunately, some people get tired of these unusual pets and others are abandoned in the fields if they are working underground and do not surface when expected. Three years ago, North East Ferret Rescue became an official organisation and a branch of the British Federation of Ferret Welfare, with 65 abandoned ferrets to re-home. Some ferrets are brought in with damaged teeth and skin problems and have to be treated by a vet, so funds are always needed. Many have been successfully re-homed with caring families.

Hooky mats and proggy rugs

May 2007

Years ago I inherited a Geordie proggy mat from my parents, and it lay in front of our Aga in the kitchen for 20 years until it finally succumbed to wear and tear from feet, children, dogs and occasional edible bits from the cooker. A lovely rug, it was made by a local lady who, my mother told me, constructed it from scraps of material, even old tweed skirts and jumpers, and with no attempt at clever design. In olden days, when the womenfolk in colliery communities made traditional hooky mats and proggy mats they were generally dark and drab in colour and design, reflecting the limited materials that people had to work with in this predominantly mining area.

I subsequently ordered another rug from a textile artist who was then working in the old pit yard at Woodhorn Colliery, near Ashington. She had a variety of rugs and wall coverings, and historical mat-making tools, crammed in a little workshop, where she was working on wall hangings for the local Wansbeck hospital depicting sun, wind, sea and earth, as well as a 'magic carpet' for a children's library. She told me that every mat she made had a story to tell. She bought material and garments from jumble sales, and also used recycled blankets, which she dyed when necessary. Wansbeck council had been supportive in promoting her work, and she received a marketing grant from them. She also ran popular courses teaching traditional mat-making techniques. This lady made me a new proggy mat with a sleeping dachshund woven into it, and this has lain in front of our Aga now for many years with no sign of deterioration. In these days of materialism and the subsequent reaction to mass production, people are more environmentally aware, and many want to recycle to produce something functional as well as decorative.

Sea kindling

December 2007

Like many of our neighbours, I still have an open fire in my living room and, although I do burn coal, I also gather wood from fallen timber on my daily walk with the dog. Wood from the sea, impregnated with salt, burns well, being generally seasoned timber from old craft, and often covered with dried tar. An expedition to our coast during winter months – when strong winds and big seas can throw kindling and the dog enjoys a roll in the sand – is one of my favourite ways of spending a morning, well wrapped up against the wind.

Alder, willow and birch wood are all worth collecting, but they do burn away quickly and so need constant replenishment. Elm must be well weathered and dry, or it will refuse to burn, and beech and larch are really only suitable for laying the fire as they are often rather twiggy in texture. Oak is the longest lasting and the one that gives out the most heat, and ash also makes a good blaze. However, wood from conifers should be avoided because it crackles and spits on an open fire. When he was a child, one of our sons loved collecting wood with me and took an old hemp bag on our walks and filled it with fir cones, which make good firelighters.

Sea coal, which was exposed from old coal layers on the sea's bottom, is now extremely rare, but it tends to be clean and smooth to handle as it has no soot in it, and it also burns slowly. However, it does often leave a white deposit in the hearth, which must be removed before a new fire is laid for the next day. Ponies used for pulling flat carts to collect sea coal from our coast used to be tethered in the dunes and on village greens in the neighbourhood of Newbiggin and Cresswell, but now they are no longer used. The few men who still glean fuel use mechanical vehicles. Regular immersion in salt water, which the ponies' work entailed, was beneficial to their limbs and hooves, and the animals were generally well cared for. I will never forget on one cold winter day watching a pony turn and swim strongly out to sea, taking his flat cart with him. The poor coalie man watched helplessly as his livelihood looked in imminent danger of drowning in the freezing waves. Rescue teams were alerted but, before they arrived, the pony fortunately revised his sense of direction, and, after swimming in a wide arc, headed back towards the shore. It was a mercy that the cart did not become waterlogged and drag the pony down with it.

Seven

Town and Country

When Audrey Insch was a teenager she was given less than 40 years to live by doctors who added that she would probably gradually go blind as well. Today, she is heading for double that span and getting as much pleasure as ever from watching wildlife and the landscape in and around her retirement city of Edinburgh. But the warning, in the days before medicine learned to master the diabetes that she developed at 14, certainly concentrated her young mind. She recalls how after the initial blow, she determined to make the most of however many years she had left. She flung herself into both her schoolwork and having fun – and especially into books. When her family's doctor wondered if she might try medicine at university, given her personal experience, she told him: 'But all I want to do is read.'

Pleasure in words started early, when her father's career as a bank manager took the family to Crieff in Perthshire, where Insch spent most of her childhood. One of her earliest memories is of encountering the word 'knickerbocker' and rushing round the house repeating it until she was thrown outside.

'I rolled down the lawn and ran about everywhere, still chanting "knickerbocker". Shocking, but what a glorious word for a small child.' Her father enjoyed word games too. He was locally famous as the man who dreamed up the town's slogan for War Week, a money-raising initiative that the government took from place to place in the early 1940s: Let Crieff Spell Grief for Hitler. Insch probably chanted that too, and certainly inherited the facility. Her conversation, like her Country Diaries, is studded with phrases that stick in the mind. She describes a lifelong friend, for example, as 'an extreme form of banker'.

Mr Insch's other gift to his daughter was time for cycle rides together in Crieff and the surrounding Perthshire countryside, on which he showed her tiny clues to the fascination of nature. Tracking a solitary bee led them to a swarm, and Insch remembers how the two of them outwitted the traditional strategy of hen lapwings, which pretend to have a broken wing to lure intruders away from their nests by fluttering in the opposite direction. 'Dad quietly led me the right way, through the heather, and there were four beautiful little eggs which we left undisturbed.'

Unfortunately, Mr Insch was also good at banking and promotion ended the idyll in Crieff with a move to Aberdeenshire that coincided with – or may have triggered – Insch's diabetes. There was still time for natural history, but she focused much more intensely on academic work and showed her mettle when she went to read English literature at Aberdeen University. She had to take history in the first, foundation year, and fell foul of a nit-picking tutor who had no sense of the subject's romantic side but kept telling her: 'Be analytical.' Triumphing in her English exams, she actually failed the history ones and went off, feeling a bit sore, for a summer holiday in the Highlands with her parents and elder brother. Back at home, she sent an account of the episode to the *Spectator*, which published it and paid her eight guineas, £200 today and a handsome publishing debut. Her title for the piece? 'Be analytical'.

In practice, she soon became a skilled analyst, helped by Aberdeen's sparky tradition of academic debate, especially in philosophy. Teachers such as Anthony Flew and Donald Mackinnon, the inspiration in part for Sir Tom Stoppard's play *Jumpers*, held open house every week for students to challenge them with questions that they then debated passionately, pitching questions and assertions across the hall to one another, and to regular questioners such as Insch, so that everyone joined in. An excellent degree followed and a scholarship to take a doctorate on the blank verse of a Scottish poet. Unfortunately, the guardian of the poet's archive at an English university proved to be a misogynist heir to those mediaeval clergy who kept women out of intellectual life. He refused access, and Insch's thesis had to be broadened, to 'English Blank Verse Tragedies 1790-1825'.

'I had a wonderful time discovering masses of them, some good, some awful,' she said. Roving the academic libraries of London, where she moved to take her doctorate, she built on her bumble bee and lapwing detective skills to track down little-known works by almost every major writer of the period. Launched eagerly on life in the capital, which seemed a place of wonders after Aberdeenshire, she also got to know celebrated writers of her own day, especially the poet Stevie Smith. Insch invited her to talk to students and became a friend, a sometimes challenging role as Smith had a curiously detached expertise in spotting friends' assets that she could put to use in her own arrangements. In Insch's case, this was a car. 'If she stayed, she could never understand in the morning that I couldn't drive her home, all the way across London, when I had a lecture at nine.' On another occasion, when Insch had managed to give Smith a lift, the poet suddenly spotted a red London bus, said: 'Look, it's a number 28, I've never been on one of those,' and got out of the car while it was still moving. Insch thinks that she spent the day meandering round London on the buses as far as Crystal Palace, miles from her home but much to her satisfaction.

Insch had meanwhile discovered that she had a vocation as a much-appreciated teacher, and this is how she earned her living, first at teacher-training college in Bromley and then at the American University in London, which brought the novel experience of Middle Eastern students whose souk culture extended as far as trying to barter up marks. One of them gave Insch a large carrier bag after an exam, which she absent-mindedly accepted, only to find on getting home that it contained a silk dress and necklace. An elderly head of department paid her for extra work by counting used notes out of another bag. She did a year at the Central School of Speech and Drama, realising a long-held ambition to take to the stage by playing May in Samuel Beckett's *Footfalls*, and took extra work at the new Open University because she fervently believed in its ideals. And then she had an idea.

She was a *Guardian* reader and she always enjoyed the Country Diary. Using one of the main metaphors ascribed to it over the years, she says: 'It was like discovering a little window on to the real world, not politics and arguments and headlines, but the eternal world that was always there, and just waiting to be seen.' She soon noticed that nobody was contributing from any of the major cities where, she reasoned correctly, most of the newspaper's readers must live. Remembering 'Be analytical', she studied the different diaries for several weeks and then wrote one about Wandsworth Common, where she lived. An appreciative letter came back from Chris Maclean, the column's editor and a fellow Scot, but it regretted that there were no vacancies in the team.

Some time earlier, Insch had met one of the Country Diarists, John T White, a sensitive recorder of Kentish life who tried his hand at teaching geography but could not cope with the young. 'His classes were a centre of noisy uproar, which could be heard all over the building,' says Insch sorrowfully. When she was introduced to him, she gave him pleasure by spontaneously saying: 'Not *the* John T White, the *Guardian* Country Diarist?' but he was already beginning to go under. A year or so after Insch had written to the paper and then put its reply on one side and got on with other things, White took his own life. Shortly afterwards, she heard from the paper again.

'Could you start on Monday?' asked Maclean, in typical daily newspaper style; and a month later he was back on the phone even more urgently, saying: 'Where's your copy?' From this, Insch deduced that she had been taken on regularly, which proved correct. She shared White's fortnightly spot with another new diarist, Roger Redfern from the Derbyshire Peak, who often strayed into Sheffield and the industrial towns of north

Nottinghamshire and south Yorkshire. Between them, they gave a new perspective to the otherwise wholly rural beat of the early 1980s diarists. Insch in particular revealed how much plant and wildlife was flourishing in suburban London. One of her many letters from readers still means a lot to her. It came from an exile in Australia who had picked up a copy of the international *Guardian Weekly* ('I didn't know there was such a paper, let alone that my diary was in it,' she says) and found his boyhood haunts in Bromley recreated by Audrey so vividly that every tree-house and bramble and willow-herb jungle foray came flooding back.

Insch attracted some attention as a 'non-country' Country Diarist, including a profile in the *Sunday Times* and as a natural activist, she was pleased to be able to promote volunteer groups that were protecting urban wildlife or fighting off developers. But then she made another small piece of history, on her retirement from teaching, by becoming the first Country Diarist to make a house move dependent on whether the *Guardian* would allow the Country Diary to move with her. She was off to a remote hamlet in the Preseli mountains of Pembrokeshire, land of menhirs and famously the origin of Stonehenge's great slabs. With a group of friends, she had stayed for years at a caravan in a local farmyard and on a visit there in the late 1980s she decided: this is where I want to stay. To her great relief, Maclean's successor, Jeannette Page, said, 'Yes, you can write from Wales instead of Wandsworth,' and a new phase of Insch diaries began.

They were marked, as the London ones had been, by an eager involvement in local wildlife work. Throughout her time in Wales, Insch was a volunteer for the Pembrokeshire

National Park and she also served as a director of an eco-centre that worked to find new and less environmentally harmful ways of life and work. She enjoyed, too, the freedom given to Country Diarists to write about their holidays. A committed Christian, she has regularly visited a Buddhist retreat in southern Spain and recorded the landscape – and dramatic weather – there. Alas, she never managed to sneak in the phrase or, still better, headline: 'Be analytical'.

She did, however, manage to use Britain's longest village name, Llanfairpwllgwyngyllgogerychwyrndrobwllllantysiliog-ogogoch, which the *Guardian* miraculously spelled correctly and I, to my secret pleasure, have now contrived to get twice into one book. And then, one day in 2005, she found herself back in Scotland to visit family and the friend who is 'an extreme form of banker'. She says: 'I was standing outside a bookshop in Edinburgh and I looked up at the castle and down at Princes Street and I knew I was home.' And so there she is. The diary could not transfer this time, being well-represented in Scotland, but Insch is busy with the Scottish Women's Rural Institute, her church, tai-chi and the daily delights of plant and wildlife that she knew in London, now in another city. With luck, her observations will find a new way into print.

The colours of spring

May 1986

Everywhere plants are bustling ahead to produce ever more flowers. Now is the time to remember banks of snowdrops, usually the first flowers of the year. The forerunners, they can go without our noticing – we are going here and there in pursuit of the original daffodil, the small wild one. On May 1 1871, Gerard Manley Hopkins observed: 'The bright yellow corolla is seeded with very fine spangles which give it a glister and lie on a ribbing which makes it like cloth of gold.' Next blackthorn and whin* blossom crowd around us. Hedges turn into super-bountiful white bubbles with sharp yellow cries from the whin. Hawthorns will follow. Now the greater celandines are standing up in green clumps with surprisingly small and brief flowers soon to turn into strong catapulting seed pods. We camped for a week in Wiltshire. On the journey we passed fields that were growing simply dandelions, a celebration of yellow. We assumed it was set-aside land gathering its strength. The effect was voluptuous. Other fields had oil-seed rape to throw a more lemony-yellow astonishment over the earth. We camped on land belonging to an organic farmer. Dove's foot geraniums were already in flower while the musk thistles are so common they have to be dug out. Their prickly rosette is the size of a large dinner plate. Next month the solitary flower head will be tumbling in the breeze. Cowslips were abundant. One piece of disturbed chalk land near Avebury was crammed with young cowslips and salad burnet interspersed with beech seedlings fallen from a tall stand of majestic trees. Very young large red damselflies welcomed us home. Nymph cases cling to the leaves of irises and rushes. The youngest have lime green stripes on

---

* Gorse.

the thorax and a body of transparent plum. They appear and disappear like wraiths. The swallows come, swooping over the water for a quick sip.

Water, water everywhere

January 1988

The west is wet, but recently it's been wettest. One night the road through the village turned into a river. Water cascaded down hillsides, streams flooded the highways. Hailstones drummed down like huge dried peas and an unfortunate fisherman held by the tide in Cardigan Bay sailed up and down all night watching the lightning flash from Cardigan to the Preselis to Fishguard and back again for five hours. At home when the lightning flashed there was no space to count the miles away because the thunder was almost simultaneous. We were left with no electricity or telephone. In some houses the phones melted.

After that our other downpours have seemed fairly harmless – unless you're a farmer. Sheep and cattle in the fields have been wet for weeks. Many farm roads have been turned into streams, which create holes and chasms in their path. As the weather's grown colder, so it's become drier. However, most walking is best done in Wellington boots, always allowing for the risk of the boot staying stuck in the mud whilst you rashly stride on. One walk took us through Llanwnda, a small settlement with an ancient church, even older stones, a farm and some houses. The church has a still centre even in the roughest weather. The path down to the sea is now one long glissade. The streams you cross have bands of flattened grass and debris. When you reach the cliffs you are rewarded with the colours of the winter sea: blues of lead and pansy edged with white. The cliffs are all wet. As the daylight goes, the experience of winter sludges up the hills with you – new, cold and damp. Then you look back at Llanwnda, where lights are appearing in the houses, small patches of brightness in the wet earth and that strange winter pleasure is upon you. Come on, dogs, get moving – home for tea. Then a huge full moon appears. At the next full moon the days will be waxing.

A London paradise

July 1989

The River Wandle flows smoothly and steadily between rounded banks, encouraging trees to grow ever taller and broader. Watercress in full flower perplexes mallards that swither between swimming or walking as they move on to it. A coot family kept fussily to the clear water while a heron standing in a little bay was so astonished by my soft-footed approach that he cried off, leaving a straight line of grey-white excrement dropping on the water. The kingfishers evaded me. I have friends who remember cycling here when it was surrounded by Surrey fields. Now, thanks to the National Trust, it is one of those city spaces which, providing aspects of the tamed country, can give so much pleasure to city dwellers both in themselves and the memories they provoke. The meadows in the extensive park land were enclosed in 1658. Fertilisers have passed them by.

Deer were followed by cattle and now there's a luxuriant hay crop about to be cut for a city farm while dozens of meadow brown butterflies dance in and out. An old circular building, probably an ice house, in the grounds has much of the original hazel wattle still in place with a primitive cement to replace the mud. The apiary that suffered so much in the October storm* has been cleared up, gained more hives, a renewed brick building and a name: The Morden Apiary. The walk to this paradise garden retains its enchantment winding through tall plants of sorrel, nettle and mugwort over hoary plantain. Back home, a fortnight's absence in Scotland had allowed three large white butterfly caterpillars to settle down in time for me to watch pupation. No amount of knowledge can remove my amazement at seeing a butterfly emerge from a tiny spotted bag. An overwintered nasturtium climbing around the back door in full bloom is the likely benefactor. F Fraser Darling's *Island Years* is another marvellous way of jolting a city dweller's experience, even if our tent at Clachtoll on the north-west coast isn't comparable to a hut on Rona.**

---

* The October storm refers to the hurricane-force winds that battered much of southern England on October 16 1987.

** Rona is a remote and uninhabited island off the north coast of Scotland where Darling stayed in 1938-39 with his wife and son studying seals and birds.

Autumn mourning

October 1989

'A mournful splendour in the brilliant gold of the sloes and the crimson leaves of the pear trees' formed part of Kilvert's observations for October 4 1871. Keats heard 'the small gnats mourn' – autumn is mourning. Here the strength, number and variety of trees allows the sadness of the end of summer, the melancholia of light loss, to be turned into necessary winter rest, needed more than ever this year because of drought exhaustion. Wimbledon common lost its marsh quality with drainage around 1880. James Thorne in his *Handbook to the Environs of London*, 1876, comments on it as 'among the best kept, and most pleasant, of the commons round London … a favourite haunt of microscopists and mosshunters'. A modern handbook, heartily recommended, *The Parks and Woodlands of London* by Andrew Crowe, 1987, notes: 'said by some to be one of the city's best kept open spaces'. It is lucky in trees and bushes, undulating ground and sudden sheltered green patches waiting for a commoner's sheep. Now there are ugly cracks in the clay ground and the gravel areas are dust dry. But the wood life carries on: squirrels dash around amongst the plenitude of acorns whilst the more ominous jays silently vanish amongst the foliage. Magpies make noise and confusion. Other birds are silent. Some great tits intermittently rehearse their spring songs. Ivy flowers emanate a strong uncomfortable smell, redolent of autumn. Bees and butterflies cluster round eagerly for the sweetness. The greenest leaves are innumerable clumps of horseradish scattered over Putney Lower Common next to Beverley

Brook which still retains the energy to flow to the Thames despite the lack of rain and the superfluity of clogging weed. My favourite charmed spot for flowers behind the railway station has sprouted a shopping trolley, various cans and rubbish. Old railway lamps are piled up beside it and the human need to dump rubbish is gathering momentum. This is a real mourning. 'And for all this, nature is never spent; / There lives the dearest freshness deep down things.'*

Crossing the river

February 1990

We started at the Richmond Riverside Development, a cheerful collection of old and new buildings, open to the river and enjoyed by people. Then on past sheep and cows to a swirl across the racing Thames on Hammerton's ferry boat. We described a huge arc on the water to defeat the current while a cormorant dived under to appear straight up the river some 50 seconds later as if to demonstrate his superior abilities. Other birds were showing off: the goldfinches, their charm; the river gulls, their burgeoning chocolate heads; and the great tits, an ability to sit still and deliver their courting song – one of them managed a plaintive flute obligato, bound to succeed. The flood-marked banks are spattered with clumps of dark-green crow

---

* From 'God's Grandeur' by Gerard Manley Hopkins.

garlic, sometimes referred to as wild onion. Some use it to flavour meat dishes, but its name demonstrates the popular opinion of its quality. Muenscher*, an American scientist, advises that a cow has only to inhale the smell of this plant to transmute an unpleasant garlic quality to her milk and butter. Trees have lost branches, high water has strewn flotsam and jetsam far and wide so it was good to encounter a group of people tackling the muddle with a cheerful vigour as well as clearing up the usual litter. Elm suckers and jostling saplings were being chopped down so the walker will have a better view of the water in the height of summer. Supplied with good tools, they were all volunteers organised by the British Trust for Conservation Volunteers in conjunction with a conservationist from the borough of Richmond. If you're interested in a well-planned day in the open air to help your environment, all groups welcome, able or disabled, then join in and have fun!

Victory for ordinary folk

March 1990

The Spring section of Vivaldi's *Four Seasons* is being played over the country. A weekend in Wester Ross brought the furious driving of heavy rain and gales while the south picked up the

---

* Walter Conrad Muenscher (1891-1963) was a German-born botanist who was professor in the college of agriculture at Cornell University from 1921-54.

delicate dreaminess of sunny spring days when it seemed as if everything is possible, children are excited, and breathing the air is like having champagne for breakfast. In Richmond Park, so accessible and welcoming, I remember John Lewis the Richmond brewer. In 1758 he challenged the policy instigated by the Ranger, Princess Amelia, George II's favourite daughter, forbidding pedestrians to pass freely through the park. Luckily Charles I had accepted that ordinary people did have to move about, and John Lewis won his case. The history of the park is worth reading: *Richmond Park*, by Pamela Fletcher Jones, published by Phillimore. The natural history is renowned for the red and fallow deer that give us a blase approach to animals gazed upon with great excitement in wilder areas, should you be lucky enough to see them. They've been busy on the fallen trees, munching up the soft tips, stripping off the bark. This is a good time for trees because so many are in flower. Close to White Lodge we saw a maple covered in small clusters of Indian red flowers while nearby a chestnut had its candles all set up ready for lighting. In among the fallen leaves fat bumblebees are prospecting for nest sites. Wasps are more interested in the old trees with their holes and fissures. Birds are pairing. Two crows delicately shared a piece of old bread. Green woodpeckers called and warbled to each other. We met two sparrowhawks, both male. Far apart they were both brooding over the landscape, demonstrating their ability to turn their heads around 180 degrees, but no female could they see. A Red Admiral fluttered past in Pembroke Lodge gardens, but this year I had one in the garden on February 21, the same day as the first frog spawn arrived.

The music of May

June 1991

Listening to music we need to be aware of the qualities of sound every minute. May and June are like that in the countryside. If you neglect the red campion, bluebells and sorrel of the banks today, tomorrow the greens are denser, colours stronger or weaker. Last week's bluebell wood has become a droopy grey, squill-covered cliffs a dark seed head. The coastal path is a profusion of flowers, ranging in size from the lowly English stonecrop through a rare and brilliant broom, the hairy greenweed, to majestic Alexanders. Clumps of sea plantains will continue flowering, the green slender drooping spike rising to produce a mass of tiny yellow flowers. Fritillaries, common blue and orange tip butterflies are vivid companions. On some dizzy patches you look down on fulmars and jackdaws gliding below you, or jump as a beady-eyed fulmar suddenly planes by close to your head. Inland, the small clear hill streams have damsel and dragonflies to delight with their colour and speed. Eels slip upstream, interested perhaps in the abundance of tadpoles to be found in some slow-moving pools. An adder slithered silently around an overhanging bank, lowering its head to sip some water before swimming strongly across to the shelter of the other bank, its mild shyness at odds with many people's wild responses. In the woodland, two young feathery buzzards fight and squabble in their nest. You can see badgers stepping out of their setts in the evening to scratch, groom and renew their bedding before setting out for the relief of their distant, well-organised latrine pits so reminiscent of youth organisations and summer camps. Walking along an old field boundary one evening with a labrador, making no special concessions to stealth, we were astonished to see two young badgers careering towards us. With their inadequate eyesight they each leapt down on opposite sides of the bank to rush away into the wood, no doubt as stunned as we were by their proximity to human boot.

Dark into light

March 1993

Whether we have the warmth of summer or cold early spring winds, the season's turn from dark to light is unstoppable. Winter flocks of chaffinches are separating to pair up for mating. Blackbirds are already busy. You see the low determined flight to some bush or other. The bird disappears, re-appears with the same single-minded purpose of finding more pieces of nest-building material. Great tits are sawing out their messages of courtship, while the pigeons strut their stuff at any opportunity, puffed-up necks glinting like rainbows in the sun. Mallards have already produced their first brood. Ducklings dash around like mechanical toys, fussing and anxious lest the little they know of life be lost. Trees teeter on the brink of leaves. The wych elm has tight clusters of green seeds whilst the alders are carrying catkins, some of them seven inches long. Huge willows growing on the north bank appear to throw showers of golden rain over the water as the sun reflects on the new fresh leaves and their radiance. Last year's traveller's joy is still looped over the branches with new leaves opening. This plant used to be called by some 'boys' bacca' because boys smoked the dried stems. There is plenty of it here. Unexpectedly a sharp sweet song and a distinctive shape registered a warbler. A sedge-warbler was announcing his unusually early arrival with clarity and grace. The other delights were more expected. A peacock butterfly landed on the path in front of us, sporting a newly minted smartness as if the months of hibernation had been spent in deep happiness. The nettles that they prefer for their eggs are still very small. A brimstone was also patrolling along the scrub looking for a mate. She will probably rely on the buckthorns for her egg laying. Meanwhile, at home, frogs surrounded by spawn sing and croon to each other through the warmth of the spring sun. Like every other living thing their enthusiasm wanes slightly when the rain falls and cold winds blow.

Magpies in the snow

November 1993

'Have you mark'd but the fall o' the snow / Before the soil hath smutch'd it?' Ben Jonson asked. The first snow of winter fell on Sunday morning so an early walk over the common gave plenty of opportunity. The flakes were fat and sloppy. However, they quickly piled up on top of each other to give a snowy effect. The sky was dark blue and grey, the daylight raw and damp. As a girl in the uplands of Aberdeenshire I was advised that the only snow to worry about was the small dry flakes which started to fall slowly and lay like rice after a wedding. This kind of fall could continue for hours, piling up 'snow on snow' until villages were cut off, school attendance threatened and hills became sledge runs. However, this is still November. Only the magpies, those black and white chancers, looked worried, as if their food supply might suddenly cease. But that's quite normal for them. They moved quietly through the trees, their plumage brilliant and gleaming purple, shadowing a human being who might just produce a bag of buns for them. A few crows drifted past. The small birds were keeping close amongst the bushes and trees. A flock of starlings swept over the branches and hurtled to some other spot where there might be food. The snow kept falling. A whin bush started to flop slightly under the damp weight. Grey squirrels appeared, tails curved over the body as they surveyed the new landscape. Their food quest set them scrabbling and digging amongst the leaves in the hope of uncovering some long hoarded treasure. As the morning unfolded the smaller birds perked up. Against the snowy background their feathers look even more distinguished. Handsome sparrows with subtle brown and fawn, proud robins carrying puffed out red chests, blue tits neat and clear. But soon the soil snatches the snow. 'Now fades the last long streak of snow' and the common looks cold and wet. On an oak tree a crow stands silhouetted against a cold clear blue sky. Winter comes closer.

A pinch of snuff

April 1994

Dark grey, indigo blue clouds loomed up. Briefly sunlight turned fresh young leaves into silver pennies before the hail bounced around, thunder bellowed, rain slashed and the wind blew. As soon as it had gone over, a blackbird busied itself tugging out a worm and mistle thrushes were poking around in the grass. The wind, straight from the north according to the weather trout, continued to cut uncomfortably, but the skies changed, the sun shone and unstoppable spring whooshed on. The park is owned by the National Trust, but its appearance was shaped by the Hatfeild family. They created a deer park, which has been undisturbed by ploughing or artificial fertilisers, relying instead on deer, cows and horses. They planted an avenue of horse-chestnut and lime trees from the house through the park to exit on Morden Road. The meadow has a variety of grasses, speedwell, sorrel, red dead nettle, cow parsley, clumps of cowslips and much more to come. The Hatfeilds also enjoyed fishing. They organised the clear chalk waters of the River Wandle to flow around the house and in diverse channels through the grounds so that many fish could be accommodated. Some of the farm buildings are open to the public, including the dairy where they bred trout for the river. There were two snuff mills still working up to the General Strike in 1926. On hot days when the smell of snuff was too much for the workers, the mills were closed and work found for the men on the estate. The river lightens the landscape, some stretches move slowly, others swirl along. In the quieter parts water birds are sorting out their spring tasks. Two moor hens displayed sharp white rears and bright red fronts as they shimmered around in the water. Two coots had settled their nest and one of them was out river sweeping. Two jays were working together. One pecked out a clutch of twigs and flew into thick ivy twining a tree. Another looked around, ripped off a twig and followed after.

Miss Hoodles' legacy

December 1994

In 1897 a Canadian, Adelaide Hoodles, started classes providing instruction in domestic science and home-making for the local women. This Victorian urge to educate and thus improve other people reached Britain in 1915, when the first branch of what was to become the National Federation of Women's Institutes opened in Llanfairpwllgwyngyllgogery-chwyrndrobwllllantysiliogogogoch, St Mary's Church, in the hollow of the white hazel near the rapid whirlpool of Llantysilio of the red cave or, Llanfair PG. So the WI of England and Wales started. Scotland developed its own Scottish Women's Rural Institute. Nowadays it has left the instructive mode, the I-know-best and-this-is-what-you-do approach to embrace shared experience and fun. The Preseli group of the Dyfed-Pembrokeshire Federation of Women's Institutes invited us to their carol service in Llanfair Nantgwyn. We had the traditional nine lessons and carols, some in Welsh, some in English. The church was full, the singing good. There was no scrimping – we sang all the verses. The candles flickered, holly berries twinkled and the little church filled with good energy. Afterwards we sat in the pews with mince pies and coffee, the sort of scrumptious pies WI markets all over the country have for sale. Luckily it was dry and calm. Other nights the pursuit of Christmas merriment has led to struggles through gales and downpours, when crossing the hills has meant experiencing the blinding conditions usually associated with snow, with headlights dazzled by the power of the downpour aimed directly at the windscreen. Then the next day the sun beams over a washed and windswept landscape. Its low rays give long shadows, which, unlike those of high summer, are easy to see into. We are fortunate to live in Nevern parish. Here the usual excitement of the carol service with candles in the dark is enhanced by the approach to the church door. Walking through an avenue of ancient yews, you pass a powerful, old Celtic cross before opening the great door to the light of Advent. May this Christmas scatter the darkness from before our feet.

Dragonflies and caravans

December 1995

Over 30 years ago, parts of the Preseli hills above Rosebush were planted with spruce trees. What was once the largest farmhouse surrounded by trees on three sides. Now the crop is ripe and 25 acres have been felled. Rosebush is a village built for the miners who worked in the old slate quarries. Although a 19th-century attempt to turn it into a resort failed, it still has the lake that was part of the grand design. Caravans and dragonflies congregate there in the summer. The miners' houses have been enlarged, but the spoil heaps still dominate the scene. Each piece of shale shows a different pattern—it's like a child's treasure house that Santa forgot. Once past the mines we were immediately walking up through pine trees. A machine, reputed locally to have cost half a million pounds, has cut down each tree, stripped its branches, left them lying in green lines, and cut each trunk into equal long lengths. Another machine grasped the pieces to carry them off to piles lining one of the forest tracks. We walked between two of those timber mountains, neat trunks exuding resin, towering more than 20 feet above us. They filled the air with a scent that made me slightly light-headed, tipsy, elated and finally keen to leave those great trees behind to clear my head. The house is now completely exposed. On the other side of the hills a house snuggles into the ground with trees for protection from the north wind. But there they have a variety of pines, giving blue and green colours, larches and birches, now glowing red – a beautiful shelter, summer and winter. Plant a tree for Christmas!

Ghosts in the fort

June 1996

Pembrokeshire echoes to the remains of a lost culture. Those early people built graves, erected standing stones and constructed protected living areas – forts, raths, castells. Sometimes during inclement weather I wonder what their lives were like. We visited one rath in a quiet piece of old oak woodland. Small oak trees, stunted by stony earth and westerly winds, have sundered the wall. Some grow in the ditch. We chose to approach it from below. Like most forts, part of its defence is based on a steep cliff. A track broad enough for a horse ascends at an oblique angle to emerge at the fort entrance between two rocky outcrops, one split by an oak which has been growing, falling, starting again for centuries. You step into a small circular enclosure no more than 30 paces across. As it hasn't been excavated your imagination can be vividly employed on the life of the small community that lived there. Now it's young oaks, bluebells and bracken. We next went to Castell Henllys, a partially excavated iron-age fort. Some of the original huts have been reconstructed. We arrived accompanied by a cold wind, scattering rain, and walked into a roundhouse with wattle-and-daub walls snugly tucked beneath a long sweeping thatched roof. In the middle a fire was burning. Sparks flew up and vanished. The smoke lost itself in the reed roof, leaving us stunned by the generosity of the fire burners. Protected from the rain and wind, we had the pleasure of a living fire, an element that civilised man usually encounters at one remove. Another delight are the two sows living in an iron-age pig house with a lineage that makes them more ancient than modern. Suddenly the lives of these past peoples seems less mysterious, and warmer. We returned through campions, bluebells, ransoms, orchids, pleased to have had a brush with the past, knowing that down the road the present called with an ace cafe.

A spell in the sun

March 2000

This area, around Tafraoute in Morocco, is famous for its almond trees, cultivated and wild. Blossom, a scented celebration of winter's close departure, is followed by soft new leaves of spring and in the Ameln valley there are villages with water springs. We walked to Aguiz, where a small boy guided us to La Source. First we saw the huge cistern where the water is gathered before the women open and close different channels to allow equal irrigation. Here we saw argan trees at their best. Peculiar to Morocco, the smaller ones might be mistaken for olives, but once they have grown to their full girth they acquire the statuesque presence suitable for a tree that provides fruits whose different parts feed animals, light fires and provide oil for cooking or beauty. Goats enjoy climbing and munching in them. In other parts we have seen how argan forests are disappearing under the pressures of overuse. Here they are majestic. As we followed the water channel upwards we saw fish and frogs in the sunlit waters and dragonflies above, some flaunting crimson bodies, others very like our beautiful demoiselle. We passed terraces where wild boar had been breeding before the villagers smoked them out, frightened of their proximity. Climbing higher we finally approached the spring itself. Towering granite rocks were producing a steady stream of clear water. In a country afflicted by dryness it felt like a miracle. Maidenhair ferns tumbled around it. Bulbuls bellowed, little warblers called and twittered, butterflies flitted by, one of them looking like our orange tip. A scramble around the side brought us to the boys' swimming pool with flickering fish and ambient rocks. We walked away past small fields of beans in flower, whose scent filled the air. The next village had a spring in the middle with women filling water pots and lower down doing the washing, before the vital resource is channelled off towards the crops. Back in Tafraoute, we looked up during breakfast and saw two Bonelli's eagles moving slowly through the thermals, their eyes probably strong enough to see the dark brown wild bees clustered on our jam. They circled round and drifted off, effortlessly.

Watched by a falcon

July 2000

The bird stood motionless. It saw a group of Pembrokeshire Coast National Park voluntary wardens, we saw pent-up speed. The stoop of the peregrine falcon is the fastest bird flight we have. Combine that with its telescopic eyesight and at that speed those deadly talons do their work. One day the warden, Ian Bullock, was sitting on a cliff edge when a peregrine whooshed above his head towards St Bride's bay, straight as an arrow. Using his telescope, the warden finally found the target: it seemed that another peregrine had dared to approach Ramsey island. The other bird was four or five miles away, but the sharp eyes of the first had spotted it. Another local joy is golden rabbits. There have been rabbits here for centuries. As they multiplied from the same breeding stock a double recessive gene threw up black (good for the bishops' gowns) and golden rabbits. This was very suitable because the high cliffs on the west side glow golden in the setting sun. Seeing their golden island, sailors knew home was not far away.

Ramsey is characterised by stone walls that gleam white in the sunshine. Their colour comes from masses of lichens, both crustose and fruticose. Traditional walls or banks were erected to keep stock in place. They are made with stone and turf, but the walls couldn't keep the rabbits in. Instead the creatures tunnelled into them for burrows. The walls fell down. Now they are slowly being rebuilt, incorporating rabbit wire into their structure. They remain for flowers to grow and birds to nest. One area is out of bounds because lapwings are nesting. We could see the adults with stately upright stance and wispy crest. We all remembered the days when the arrival of flocks of lapwings marked the spring with their joyous gyrations. Young chicks dashed about, trying out little fluttering runs. What a good day out! A herd of red deer, a remnant from the days of venison farming, is another unexpected pleasure. We note a proud display of antlers sported by the two leading stags.

Trees with wet feet

November 2000

The Vikings invaded a few weeks ago, intent on pillage. The first fieldfare was alone, busy on a cotoneaster. In amongst the rain and wind we visited holly trees and rowans before the backup force arrived. Now they are swooping and clattering, each day the holly berries diminish in number. Watching birds during these hard times you cannot help but be impressed by the neat ability of small birds to keep low and vanish into the shelter of any leaved bush. On one particularly lashed-about walk we sought some shelter by creeping under a low holly. Saved from wind and rain, we could catch our breath and look around. The ground was covered in berries torn from the tree:

what will eat them down there? When we emerged we were dazzled by yet another rainbow. Days of non-stop rain become tedious, but the rainbows seen on showery days have been triumphant, soaring arcs of colour. Another delight is the varied hues of the tree leaves in sunshine. Oaks are providing rich marmalade while the beeches flame into gold. Whether the sky is pale blue or dark indigo, behind them the trees sing, 'What is this life if full of care ... '

Admittedly, if you stand around to stare in some places you may lose your boots. In the gales you can see the underside of the leaves. Alders and willows are noticeable for their steely grey tones, which gleam when caught in the sun. Both trees need wetness. Venice was built on alder piles because the wood does not rot easily in water. A pertinent tale for current weather conditions concerns the alder and willow. They both attended a great feast for the fertility deities, when all living creatures celebrated together. However, these two were so mesmerised by flood waters that they stood gazing upon them, quite ignoring the mighty gods, who then decided that, if that was what they wanted, that's what they would get. Since then, they have stood by the waters, traditionally holding their banks to maintain the steady flow of water, without which the land dies.

A special countryman

June 2001

The day of the funeral was lovely. May suddenly stopped batting us back into winter. No cold north winds, but a rich abundance of spring flowers. Bryn was a leading farmer in Pembrokeshire and beyond. What made him special for me was his delight in the countryside and its inhabitants. As the practical work on the land grew beyond him so he had turned to the smaller stock, the cats, dogs, puppies and kittens. A byre without a few cats soon pulls in another sort of quest. A shepherd without a dog is a man without an arm. They all need feeding. The farm has New Zealand contacts from young farmers who come over here to help the sheep shearing. Eventually a New Zealand back runner appeared on the farm. This fleet, sturdy, chestnut-coloured hound can run lightly over a flock of sheep to move them forward from behind.

As the farm jobs are redistributed, one son going to feed the little ones was amazed by the response of the wild birds to his appearance. They flocked in to take titbits from his hand. I remember a friend's small boy, glowing with pride and excitement, going hand in hand with Bryn to inspect the lambs and ewes. When he returned he was a bigger boy, as if the gentle delights and concern of his shepherd had cast a good spell on him. By the day of the funeral, the village was immaculate. Strimmers and lawn mowers, spades and wheelbarrows were all used to honour the man we'd lost. Built in 1690, the chapel has a graveyard dating from the same time. Grasses are in flower along with herb Robert, Canterbury bells, bluebells, wild garlic, speedwell, buttercups. From there you look out over the sweep of the Preseli hills. On the grave, from the immediate family were dextrously woven wreaths in white, gold, bronze, yellow, blue and green, with a rectangular one from the grandchildren: a plump little white lamb on a field-green background.

Peppers and pumpkins

November 2001

Back to Cortija Romero for the autumn, colour focuses on the trees. Poplars point saffron heads to a blue sky while the leaves are pulled by the earth littering the air with gold. Cherries give a fiery rust-red to orange. Chestnuts are surrounded by spiky balls of tired green, split open to show the dark nuts. The olives persist in their green and grey but the ripening fruit gives a smart fresh green. Bracken is the same colour as that on Carn Ingli at home, and self-sufficiency is truly possible. We are invited into the home of a 74-year-old who knows our guide. We sit in a room open on one side. The roof is made of tree trunks, bamboo canes, odd bits of wood and plastic. Strings of peppers and onions hang from the ceiling and dried pumpkins lie piled on the floor; this year's crop is still growing. The tourist board has supplied sturdy wooden chairs with rush seats for visitors.

The old man entertains us with a guitar, an accordion and a tambourine. His hospitality is generous in grape juice, which has been pressed and intoxicated by its own yeasty sweetness into an organic astonishment. Dogs, cats, hens, pigeons, goats and donkeys complete the household.

Another walk takes us to an old olive press built in 1779. Driven at various times by river, mules and generator, it is now returning to a family home – the retiring presser has five daughters. We see the place where the olives are first pressed before the mixture is spread over great wheel-shaped mats to form huge sandwiches on which the great weight is lowered to create extra-virgin olive oil, cold pressed. Finally we go up to the Buddhist monastery, O Sel Ling – place of clear light – about 1,600m above the distant blue Mediterranean. It is cold, and thunder growls around the Sierra Nevada. We watch with astonishment as a tornado starts to spin above the sea. Hailstones ping down as we walk around the blessed stupa. Lightning crackles and jumps – purple, red, pink, orange, white lightning, close thunder. We walk down the zigzag path. Hail turns to rain, we descend into a cloud that seems to carry lightning zip fasteners all around us. Finally we emerge, see the track again and move further down to tarmacadam and a waiting bus. In the morning the mountains are covered in snow. It's cold and the Spaniards rejoice – they may be spared a drought next year. Hundreds of little flies vanish overnight. A date palm usually buzzing with bees is silent. A flock of goldfinches follows us along the track, gratefully sipping from the puddles.

Moths and a snake

June 2003

Today hummingbird hawk moths have arrived from the Mediterranean. Wherever they go, they create excitement – 2cm long, the brown bodies remain still, while the brown-orange wings fly at such speed they become invisible. Meanwhile, the proboscis reaches the inner sweetness of the bloom. It moves with a neat exactitude, visiting flower after flower. As suddenly as they have come, they go. Gardens settle down into summer heat. The young tits have almost grown up. For weeks, these fledglings have been feeding themselves at the bird table, but as soon as an adult bird appears, they collapse into fat fluffy cheeps, with quivering wings, open beaks and an urgent need for food. Watching this pantomime, I am reminded of a young cuckoo I once saw being fed by its exhausted mother. All these small birds produce plump offspring. That the cuckoo ends up so large just happens, and you feed it till you drop. A friend presented me with a grass snake. It had entangled itself dangerously in some pea netting. After carefully cutting its shackles, which had dug into the body as it struggled, we carefully carried it over to my large compost heap, hotting up for next year. I pushed a stick in, and the snake slid into the hole.

Living in a holiday location county is an excellent way of prolonging your own holidays. We visited Little Haven in the south, the kind of place children remember for ever. Looking at the sandy beach, it was hard to believe that this was once used to export coal. Small boats beached at high tide would be laden with coal brought in by horse and cart, and sail out on the next tide. In the cliffs between Nolton and Little Haven, you can still see traces of the coal levels.

Wales' highest frogspawn?

February 2005

You can climb Carn Ingli to find frog spawn in the small top pools, drop down into Ty Canol wood, where there's more spawn in the gully, or take the simple path up Foel Eryr; but wherever you go you'll be slipping and dipping into mud. There's been a lot

A hummingbird hawk moth hovers as it feeds

of rain. So when Sunday came with overall sunshine, we used the car to go to the city. You don't sink into pavements. St David's cathedral is built from the countryside. Its solidity and lightness come from the Cambrian sandstone used in its construction. Sunlight pours in, picks up the grey and purple tones to suffuse the building with a thoughtful serenity. Irish oak used in the roof adds another lightness. And it is dry. On to Solva for lunch. This is a creek village, busy with people having a good day out. In the mid-19th century it was the start of a direct shipping line to New York. The hillside above the village is glowing with gorse in flower. Onwards to Newgale, a small settlement beside a beach almost two miles long. The sun was ricocheting off the sea to give us double rations. Children were running and writing on the sand. People were walking, stopping, launching their canoes, exercising their dogs; and everyone was smiling. Canoes were launched and paddled. Kites in various styles swooped and soared above us The only thing they had in common was that they'd all been bought. Remembering the delicacy, delight and potential despair of making your own kite, adjusting the tail and cheering it upwards, I was almost happy to see them.

Then home, where the next-door farmhouse has wallflowers in flower.

Sunlit patrols

July 2005

Peace and heat – the dragonflies love it. Golden rings* were patrolling their territories along one of the small Preseli streams. When they met, the clash of wings held an ancient resonance; how long has this sound echoed over summer waterways? A few chasers added another ferocity. Lower down, above the water, we spotted a local rarity. Two small red damselflies were flying together with a delicacy denied to the more robust dragons. The sluggish water is furring up with weed. There are whirly-gig beetles and water measurers, but no fish to be seen. The banks are colourful with the neat, violet, ivy-leaved bellflower, blue speedwell, yellow spearwort and bog asphodel. Closer inspection reveals the small white flowers of the sundew unrolling on delicate stems, the red cushions they spring from almost obscured by surrounding growth. A grasshopper sprang up and plopped into the stream. Even as I scooped it up, it collected its legs and sprang on to the bank. All around were gorse bushes. The sheep give them a steady topiary clip, which produces smooth dense hummocks, especially with the softer western gorse. Meadow brown butterflies flopped about. High above, three buzzards hung in the air, calling.

---

* Golden rings refers to the golden-ringed dragonfly.

Eight

Poet in the Limestone

Sarah Poyntz is a poet from a beautiful part of the world, but although she was raised in a house called Tranquilla, it had recent bullet holes in the back wall. The *Guardian*'s only Irish Country Diarist was born in 1926 towards the end of one of her country's many times of troubles, and her parents came from opposite sides of the political divide. Her father, Frank Poyntz, was a well-known solicitor in New Ross, County Wexford, with his own father and brothers in that pillar of union with Great Britain, the Royal Irish Constabulary. Even so, he was blackballed from the local tennis club because he was Catholic, until a Protestant friend challenged the exclusive system on his behalf and broke it for ever. Sarah's mother, Nellie, was the daughter of Capt Larry Murphy, a skipper of tea clippers sailing between Liverpool and China, and she supported the executed 1916 Easter Rising rebels, welcomed Irish independence and quietly voted thereafter for Fianna Fáil while her husband backed Fine Gael. The different traditions did no harm at all to a close family. Poyntz describes them positively as making life more interesting, because both parents put humanity far above political divisions. 'The house used to ring with arguments,' she says, going off into one of the gales of laughter that punctuate all her conversation. 'There were the two sides laid out straight in front of you. Very useful.'

The Poyntzes, whose name is an Anglicised Gaelic version of Norman and so an encouraging mixture in itself, were lucky to live in a community that shared their tolerance for the most part. When pupil numbers at the Protestant school dwindled after Irish independence, the Catholic priest 'lent' children from his own school to the Church of Ireland rector on the day of the annual inspection, so that the Department of Education in Dublin would not close the Protestants down. On another occasion, however, Poyntz recalled her father coming home from work white-faced and tense after the local Catholic hierarchy tried to impose a boycott on Protestant businesses after failing to get parents in a mixed marriage to send their child to a Catholic school. Frank Poyntz had ordered a curate who had come to ask him to join the boycott out of his office, telling him: 'Go home to your church and look after it, and leave me to look after my affairs.'

Not surprisingly, Sarah Poyntz was a bold little child. Before she was five, she pre-empted her many later expeditions into the countryside for her *Guardian* Diary by trying to follow a much-loved nanny called Lily who had emigrated to the United States. Equipped with a penny and a reefer coat whose brass buttons were decorated with anchors, Sarah left Tranquilla for New Ross docks where she walked up a schooner's gangplank, gave a sailor the penny and said that she wished 'to go and find Lily in America'. The kindly crew treated her to plumduff cake while her parents were fetched, taking her home in floods of frustrated tears.

The other great gift of Poyntz's childhood, which she evokes with great skill in her memoir *Memory Emancipated*, was the flora and fauna of social life in New Ross. Apart from large numbers of relatives, she mixed daily with a cast of neighbours whose names read like a version of botanical or ornithologists' specimen lists. Crackers Murphy, Phil-the-Randy, Dunphy's Blah and Mother O'Sorrows, a specialist in conveying (and enjoying) bad news, usually with the introduction 'Did ya hear … ?' which became her other nickname. None of these people intended any harm or represented any threat to Sarah and her elder sister, Kitty, and brother Jack, and as she says, 'They enriched our lives, made us aware of the great variety of human life and encouraged us to take a delight in these differences.' One evening during a power cut, her father and an auntie whiled away the time by listing every nickname they knew, while Sarah wrote them down by candlelight in her schoolgirl journal.

Bursting with life and curiosity, she was well-educated at Loreto Abbey at Gorey in County Wexford, a convent school run by the Loreto order, named after the Italian shrine that is said to contain the Virgin Mary's house. Orthodoxy has it that this miraculously left Palestine first for the Balkans but then, after problems there, for the small Italian port on the Adriatic coast. Not surprisingly, the virgin of Loreto is the patron saint of Italian aviators. Absorbing these riches, plus a great deal of Shakespeare, Poyntz decided to be an actor. Very well, said her mother, but go to university first. 'I did,' says Poyntz, 'and I soon

learned about something called the need to earn a living.'
Relishing the teaching of experts such as Dr Lorna Reynolds,
her English professor at University College Dublin, she
decided to teach herself, starting like so many of her generation
over the water in England.

There had been one dreadful tragedy during her happy
youth in County Wexford. On a July day in 1938, her sister,
Kitty, was drowned on holiday with friends at Fethard-on-Sea
on the Wexford coast. Family life was never the same again.
She invokes the tragedy in a poem that imagines the 15-year-
old, 'Willow slim, only a bit / Of a girl, struggling to be', and
as well as her own suffering and that of her brother she had to
witness her parents' terrible pain. The grief never left them. With
it, however, came consolation in the way that the community
of New Ross and the Poyntzes' extended family gave sympathy
and practical help. It was an unlooked-for lesson in both the
harshness and nobility of life, which was to lend its own
understanding to Poyntz's later writing.

She also put it to use in many acts of kindness to pupils, both
in London and then at Callington in Cornwall, where another
future Guardian Country Diarist, Virginia Spiers, was one of the
girls in her class. 'We were all very excited,' Spiers remembers.
'Everyone was going round saying "We've got this new teacher
coming from Ireland called Miss Poyntz." It sounded most exotic,
and we weren't disappointed when she arrived with her red hair
and passion for books. Everyone wanted to please her.' Poyntz
scored another hit when the school staged *Juno and the Paycock*
and the girl playing Juno had to drop out at the last minute
because her father had a stand-up row with a teacher. 'It was my

chance to act at last,' she remembers, and her stand-in Juno won over a very fierce teetotal JP on the board of governors who tutted loudly whenever a bottle of stout was produced on stage – which, this being *Juno and the Paycock*, was often. 'At the interval she went up to the head but instead of complaining, she said, "Well there's one thing I will say and that's that the girl playing Juno has a wonderful Irish accent."'

Poyntz settled in a small cottage in St Dominic and was often seen out on countryside walks. She also befriended her students and their families. Spiers remembers that when her father was killed in a riding accident when she was about the same age that Kitty Poyntz had been, Sarah unobtrusively befriended and comforted her mother. 'She used to come round for a chat and they loved watching period dramas on TV together.' Her academic qualities were meanwhile recognised in 1971 when she won a schoolteacher's fellowship to Girton College, Cambridge, *alma mater* of Swanwick, Case and Enid Wilson's mother. She took the place by storm, not just academically but as an organiser of races along the corridors on kitchen trolleys.

She made many friends at the college, prime among them Mary Ann Radzinowicz, an American with Irish roots who was Girton's head of English literature and also held a university lecturership. She was someone Poyntz could talk to about the violence that was racking Ireland, and Radzinowicz's children, Annie and William, became part of the circle too. When the family moved to Cornell University, where Radzinowicz was appointed professor of English literature, Poyntz went with them. It was an ideal move after ill-health following major surgery put an end to her full-time teaching career. This was cruelly timed;

she had just been appointed head of the high-flying Perse school for girls in Cambridge. Instead, she could only physically manage part-time work preparing girls for university examinations and teaching supplementary Shakespeare to students at Girton.

And then paradise was regained. In 1986 Poyntz decided to return to Ireland to help look after her ageing father before retiring to Ballyvaughan on the coast of the Burren, the internationally famous limestone landscape of County Clare. Mary Ann Radzinowicz followed in the early 1990s on her own retirement, and has become as familiar in the Country Diary as the Burren's white goats and Poyntz's habit, ingrained by her years of teaching, of scattering quotes from the classics, each with the briefest of attributions such as simply (Shakespeare). Celia Locks, the diary's current editor, who enjoys regular cheerful postcards from Ballyvaughan, has managed to limit this informally to one quote per column in recent years, but she has been indulgent to the role of Mary Ann. Another (male) diarist who introduced someone a bit shadowy called 'my Brazilian friend' was reined in. But Mary Ann is interesting, busy and well-used as a foil by Poyntz. 'She sees so much that I miss,' says Poyntz, who may be bent over her hobby of building model boats when Radzinowicz – the keeper of the cottage's garden – spots a swarm, a shoal or a flock of something interesting.

Poyntz joined the Country Diary team in the simplest of ways. Looking out over the limestone and the Atlantic, she thought: 'Now wouldn't it be grand to be in my own newspaper.' 'So I wrote in and said, "I'd love to write a Country

Diary." They had a slot at the time and though they warned me that they had quite a list of applicants, they said: "Send in a sample." I did and they liked it, and now here I am celebrating 21 years.' But she has an agenda too, a touch of Helena Swanwick's campaigning, in the poetry. Both she and Radzinowicz are in a sturdy local band of guardians of the exceptional landscape of the Burren – derived from Gaelic meaning 'stony place'. In her own collection of diaries, *A Burren Journal*, Sarah describes the effects of 'the pawmarks of the Celtic tiger' on the landscape; the way that a revived Irish economy is leading to second homes and rabbit-hutch retirement pads alarmingly close to the most sensitive areas. 'The threats are real and many,' she says, and 300 words a month of love for and delight in the beautiful region are a way of countering them. Hers is a diary with a mission.

Orchids and islands

June 1989

Here in the Burren, it is now orchid time. On our walks, in this long hot spell, we see pyramidal, O'Kelly, fragrant dactylorhiza majalis. Later, in one of the boats of Aran, the currach, tarred canvas between us and unfathomed ocean, we rush, seemingly straight towards a great, grey stone wall, barren and terrible in its isolation. I remember in 1961, arriving at Inishere by steamer to see a cow, held by its horns at the back of a currach, swimming out to the ship, being hoisted by a crane. Everyone gazed up until warned: 'Would you mind now and not be underneath the beast for 'tis showered you'll be with primroses and violets!' Today, the same great stone wall is seen for what it is, terraces of grey walls dividing the fields as, on Inishmore, we climb to Dun Aonghasa on its 270ft-high cliff-edge and later as we revisit Celtic Crosses, ruined 6th- to 15th-century churches. There is a dignity in the islanders that is special. Perhaps it comes from their closeness to and humility towards elemental seas and winds. The islands affect non-islanders. I think of Bob and Carol Kaske from Cornell University, United States. Aran brought out all their openness to and humility before a brave community, still epitomising an ancient civilisation. Their visit drove us to read together that truly tautly beautiful tragedy of Synge's, *Riders to the Sea*, set on Aran. For anyone, open to Aran's three islands, the words of Synge's character Maurya will echo forever, 'wind is raising the sea, and there was a star up against the moon, and it rising in the night.' The prose lifts, falls with sea, wind and the old language, Gaelic, spoken so purely and beautifully by the islanders.

Shadows in the fog

January 1990

It is always strange to see at sunrise the great Burren rocks, drystone walls, holly leaves rimed white with frost and to witness its rapid disappearance when the sun exerts its power. The frost makes the earth friable – a boon for our digging and delving. Outside my window is a large Burren rock shaped like a face

– just chin, mouth, nostrils, rough hair trailing to one side. The lips are slightly open. It lies seemingly gazing at the sky and, covered with hoar frost, it is the sculpted trunkless head of a Greek god. Then, changed by the light of dawn to grey, streaked with white, it assumes the familiarity of the region, a Celtic deity, fallen and long since abandoned. On a recent morning of white, impenetrable fog, our house apparently isolated, when our neighbours' lights three fields away and the sea and bay but 600ft distant, were all invisible, perched on the nose-tip of our fallen god was a song thrush. It hopped down to feed, flew back again, raising its head to utter notes of perfect phrasing, repeated once: 'What seas what shores what grey rocks and what islands/What water lapping the bow/And scent of pine and the woodthrush singing through fog.'* Strange and indeed it has been a time of strange weather – one day Ballyvaughan village and bay walled in fog yet not two miles along the coast road where our fields begin, perfect clarity. Another day, our friends Mary Lou and Frank reported dense fog to beyond Black Head with the fog apparently sitting on the ocean. Further on all was clear with sunlight on hills and sea. Fog came often 'on little cat feet'. In clear spaces in these sheets of fog we saw five curlew fly overhead, their long curved beaks distinct while bay life continued with heron, oyster catchers, redshanks and gulls working close to the shore.

---

* From Marina by TS Eliot.

Saving the school

September 1990

It was a relief to see the rain falling after weeks of near aridity with dust being flung on to the hedgerows and their wild flowers. To breathe was to feel the delicate freshness of the renewed air: to gaze was to notice the renaissance of the wild fuchsia which, so to speak 'palely loitered' during the heat. Now it is vivid with colour beside orange hawthorn hips, above flaming montbretia and, in our own Burren garden, lavender. Soon we hope to make crabapple jelly and blackberry jam. This may even be the year of the sloe gin! Four years ago we had some fruit trees planted, two of them being apple. Unfortunately they were sited in an unsheltered, open space with the result that only the apple trees bore fruit, just one apple each year, always knocked before ripening by the birds. However, we were lucky this year. We watched this beautiful, perfectly round apple reddening. Then one morning at about 6am the fruit was gone. We rushed out before the birds could get too busy and there our apple lay on a nest of grass. We ate half each and it was delicious, just as I'd always imagined that original Eden apple to have been! There was great excitement in the village of Ballyvaughan recently when news came through that a grant of £8,000 had come through to help renovate the old school as a community centre. This added to more than £17,000 collected by the Ladies' Club (the population is about 400) brings construction a great deal nearer. This is but one example of the kind of people who live in this landscape, decent, caring of the beauty they live in and so very anxious to preserve it. As Ibsen said, 'A community is like a ship'; in this one the ladies were 'prepared to take the helm'.

A high opinion of women

June 1992

Flies, Flick and Paint Job. I am standing by the River Nore in the pretty village of Inistioge where my family spent many afternoons and in spring and summer many long, light-filled evenings. It is strange to return and find such little visible change. Behind me is the grey, lichen-crusted Brown's Barn's bridge, through which the water rushes, making whirling pools that disappear and reform unendingly. Here my father came, adapting the fly he had so carefully made at home in New Ross, to river conditions of speed and light. Here he stood but in the middle of the river, loving, as he said, 'The flick of the wrist with the arch of the line'. We joked that he 'had laboured all night and caught nothing' until he confessed that he kept putting back the brown trout he caught: 'They are such gallant battlers for their lives. Who am I to deprive them of it?' I walk along the river bank, lush water meadows, trees everywhere, Mount Brandon in the distance effulgent in the last shadows before dusk settles. In a still inlet, water boatmen are busy, a ramshorn snail rises to the surface to gulp its air supply and descend. Apart from gnats, the only visible creature is a pied wagtail looping, hovering, catching its last meal. It is inevitable that I should remember my father saying, 'This is the most beautiful place in the world for me. If France were the other side of the river it couldn't be more lovely.' The countryside filled him with happiness. I think it helped him to keep growing – towards the end of his life I remember his words, 'Your mother and life itself have given me a very high opinion of women. I have always fought hard for good settlements for wives [in legal separations – he was a solicitor]. They deserve the best from us.' The same man was little affected by monuments. On seeing the oak-studded church door in Llanreath, Cornwall he exclaimed, 'It could do with a lick of paint!'

Bats in the plumbing

April 1994

A warning for those of us who live in Ireland's Western World! Doctors have cautioned against sunburn and sunbathing (without a barrier cream). The air is so pure here that it is unable to filter the skin-cancer-causing sun rays. In most other areas of the planet, pollution and smog act as barriers. One pure, unalloyed region and there's a huge fly in the ointment. This March day of sunshine, still Atlantic waters, soft spring breezes, casts the mildest of spells on birds, creatures of the wild and ourselves. Tons of sand have been pitched up on the Rine during the almost ceaseless winter storms. Each springing grass leaf glitters against golden sand crystals. Brent geese, oystercatchers preen themselves while dippers rush here and there and curlews stalk slowly, pausing occasionally to excavate with their long curved bills some delicacy. All, however, was not well in our attic. Our clever electrician, a young, strong man, a great player of our Gaelic games, climbed up to wire for extra lights. After a few minutes he scuttled down the ladder, white-faced. 'Something flew at me.' We climbed up and shone torches all over – nothing. Our electrician finished and departed. I ventured up to the attic several times afterwards – nothing. About six months later I saw a piece of fur emerge from a tap. After another six months, just recently, our excellent plumber came to check everything. He showed me what he had found in the attic, in the water system – at the bottom of his red plastic bucket was a drowned pipistrelle bat: fur brown/red, lighter coloured underneath, the face and ears almost black. It, six centimetres wide, is about the same size as our smallest mammal, the pigmy shrew, and it certainly frightened our six-foot-tall electrician! Our poor little bat 'hath flown / His cloister'd flight' (Macbeth) and will no more 'With short shrill shriek' flit 'by on leathern wing' (William Collins).

Nanny comes calling

August 1994

As often happens with a very important visitor, she arrived just as we were about to depart for dinner at our French friends. Mary Ann phoned our hostess, saying, 'We may be late – we have a problem here.' Our hostess replied, 'Do not worry – I send Alexis,' her grown-up son. Within minutes Alexis arrived with a young French girl, Benedicte, from Paris. They greeted with gentle words our visitor – a wild mountain nanny goat. Her hair was white and long, her horns easily 15cm at the forehead, tapering back behind her head. Her rapport with Mary Ann was instantaneous – everywhere Mary Ann went the nanny goat went too (munching ivy and blackthorn). However, she then made a dart for our shrub, *Elaeagnus x ebbingei "Limelight"* and proceeded to nibble it. Up to that critical moment we had been wondering if we could keep her. Now we realised she would have to be kept tethered if we did and what kind of life would that be for a creature of the wild? The four of us decided that our young friends would walk the nanny to the nearest path to Cappanawalla hill behind our house. Alexis asked for a rope and Mary Ann gave him a dog leash. He put the leash on and Benedicte led the goat off, Alexis walking beside them and what a lovely sight, the beautiful young girl, the white goat and the handsome man! After giving them a headstart, we followed in the car up the lane to Newtown Castle. On this lane with access to the hills we left the nanny goat – with great reluctance and a sense of awe, of wonder at her friendliness, as Mary Ann described her, 'her eyes were so innocent, her ba-a-a so gentle.' We wondered greatly what 'our' beautiful wild nanny goat did or what was done to her, in her awful vulnerability. We need not have worried – she found shelter and kindness with our German neighbours who live by the sea near us. Truly a European venture, French, German, Irish, even international with American Mary Ann. For the gentle goat, 'Fortune' was 'more kind than her custom' (Shakespeare).

Marching for peace

February 1996

The dawn came slowly, pouring silver light across the sky, over the quiet waters of the bay. As the light strengthened, multiple shades of grey spread everywhere, toning in with the Burren's grey stone wall, its hills with their patches of morning mist. The peace was tangible, 'dropping from the veils of the morning' (Yeats), the peace of natural things. However, the people of the village (population 400 about), like slightly over 98 per cent of our Republic, resolved to make a stand for peace. We decided that we, like those in the big centres, would march for peace on February 25. So, at 3pm, we gathered with others from surrounding areas in the centre of Ballyvaughan – we, the people, elderly, middle-aged, young and children, with our home-made placard: Give Back Our Peace – Stop Killing. One little girl had designed her own poster: the Union Jack side by side with the Irish tricolour, a hand from each flag reaching to clasp the other. With Father Kelly we marched, on a cold, glitteringly sunny day, standing for a minute's silence for the victims of terrorism (Canary Wharf and the Aldwych bus bomb in all our minds). Then the Lord's Prayer was said and we dispersed. Yet again this marvellous region on Ireland's western coast manifested its worth, its mettle in the grand numbers taking part, in the openness of our demand for peace, our hands carrying nothing but paper posters. There was a lovely, easy unity among us. The intelligence to uphold our democracy – allied to hearts full of concern for the innocent dead and wounded – impelled us, minds and hearts beating as one, to walk for peace. 'Still in thy right hand carry gentle peace' (Shakespeare).

In praise of the lasso

January 1998

There is, I think, much to be said for the lasso. Recently I watched a garden spider jogging around its silken web, which was hung with raindrops. As I stood, fascinated always by spiders, bits and pieces of information gathered over the years came back to me, for example that the silk contracts under wet conditions, thus preventing the breaking of the threads; that of two strands with exactly the same dimensions, one of steel and the other of spider-silk, the latter is the stronger. I knew, of course, that spiders use their webs and silken cords to catch prey. Some species even manufacture a sticky ball attached to a thread. This they aim at passing insects, effectively lassoing them, thus leading us to the great question: who used the lariat/ lasso first – cowboy or spider? Recently, in my home county, Wexford, I heard a true story of an appearance on a farm. Farmer Pat Kehoe noticed each morning strange hoof marks near those of his horses. He kept vigil and one night, with a friend, Ned Cullen, he managed to lasso a strange beast which, from its tracks, he'd thought might be a deer. Not at all – it was much stranger. Pat had lassoed a nyala, a native of Zambia! It is the size of a stag with straight 50cm horns, bent towards the end. Pat has rejected many offers for the animal, the Kehoe family having become attached to their nyala, determined to keep him.

He gets apples, carrots, five pounds of oats each day. The mystery – how did the nyala get to Pat's farm? Wexford boasts of more than the nyala. Near Wexford town, on the North Slob (with its centrally heated observation tower) among thousands of Greenland white-fronted geese and wigeon, the rare American wigeon and green-winged teal can be seen. 'And still we gazed, and still the wonder grew' (Goldsmith).

Battle for the limestone

April 2000

Nine years is no short stretch in human life. It took our local Seven Samurai (the Burren Action Group) that long to gain a splendid environmental victory for our lovely Burren. Last month, March, our highest planning authority, An Bord Pleanála, refused a government minister's appeal to build visitor facilities at Mullaghmore, one of the more remote areas of the Burren. It is a region of great fragility, an area in which to be solitary with its beautiful, thought-provoking and extraordinary shaped mountain, its turloughs (lakes that dry out in fine spells and refill in wet weather), its wild flowers and wild creatures. The Burren Action Group fought the power and limitless funds of the state. They scraped money together from collections and they put on the line their own financial security, their farms, their homes. They owe about £150,000 in legal fees, which could be waived (though there is no sign of this). The minister is having her team search for a technicality on which to appeal the decision.

Mullaghmore, one of the more remote areas of the Burren

Early this month I walked into the Ballyvaughan village, stopping now and again to watch birds – curlews, a heron, a great flight of Brent geese, sanderlings. But pride of place I must give to our pair of resident mute swans. I watched them sail in beauty, away from seaweed, out into the little harbour by Pier Road. Then in perfect synchronisation, side by side, each head was buried deep in the water and raised four times. In alternation, six times each bird buried its head as the other raised it. The timing and the rhythm were perfect, completely stylised. The cob, after this, stroked the water between them with his beak and then they mated, the female sinking with just a small loop of the neck and the tail visible. Then they sailed on. It was truly one of the most lovely sights I've ever seen. Mimi, in Jennifer Johnston's novel *Two Moons*, weeps on seeing a dead cormorant, 'Its feathers dark and stiff with oil.' Her spouse remarks: 'Why waste tears on a bird?' and later, 'Oil is more important than birds.' Ah!

Marking the Millennium

January 2001

Cheese … It was nothing like cheese. The night following its eclipse, splendid here, it shone above Finnavara and our bay like a beautiful peach, one just plucked from the tree, with a delicate bloom, a perfect moon. It cast its light on hill and sea, warming their cold and icy look with its 'sprinkled blush' (Marianne Moore). So the first year of the millennium has ended, though for many it now begins with 2001. What has our small country done to celebrate this past year? Each baby born on

January 1 2000 received a silver salver, and silver tokens were given to those who turned 100. How, it might be asked, did the environment fare? – it got the biggest grant. In 14 forests, 1,200,000 trees (oaks and other broad-leaved varieties) were planted, one for each household, with a certificate issued of the location and species.

To match this, people here paid ten punt each to plant a belt of trees beside the new playing field. As the old Irish poem Cill Cais asks, 'Cad a dheanfaimid feasta gan adhmaid?' (What will we do without wood?) Brigid was released on Cullenstown Strand, the 100th seal cared for and then freed from the National Sanctuary. Golden eagles, extinct here for years, will, it is hoped, fly over Donegal from their new breeding sites in Glenveagh National Park. Dublin's River Liffey was enhanced by a new pedestrian bridge and a short boardwalk. Amy Sweeney, aged 11, wrote of her hopes for the new millennium. 'That all the problems of the world – war, famine, poverty, pollution – will be solved. I also would like Sligo to win an all-Ireland football final.' (Gaelic football)

Bellissima Italia

April 2001

Kilometres of arcades with mosaic or tiled floors, some with ceilings of paintings: we were in Bologna, Italy. Such a gracious city, younger people giving us their bus seats, and faces in the crowd from the Italian Masters: Caravaggio, Da Vinci, Michelangelo, Raphael. And again, in Ravenna, to notice a face similar to one in the beautiful mosaics of San Appolinaris in Classe is to be transported back not only to the sixth century but also to the 1960s when I first visited this magnificent church, having walked from Ravenna – I had little money. On my return, a farmer and his wife gave me a lift. I sat among straw in their Cinquecento exclaiming, 'Bellissima Italia', in an atmosphere of infinite goodwill. The church then rose out of seemingly limitless green fields. There were but four other people gazing at … paradise. To visit Italy always makes me aware and proud of our European heritage. To return to England is to see faces from the National Portrait Gallery in London's streets. To come back to the Burren is to see faces from the Book of Kells, Jack Yeats, O'Conor, Lavery. What a fullness of ages in faces!

This morning, furze, daffodils and primroses tumble in the gale. The mist rises, disappears and the sun strikes beauty from limestone, sea and fields. Forbidden fields now that we are trying to limit foot-and-mouth disease to the one case in the north-east of the Republic. We are still able to walk the Flaggy Shore, the lanes and public roads, while blackthorn blooms in hedge and field. Brent geese are plentiful – I counted 20 in Ballyvaughan Harbour. We are lucky that they spread 'gray wings' on 'every tide' (Yeats).

Bringing art to Ballyvaughan

August 2001

Guardian readers who know Ballyvaughan will be sorry to hear the news that one of the village's most beloved sons has passed away. Michael Greene died suddenly last month at the age of 44, playing the game he loved, Gaelic football. As a young man Michael had a dream for Ballyvaughan, the village of his birth. He saw the incredible beauty of our landscape and believed there should be an art college among the hills and valleys, a place where young people could relate to their natural surroundings and, in their turn, create things of beauty. Now Michael's dream has been realised, and recently I toured the Burren College of Art with my close friend, Jane, just retired from her headship of an art department in Cambridge. We watched a group of young New Yorkers render their visions of the area in painting and sculpture. Michael's vision was eternal and universal. For as long as people value the things of the mind, of the heart, they will continue to come here to give form to their inner selves, to dwell in the beauty of life. Visitors to the village may also tour Newtown Castle, which adjoins the college, and was restored by Michael and his wife, Mary. They cannot but wonder at the testament to both the history of the Burren, and to the vision of a remarkable man. What more could a man do for his village? Well, Michael did much more, chairing our development committee with wisdom and insight through difficult times. Because of the college, Michael's work was celebrated internationally, but his renown never went to his head. He remained rooted in the village of his birth, in the Burren.

Hypnotising hens

December 2001

William Butler Yeats, the poet, had a habit of hypnotising hens, as related by 'Y' of the Irish Times in his recently published book, *In Time's Eye*. A collection of his daily nature columns for the *Irish Times*, it is a wonderful read. Nature diarists can illumine the lightless stretches of winter evenings. I remember an opening line by the late Enid Wilson: 'Cloud can do strange things in quiet December weather.' As ever she was right. We walked the Flaggy Shore on a mild and misty day. The clouds were grey and low. The mist thickened until, on reaching Loch Murree, it lay outstretched like a silken scarf above the grey water and over it the now darker clouds accumulated, massed and dense. Below the cloud and mist, eight whooper swans and three cygnets glided on the water, necks upright. It is scarcely surprising that human creatures used swans for myth and poetry making. Leda was visited by Zeus in the form of a swan and Yeats wrote The Wild Swans at Coole, ' … now they drift on the still water, / Mysterious, beautiful'.

One morning, before light spread, I gazed out on fog and, on furze gorse seemingly white with frost although it was very mild. I immediately went to investigate and found every furze-bush layered with webs of crystal drops as small as seed pearls. 'Ah! The family Linyphiidae have been busy,' I thought. The money spiders had made such loveliness and, for unwary insects, deadly traps. The webs were flat and above each were silken lines holding the structure in place. Insects bump into these, falling upon the web under which the spider lurks.

Sarah in Wonderland

March 2003

I think I will write a book and call it Sarah in Wonderland, for marvels keep occurring. I went out to feed the birds on a morning full of dazzling gold – the hills and sea were spinning in gilded twists of light. As I filled a peanut feeder, I saw an *Apodemus sylvaticus*. He, the wood mouse, was caught in the double strands of wire from tree-branch to feeder. I am sorry to say he was dead, having died trying to reach sustenance. He was beautiful, his eyes bigger than those of the house mouse, his hind feet longer, his back rich brown with a little yellow throat patch. That was one wonder, and recently a Galway fisherman caught a mantis shrimp, *Meiosquilla desmaresti*, which is now on display in the Atlantaquaria in Salthill, Galway. Its claw, astonishingly, has a speed of up to 100mph and is capable of shattering aquarium glass. The aquarium manager said it can 'pack a bigger punch than Tyson'.

Third, a white stork with black wing and tail markings came here instead of wintering in Africa. Nightly, for weeks, he returned to the same place, the Moriarty farm near Portmagee. There he perched on the gate pier, sleeping on one leg. Of course there is the wonder of the human animal, too. A local friend told us nettles were good for rheumatism, taken in soup, tea or by beating oneself with a bunch. The latter reminded me of an old man who so beat himself in beautiful Cornwall when I taught there that I feared to pass his house lest I'd hear him roaring. And then there is the marvel of language. Of a non-stop talker, our friend Emily said, 'She's a STORM, you'd be clattering around in the wind of her words, having to take a boat to Alaska to escape drowning.'

The blackbirds flourish

April 2004

Readers will be pleased to hear this news – the blackbirds that built their nest in the Christmas tree in Limerick successfully reared one chick. It flew the nest more than a month ago, many suitable, daily Christmas gifts having been laid out for it. Now we wonder if the parents will build another nest, because our spring is colder than the Christmas season. What a strange sight it must be for Toni Droney (Bell Harbour) and her family to look out and see stretched out on their lawn a large bull seal. Toni once walked with her small children quite close. The seal was unperturbed, nonchalantly raising a flipper – in greeting? He comes quite regularly, resting on the grass until the returning tide and probably hunger, lure him away. As a result of reading *Ireland's Mushroom Stones* (L Dunne and J Feehan) we went to Mullaghmore to see them. After much poking about we found, with the help of field glasses, one at Gortlecka and another at Rinn na Mona, and truly wonderful they were. Even their names; mushroom or wave stones are not only descriptive but also imaginative – much of their present shape being caused by wave action over thousands of years.

Now they stand stranded in their limestone landscape because of either a lowering of the water table or of isostatic uplift (the earth responding to the lifting of great ice-masses). They are markers of our remote past and embellishers of our present. Their limestone grades from dark to light, their crevices from circular to long knife-edges, their surfaces adorned with white, black and green lichen. Above them, reaching to the sky, are the undulations and great sweeps of Mullaghmore Mountain.

A wonder of paper and glue

August 2004

I am following a paper trail and learning a great deal. It was almost by accident, well, serendipity, that we made our discovery. We passed it many times a day, totally unaware of its existence. We opened the door of our boiler-room and there it was – attached firmly to the inside of the wooden door. It measured about 15cm wide, 16cm in length and 12cm in depth. Its colour was a rich cream, its construction layered, each layer composed of many, thumbnail-sized scallop edges. Readers will have already guessed – it is the nest of *Vespula vulgaris*, the common wasp, which by its own invitation has become our house guest, by building its most uncommon dwelling in our boiler-room. Of course by the end of the summer we may have sheltered more than 6,000 house guests. This does stretch the hospitality instinct! The nest is both beautiful and wonderful, its construction a marvel of engineering and architectural design. To think it all began in the mouth of the queen wasp. She, with her mandibles, scrapes off fragments of wood, paper, even fabrics, mixing them in a ball with her saliva, and thus into thin paper – major recycling! Out of this she begins the stalk of the nest, then the layers, building from the top down; each layer is attached to the one above by little pillars. Into the cells she glues her eggs. The queen confines herself to reproduction after the eggs hatch into workers. These become the babysitters even providing central heating (about 30C) by contracting and extending their abdomens rapidly and air-conditioning by vibrating their wings. We can only gaze in wonder at this paper world, 'a little world made cunningly' (Donne).

But it has to go

December 2004

Absolutely mesmerised I was, for I have discovered a whole new world – to misquote Shakespeare's Miranda, 'O brave new world, That has such creatures in't!' I am, of course, referring to the world of wasps. Readers will remember that we were unable to open our boiler-room door and that therein was a wasp nest. Well, our friend Ben Johnson, our local expert on bees and wasps, came to our help. He got the door open to reveal a wondrous object. When I wrote in August the nest was 16cm long; it was now 79cm long. It stretched from one side of the door, over the door-handle to the opposite wall. It was beautiful, a masterpiece of architectural design. But joy soon turned to sadness. Ben explained that the location of the nest in such a warm space would enable the wasps to over-winter, ever-increasing the size of their dwelling and assuring the survival of almost every larva. In addition we could never ask our plumber to service the boiler. It was with the utmost reluctance that I asked Ben to use the gas on our wasps. The creatures had not harmed us – they had, in fact, because of being carnivores, disposed of countless insects harmful to plants and flowers. After the slaughter Ben took the nest down, and it was even more wonderful to see the inside: cell after cell, perfectly fashioned to fit each larva. I suppose our nest contained more than 25,000 larvae. I miss the wasps flying about and, another marvel, they can fly in light rain and can fly forwards, vertically, both down and up and even in reverse. I am substituting 'wasps' for Emily Dickinson's 'bees' – wasps 'are Black, with Gilt Surcingles / Buccaneers of Buzz'.

Turtle power

December 2005

As I write, she may be resting at or departing from the Canaries. She was caught in a lobster pot and brought back to Dingle, Co Kerry, where she was fitted with a satellite device, powered by a three-year battery. Cork and Swansea universities are carrying out this female leatherback turtle project, and are logging all the information gained from tagging about her whereabouts, dives, diving depths and temperatures. She swims about 40km a day, diving to 160 metres. The researchers hope that this turtle will identify her breeding grounds for them. I never knew that Irish and Welsh coasts are homes to this species, *Dermochelys coriacea*, which dates back about 60m years. This leatherback is about 2m long, 30 to 40 years old and weighs approximately 400kg. This particular species has, compared with all other turtles, one unusual feature – it is warm-blooded.

Without the slightest error, barring accidents from ships or fishing, she will navigate her way to a warm, tropical coast where she will lay 80 eggs, returning after ten days to lay another batch. This is repeated for more than two months. Her navigational prowess over thousands of kilometres is astonishing and wonderful. It is thought she uses the Earth's magnetic field lines and ultimately her senses of smell and taste.

This is the first attempt to track leatherback turtles in European waters and I so hope it will be successful. All being well she will return to Dingle. She will never know her young and not many of them will survive. However, leatherback turtles are not the only migrators at this time of year. Here, during the recent cold snap when there was a sparse sprinkle of snow on the Burren hills our garden and fields welcomed migratory birds, fieldfares and redwings.

Murder on the moor

February 2006

He used hair gel to make his hair stand up, probably to give an impression of height. He was a little man, barely 1.6 metres, in his 20s. A murder victim whose torturers and murderers will never be known, Cloneycavan Man (discovered in Clonycavan bog, Co Meath in February 2003) is more than 2,300 years old. Only a few months later another iron-age body was discovered: this one, headless, was in Croghan bog, Co Offaly. Old Croghan Man, a giant 1.98 metres tall, was a torture and murder victim from about the same time. The lonely bogs were simultaneously these men's graves and preservers. We now know that hair gel was imported into Ireland from either south-west France or Spain and was very expensive, revealing the haut bourgeois or noble status of Clonycavan Man, also shared by Old Croghan Man, who never did a day's manual labour – his hands were unroughened. His fingerprints are like those of today's population – as is the reconstructed face of Clonycavan Man, even down to blue eyes.

So to 'our' giant leatherback turtle, who was tagged in Dingle, Co Kerry last year and is now swimming off the coast of Senegal in water of 24C (the sea here is 9C, so you can see why she migrated). She recently dived to 500 metres, her deepest dive yet. Long may she survive. Today we watched Brent geese surfing, six riding each wave as it crested, borne in, only to begin again. They were not feeding. Were they enjoying themselves?

Remembering Enid

October 2006

I was sitting on a stone in the little deserted village of Formoyle, above the Caher river in Lochrann, known locally as the Khyber Pass. The village was abandoned in 1848 during the great famine. The walls of the small houses still stand but the roofs have long disappeared. Over the years I have shown this village to friends from abroad and always with the same result – we have arrived as a group but almost immediately have separated, each to seek solitude, a solitude that the place seems to impose. There is a sadness, of course, but also a great quietness and peace. There is no place here for vulgar brashness, for the loud and boastful. We do not know where its inhabitants went. We can but suppose that the few survivors migrated, leaving us this legacy of stillness, of calm. As I sat there I remembered Enid J Wilson, that former great Country Diarist, describing her visit to a deserted farmhouse in North Westmorland. The house, she wrote, has 'such an air of common goodness that I half expected to see smoke in the cold chimneys'. She might have been describing this village. As I wound my way down to the road, and a steep descent it is, I noticed house martins swooping and then gathering on the telephone wires. Perhaps they were about to migrate. If so, it would be our second migration of birds seen this autumn. In France we witnessed a wonderful gathering and flight of swallows. Down in the valley a sharp little breeze sang among the tall grasses forcing them into a wave-like dance. The whole vale had a golden sheen from mountain summits to foothills, the Caher river, swollen with recent rain, tumbled over its stony bed. A few grey fish sheltered in the lee of a large rock, their delicate fins beating the water, their tails moving to keep them in place. Indeed, as Wilson remarked, 'October days often have a feeling of hope, of next year's promise.'

Speeding butterflies

June 2007

I am somewhat wary of butterflies and moths. This wariness originated in upstate New York while following an Indian trail.

I reported my sighting to Mary Ann of a butterfly, 'large, wide wingspan, coloured black, yellow and blue'. I asked her its name and she replied: 'It is the Great Bruise.' I was silent but thinking on my first visit to this huge country, and trying to understand different customs. 'Well, Americans are a very down-to-earth people; after all, they named a town Mechanicsburg.' (I later, in France, found a town named La Machine!). Some time later I tentatively inquired: 'Is it really called the Great Bruise?' Laughter. One of the astounding things I find about butterflies is their speed. We were overtaken by myriads of them on our recent French trip. I also find them much harder to identify than birds. They come much nearer but close their wings as soon as I focus on them or go tacking off across the river or over a hedge. However, I did see in France a most delightfully coloured caterpillar: black body with speckled yellow and a long, red back stripe, the sides having red lines with red and white spots and yellow dots. I had discovered the spurge hawk-moth, family Sphingidae. I believe it is named after the Sphinxes of Egypt because it can pose like one, with its head and thorax raised. Later I was lucky to see a beautiful butterfly that I later identified as the poplar admiral with its 60 to 80mm wingspan. This is a wonderful year for butterflies here in the Burren. Today, walking by copses and meadows, I saw small and large whites, and common and small blues. In our front field I was almost swarmed by little Burren blues and six-spot burnets, but never have I seen the Burren green moth, unique to this region.

Thieves from the sky

September 2007

They came in a pack, the thieves, stealing everything they deemed to be of value. It was a perfectly organised operation, nothing was left to chance. We watched thunderstruck, noting their legs clad in what looked like baggy trousers. Except for about four they were all dressed uniformly in black. The four were hooded. What you might call 'the attack' was very professional. We were rooted to the spot and quite helpless, such was their speed. We remained hidden until all was over. Then we surveyed the damage and our losses. You could say we were well and truly 'rooked'. Twelve rooks and four hooded crows relieved us of 16 beautiful red apples and a tree full of rose-coloured pears. The rooks took it in turns to land on the fruit trees. They then, with their great, strong beaks, broke off the apples, flopped down on the ground to contest with their fellow robbers for the fallen fruit, the successful bird spearing it and flying away to isolated rocks or walls.

The hooded crows were adept at nipping in to steal the ill-gotten gains, leaving the hard work to the rooks, although the latter made a real battle of it. What began as blatant robbery became in the end a kind of game – see who gets the ball, in this case, of course, the fruit.

Sometimes a rook in flight was forced to drop his load. Then the *ruaille-buaille* (pronounced 'rewlah-bewlah' – pandemonium) started with three or more birds scrumming, only one scoring a try. Once a rook flew to a rock with a large piece of apple and was joined by two juveniles. The apple was shared. At last they all flew away. To tell the truth, we didn't mind this theft very much because the apples are tasteless and the pears never seem to become soft and edible, unlike our delicious plums.

The blackbird's singing lesson

November 2007

'A Garden is a lovesome thing, God wot!' wrote the 19th-century poet Thomas E Brown. A statement worth considering. Mary Ann was in the garden singing away, Smoke Gets in Your Eyes. She finished and had just begun, O Shenandoah … when I was about to issue forth. I had barely taken a few steps into the 'lovesome thing' when suddenly her singing ceased. Our resident blackbird had arrived on the scene and proceeded to show how it should be done. The trilling, chords, arpeggios went on and on, now sounding like a flute, now like a violin. Neither of us could compete. It certainly was a performance, glorious and wonderful. How lucky we are to have a resident tenor. At the end he looked about as if awaiting applause, flicked his wing feathers – perhaps in disdain – and flew to a tree, still looking down on us.

At least he was harmless, unlike a tree branch some hours later on that windy day. A branch from a hawthorn tree pierced Mary Ann's hand. Four stitches were necessary – a garden lovesome and dangerous. Our wasp's nest was showing activity up to October 23. Now all is quiet and the beautiful nest lies unseen, uninhabited beneath the earth. The queen has fled, waiting dormant until next year. On a walk towards Feenagh we stopped to watch a farmer, his wife, their two dogs and a cat. The farmer was bent over his tractor, fiddling with something mechanical. The others were all waiting. The dogs were barking impatiently. The farmer's wife said all five of them often do jobs together. The cat always likes to accompany them, although she sometimes slopes off to have a short nap in the sun. What would our world be like without the foibles of ourselves and others, without the unexpectedness of creatures?

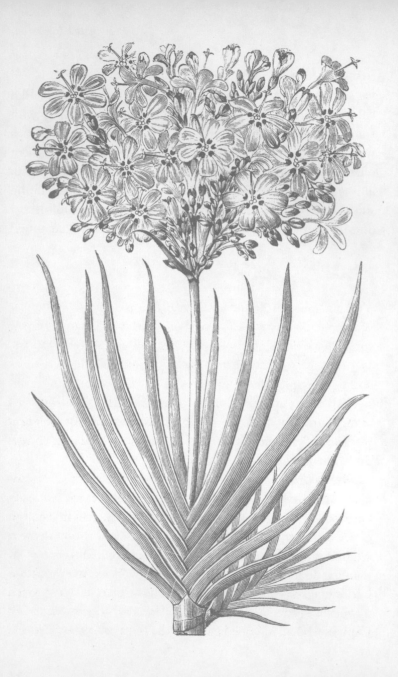

CHAPTER
Nine

A Walk With Jinny

Virginia Spiers suggested to me that warmth was a characteristic of female Country Diarists, and on an idyllic day of pottering round her native Tamar valley in Cornwall, she proved the point. Is there anyone who doesn't know Virginia between Calstock and St Dominic, where she lives with her husband, Jack, plus her two sisters and their husbands nearby? The six of them get along famously and go for long, diary-inspiring walks at weekends, Virginia with a notebook so that she doesn't forget the endless suggestions everyone makes.

She has the pen; her sister Mary Martin, an artist well-known in the West Country, has the brush. Unbeknown to me, I already had both of them tucked away in my kitchen shelves in the form of *The National Trust Book of Picnics*, whose cover shows a young woman preparing a harvest picnic in a cornfield. It is a vivid painting done in swirly Van Gogh style by Mary; the model for her picnicker was Virginia. Guardian diarists have been immortalised in many places; Ted Ellis on a beer label, Bill Campbell on an inscribed park bench, Thomas Coward, Arnold

Boyd and Lance Samuels by three memorial bird hides and a reed bed in Cheshire. Here is another to add to that distinctive collection.

So when Spiers' soft Cornish voice invited me down to the Tamar, I didn't hesitate, even though the chances of a picnic in January were slim. As soon as I changed at Plymouth into the one-car diesel that rattles up the river to Calstock, the Spiers' world sprang to life. Everyone knew everyone and the chatter was riveting. 'I tidied his Lordship's bedroom while he was away – he's got rows and rows of ornaments in there. He's got 16 clocks.' 'I always rely on that cream, you know, the one, what's it called, comes in a blue tin, oh dear, I can't remember the name.' I even joined in, correctly suggesting Nivea.

The train crosses the muddy estuary of the Tavey, slides past gorse hedges and through tangly valleys with odd signs of terraced cultivation, now abandoned, then creeps across the slender Tamar viaduct into Calstock. It's dead on 14.09, as promised hundreds of miles north when I started in Leeds, and Spiers, with her own tangle of greying hair, is waiting on the platform; clearly scarcely able to wait before launching into our tour.

She is hugely knowledgeable. That viaduct, for instance, is one of the country's oldest concrete structures. This pub was nicknamed the 'Sheffl' because knife-grinders from Sheffield used to put up there. Calstock churchyard, which we ramble through, has celandines, lovely views and monuments to men killed in quarrying, mining and shipping disasters, which once plagued this deceptively rural backwater. We carry out a mini-census of bumble bees (numerous) and Spiers scoops up and analyses a handful of soil. A farmer's daughter from St Dominic, she went straight from Reading University into the government's 1960s soil survey, which graded the whole country from one (prime agricultural land) to five, largely to stop builders grabbing grades one and two. She is eloquent on the subject, so much so that Jack fell for her when he attended a lecture she gave on land classification at the Ministry of Agriculture. 'You don't need chemical tests to know your soil,' she says, crumbling the rich black earth between her fingers. 'You get to be able to tell the quality by look and feel.'

The tilth round Calstock is grade one, which explains those abandoned terraces above the railway embankments. In Victorian times, paddle steamers used to take trippers up the Tamar in spring to admire the froth of cherry and apple blossom with daffodils growing wild beneath. Growers teetering down the slopes, sometimes on ropes, supplied markets from Covent Garden to Manchester with fresh flowers. 'There's a pittosporum gone wild,' says Spiers, pointing out a leggy shrub that was fashionable for flower arrangers in the 19th century. 'And that's a hemp agrimony. And look at those ferns!' The flower trade is minimal now, but every farm has a roadside stall of produce with an honesty box, only recently fitted in some cases with a lock.

It was the Cornish bank of the Tamar that prospered most, as the adret, or sunny side of the valley, as opposed to the ubac, its shady counterpart. Spiers enjoyed such geographical terms as a student and has never forgotten them. Criss-crossed by narrow lanes where cars have to back and squeeze, the landscape is like a Greek island or Spanish hill village, with vast amounts of added lichen and ferns. 'I miss the lichen when I'm out of Cornwall,' she says; it is such essentials of this small and specialised landscape that fill her diaries, based on a lifetime's familiarity. As a girl she took short cuts across the beautiful grounds of Cotehele, the local mansion, and remembers the garden's tree-sized Cornish Snow camellia seeming even taller, because it was big and she was small. The field beyond is where the family had real-life harvest picnics, with Mrs Martin sticking an apple on the end of the kettle spout to stop the tea spilling on the walk from the farm.

Down by the river is where Spiers' uncle Stan ran a salmon fishery, and in a narrow side-valley, more ubac than adret, her grandfather's mill with its waterwheel still turning, albeit now as a tourist attraction. In the kitchen, her grandmother made cherry pies from fruit grown up in the sunshine at the top of the hill, serving slices with dollops of clotted cream. Later on, as the trade succumbed to foreign fruit, many of the trees were felled and Spiers remembers their distinctive orangey-red logs burning in the mill's grate.

There would be several lifetimes of Country Diary material in reminiscences about this, but Spiers has another arsenal in the fruit tree breeding work that has engaged Mary and her husband, James. Around their house near the mill and in the grounds of Cotehele, the couple are reintroducing cherries and apples with evocative names. Cat's Head, Bottle Stopper, Onion Redstreak and Cornish Mother. They hunt everywhere for traces of original stock; on the day of my walk with Jin or Jinny, as everyone calls her, they had gone to France to track down some cherry trees in the Ardeche, which they were convinced were the same stock as plants brought to Cornwall in the 17th century by Huguenots fleeing persecution. They found them last year and tied bits of white cloth round their trunks, to help rediscover them; like Hansel and Gretel with their crumb trail.

Ending our tour at her and Jack's home on their own steep hillside in St Dominic, we explore the Spiers' mini-jungle where orderly lines of daffodils are starting to spike through the soil, remnants of another abandoned market garden. More names: Lucifer, Croesus and other bright, shining figures from mythology. There are willow warblers in the wood, swallows due back in the barn in late spring, and the click-tock of a complex system of rams and waterfalls that Jack has installed to feed a succession of ponds. Abundance everywhere; and needless to say, it turns up in the couple's warm kitchen, surrounded by more of Mary's bright oil paintings, where home-made scones follow home-made soup, home-grown salads and home-baked bread.

It was all this home-working that landed Virginia her place in the diary team. She had been urged to try by Sarah Poyntz, her inspirational teacher at the high school in Callington, who came back for a nostalgic visit in 1994. The two women sat admiring the view and Virginia, who has published books on the valley and its history, said how much she enjoyed describing its beauty. Why not have a go for the *Guardian*, said Sarah, who was well into her own stint on the column. Virginia sent a couple of samples and the then editor of the section, Jeanette Page, liked them. But there was no vacancy.

'Then, more than a year later, the phone rang here, and luckily I had just had to come in from the garden to get something done,' says Virginia. It was Page, asking in typically last-minute *Guardian* fashion if there was any chance of doing a diary … for the following Monday. Cotehele's great hall had just been decorated sumptuously for Christmas, so Virginia scooted round and described it. Page was pleased and asked for another, then a third. Spiers has carried on ever since.

She keeps a routine: the walk (sometimes up in Northern England or on holiday overseas), a week to mull, write and email the piece to London, a week not thinking about the Guardian or the diary at all, and then a week getting ready for the next walk. 'They once asked me if I would go fortnightly instead of one diary every three weeks, but I said no,' she says. 'It wouldn't have suited my pattern.'

Spiers notes the number of women getting involved in gardening today, particularly professionally at National Trust properties such as Cotehele. She has her theory about warmth in women's writing. And she wonders if women have, or have had historically, a particular interest in linking things and making connections. 'Only connect,' she says, quoting EM Forster. 'That's another thing I remember being taught, by Sarah.' An apple variety's name links to the Victorian river barges, which may connect to a recent controversy about breaching the Tamar's flood dykes to flood hay meadows and turn them into saltings. And in that way, a Country Diary is born.

Decking the hall

On a mild, grey, late November morning, branches and bunches of dried flowers are brought into the courtyard of Cotehele House. Inside the Great Hall the long polished table and carved chairs are shrouded with dust sheets. There are piles of greenery on the floor and above, standing on a scaffold tower, two men work, threading and weaving flowers into the Christmas garland, which is looped between the chandelier chains and extends the entire length of the 16th-century hall. A wan light from the mullioned and transomed window casts pale shadows on to the walls, where the delicate tracery of decorative beech and bracken fronds belie the deadly nature of the old weapons and armour. The doorways have yet to be edged with evergreens and berries and the massive granite fireplace is black and empty. But, come December, logs will flame and smoulder and candles will be lit on dull afternoons as visitors pause in this peaceful space. Until 1947 Cotehele was owned by the Edgcumbes, who first acquired it in 1353 through marriage with Hilaria de Cotehele. The original medieval and Tudor character of the house has been retained because the family's main residence, since the mid 16th century, was Mount Edgcumbe, lower down the River Tamar and overlooking Plymouth Sound. The Great Hall, as in earlier times, was an important gathering place. My grandfather attended the Michaelmas rent rolls when he paid for his corn mill in the valley leading to Cotehele Quay. In the 1950s, after the National Trust took on the estate, there were Christmas carol services – a tall spruce

was brought in from the woods and the walls festooned with holly
and ivy. Recently, the hall has been decked in medieval style,
without a Christmas tree but with the long garland. This year
the thick rope of glistening pittosporum foliage and interwoven
starlike flowers is hung higher than usual. The spectacular arch-
braced roof with its moulded wind bracing looks down
impassively on the advent of yet another festive season.

Flowers in the lanes

April 1995

In April, our sunken lanes and minor roads are remarkable for
a magnificent spread with masses of palest yellow primroses
full out in sunshine. Bluebell leaves grow thickly and the broad
hedge-tops, cut hard by tractor-driven flail, have honeysuckle
leafing up between dead bracken stalks and jagged stumps of
oak, ash, hazel and holly. On the reverse side of these
roadside hedges, a pared thicket of bramble, hawthorn and
blackthorn often encroaches towards guard fences, which keep
cattle and sheep off the banks and here there are fewer flowers,
probably due to fertiliser and spray drift. Despite annual
battering and shredding by hedge-trimmers, old earth and stone
Cornish banks still resemble miniature linear woods and many
have existed for centuries since early clearance of woodland.
Apart from steep remote areas, lengths with fully developed
strands of trees are rare, unlike earlier days when hedgerows
were coppiced and 'plashed' on a seven-year rotation for farm
wood-burning supplies, a tradition then obligated by tenancy

agreements. Today's shorn twiggy tops provide no logs and little cover for birds, especially in early spring when many are cut. Along and across the banks is a network of fox and badger tracks, through bluebells, around deformed trunks and under stunted twigs. Burrowing rabbits wreak havoc in places, making banks no longer stockproof without supplementary fences and although foxes prey on rabbits they are likely to be shot by farmers worried about lambs. Linesmen, responsible for the care of specific roadsides, used to shovel slumped earth from 'footings' and heave it to the top of banks but modern mechanised maintenance scrapes and removes it to a dump. Wide lorries and tractors cause more destruction, knocking off chunks and eroding the bottoms as do increasing numbers of cars manoeuvering past one another. Yet these ancient narrow ways, with their high banks and stunning succession of wild flowers, continue to amaze.

A windy walk

June 1996

Pink thrift and dazzling yellow gorse are intermixed on the cliff edge, high above a roaring sea. Creamy spume is driven onto boulder beaches and wisps of it whirl up the cliffs in eddies. This stretch of coast, running south from Hartland Point, takes the full brunt of westerly winds. Hedgerow trees in the sparsely populated hinterland are severely stunted, shrinking away from prevailing weather and, along the coast, natural vegetation hugs the ground. Short streams, with headwaters rising just west of those flowing to the Tamar and Torridge, have cut out deep valleys, often with rocky gorges and waterfalls before the shore. The coastal path climbs and plunges precipitously up and down between cliffs, many looming more than 400 feet above the narrow valley mouths. After a bus ride to Hartland, we walk through bluebell woods on a muddy path strewn with hawthorn petals, past the landmark of Stoke's tall church tower to an isolated ruin, and then on the coastal path to Bude, more than 12 miles south. Clifftop fields are green after a fortnight's rain, contrasting with the bald cliffs of folded strata, sheer rock slabs and crumbling, slipping earth. Coastal valleys have remarkable flowery turfs carpeted with pale blue vernal squill, yellow vetch, daisies and silvery-pink thrift. White bladder campions, fragrant burnet roses and tussocks of thrift cling to rocky outcrops and, on damp sites, primroses and violets are still flowering after an exceptionally late cold spring. Drifts of bluebells and uncurling ferns grow amongst dwarf thickets of sloe, bramble, ivy and honeysuckle, which harbour boisterous wrens and blackcaps. On the last lap, south from Morwenstow, we are overlooked by the huge, white dishes and spheres of the incongruous listening station.

A world of white

May 1997

Drifts of foaming white cherry blossom have been succeeded by an equally fantastic display of apple. In Cleave's old orchard, above Glamorgan Hill, Burcombe cherries have already set, bunches of hard, green, olive-like fruits emerged from delicate petals and sepals, now withered and blown away. Apple blossom is fading, overtaken by leaves, but an old Jubilee's lichened twigs are still thickly covered in perfect pink and white blooms. Under encroaching oak, elder and hazel, amongst bluebells, uncurling ferns, campions and brambles, rows of Double Whites extend up-slope. Greenish, blunt-ended buds are opening to richly scented, pure white, narcissi. Pheasant's Eye, with white re-curving petals these, the latest narcissi, once formed a valuable crop for growers. Flowering often coincides with Whitsun and, until 30 or 40 years ago, they fetched high prices in the first few weeks of May. A preserved duplicate order book for 1953 records the first boxes sent to Mr A J Willis in Leicester market, selling wholesale for 2s/9d a bunch. With blue irises and lilies-of-the-valley, Double Whites provided income in the period between spring daffodils and cloched strawberries picked later in May. Reputed to have originated in Bere Alston parish, growing semi-wild in hedgerows on Clamoake farm, they were first sent to Devonport market in 1880 by Mr Jackson. With other Poeticus varieties, grown under fruit trees, they were the mainstay of the valley's first commercial flower producers. Difficult to establish and only thriving where undisturbed, surviving stands are now rare. This orchard, reverting to woodland, is an ideal site and the undergrowth also shelters blackcaps, chiffchaffs and willow warblers. Their persistent clamorous songs, mingled with the cool green fragrance of bluebells, blossom, new leaves and recently dampened earth signify 'Summer is a-come today'.

The flying duchess

February 1998

Upstream from medieval Horse Bridge, beyond the northern flanks of Kit Hill and Hingston Down, the Tamar meanders through a pastoral landscape, flat meadows extending from riverbank trees towards gently sloping hills. Easterly winds and frosty nights have cut back unseasonal January growth, grass has shrunk and fields are drab. Pared hedges show little sign of new greenness, shorn forms contrasting with those, as yet unflailed, tangled with last year's woody growth – slender wands, spiny spears, arching strands of briar and bramble sheltering underlying ferns, foxglove and emerging primrose. Snowdrops spill over a garden hedge opposite the round of lime trees at the entrance to Endsleigh. The letter B, carved on the lodge wall, marks it as part of the old Bedford estate. Down the long driveway, through thick-trunked, spreading rhododendrons, under oaks and tall conifers, the big house is a private hotel. The grounds are part of a charitable trust, no longer visited by the Bedfords. They used to come regularly, accompanied by retainers, and older locals remember tales of the flying duchess, piloting her little aeroplane, and the duke's rides, brushed clear of leaves before he drove through his woods. A syndicate now controls the salmon fishing and a trust lets the cottages to tourists. Extensive coniferous woodland is managed for commercial forestry, and the walled kitchen gardens are used as a nursery and garden centre. Within those high, crumbling brick walls, which once contained fruit and vegetable beds, melon, peach and strawberry houses, are local varieties of apples and cherries amongst ranks of container-grown shrubs, poly-tunnels and netting screens shielding young camellias, magnolias and azaleas from desiccating cold.

Ice and ice cream

January 2001

On a cold Sunday morning, scores of cars park by the dam of Burrator reservoir – navy-blue water surrounded by mature plantations below Sheeps Tor's sunlit rocks. People stroll and jog and an ice-cream van has already set up pitch.

Nearby, the dismantled Yelverton-Princetown railway winds through the wood beside Devonport leat, towards exposed pastures on the wet Dartmoor fringe, where shaggy ponies huddle in an old droveway from Walkhampton. Beyond the Tavy, across the Tamar's sheltered domain, landmarks such as Kit Hill, Sentry Hill wood and St Dominic's alstroemeria glass houses are discernible and, on the skyline, Bodmin Moor lies under a cold haze. The former railway meanders upwards through deserted moorland above lichened woods in Walkham valley.

Black-faced sheep graze among granite boulders, orange bracken, dark gorse bushes, stunted hawthorns and ancient boundaries, all vivid and clear-cut beneath blue sky. As the track gains height, doubling back around Ingrator and its derelict quarry, views become ever more expansive northwards to Cox Tor, Great Staple and Great Mistor.

In the bitterly cold east wind, ground is frozen hard, with

ice-crazed puddles in Eggworthy cutting. One can imagine the engine and single coach with eight passengers stranded, buried up to its roof in snow, during the great blizzard of March 1891. Another tortuous loop around King's Tor must have added to the sense of desolation experienced by convicts en route to the prison, remote and hidden behind the blasted tussocky slopes of Hessary Tor (517m).

Circling the parish

June 2002

Beating the bounds on jubilee Monday began in drizzle that enhanced the green of Cotehele's woods, reed beds and tidal water. Trees dripped along the millstream and muddy Duke's Drive, once a carriageway to St Dominic church. A heron flew from a clearing of buttercups and ragged robin and we climbed Bury Hill, bypassing a stream cut off by modern fencing. Triticale grows amongst pastures off Summers Lane and, from Cornele, we looked north of this agricultural parish to old mines beneath Kit Hill. Over post and wire, using plastic chairs provided by a new owner near Dupath, we followed pollarded ash uphill to the A388 – turnpike and ancient ridgeway. Two stones and a medieval cross are markers, and in Westcott farmhouse, straddling the boundary with Callington, the youngest walker climbed through a window.

Sun comes out and a westerly blows from Bodmin Moor. Under Viverdon we are escorted past a herd of cows and Limousin bull with distant blue views east to Dartmoor. After plunging from Vernago there are sunlit glimpses of foxgloves in Birchenhayes's old market gardens opposite shady Crocadon Wood, and in Brentswood unripe stones litter the ground around surviving cherries. Facing Pillaton parish, above Ornivers marsh and through a weedy set-aside field, we reach Halton Quay. There, cottages of former growers, farm-workers and the manager of Co-op's coal and corn depot are now desirable, freehold residences. Past the holy well and recently converted barns at Chapel farm we return upriver, along the Tamar levee, knee-high in lank grass.

A lonely quarry

December 2002

Up in the mist, the back cliff of Kit Hill quarry is barely visible, gloomy above the deep pool and boggy fringe. The wet southerly wind smells faintly of sewage waste, spread on fields below the stack, and also of Callington's modern pasty factory. The outdoor production floor is derelict, closed since 1955. At its peak, between the wars, up to 100 men walked uphill to work in this isolated quarry. They bored and blasted, loosening raw granite for mechanised cutting, shaping and dressing. Finger dumps are piled with discarded blocks, now colonised with lichen, moss, polypody ferns and scrub. An incline plunges straight down the northern slope, through flowering gorse, soggy ginger bracken, dripping oaks and mountain ash. The pastoral vista towards the Inny and upper Tamar from Bodmin moor to Dartmoor is obscured by drizzling cloud.

Tons of paving setts and finished blocks for embankments, bridges, parapets and lighthouses were once sent down this hill in trucks, destined for Devonport, London, the Scillies, Guernsey, Gibraltar and Singapore. Sidings joined the mineral railway, winding from Kelly Bray to Hingston Down, which opened in 1872. Early traffic also included ores, arsenic, Phoenix bricks for Russia and Pearson's granite. Another rope-worked incline dropped trucks from the Butts to Calstock quay where stone was unloaded for shipment in 500 ton 'flats' – steamers for transport down the tidal Tamar. Once the viaduct was completed in 1908 river traffic declined but, for a while, a steam-operated lift linked the south-western line with riverside quays.

An abundance of apples

November 2003

Beauty of Cornwall, Devon Crimson Queen, Early Bower and Venus Pippin apples were made into sorbets, sauces and ice creams included in menus celebrating the diversity of local food and traditional apples at the Dartmoor Inn near Lydford. James and Mary gathered 60 varieties for displays and tastings there and at Cotehele House, staggering the picking to coincide with optimum ripeness. Trees in the 'mother-orchard' are now mostly bare, underlain with the sweet, cidery smell of fallen fruit. Little green Cornish Longstem apples still cling on and King Byerd will be picked and stored for winter use. Water droplets, cobwebs and fringing nettles reflect low sunlight slanting beneath branches but, in this tightly planted reference orchard, the

*Calstock viaduct which links Cornwall with Devon,
crossing high above the tidal Tamar*

collection of labelled trees grows spiry, restricted from developing characteristic shapes.

Alongside the adjoining and more widely spaced cherry orchard, sheltered by a sunny hedge of berried hawthorn tangled with flowering ivy, a spreading tree is loaded with shiny yellow apples flushed pink. These Longkeeper apples will remain juicy and crisp well into next year but the Hockings Green, once widely grown in east Cornwall, is surrounded by fruit dropped early and small after the unusually dry summer and autumn. Earlier in the day, on the Tommy Knight (grafted from a rare survivor at St Agnes) bright red apples were glazed with ice and the leaves edged with rime. Cold mist lay in the valleys below white frosted fields and Jeff's Limousin suckler cows stood side-on to the warmth of the sun rising above Dartmoor's clear skyline.

Daffodil valley

April 2005

A startling primrose slope shimmers through bare trees at Cleave where a regime of summer strimming has allowed plants to seed out and thrive on the sunny ground. By the millstream survive ragged rows of once-commercial Croesus and Lucifer daffodils, both with orange cups and creamy-white petals. The millpond, where I used to swim with my cousin towards the waterwheel, is truncated and dammed off from the converted mill. The wooden launder to the overshot wheel has long been demolished but, after more than 30 years in store, its thick oak planks are being recycled as benches in a nearby farmhouse.

In the converging valley, a plot of fragrant white Ornatus, with distinctive pheasant-eye centre, still flowers profusely among hazel scrub. This *poeticus* type of narcissus was once widely grown as a follow-up to the slightly earlier Actea and Horace. As long ago as in 1927, a neighbouring grower noted in his diary that he had purchased four hundredweights of Ornatus bulbs for £20 but this particular garden was probably planted more recently. On surrounding hedges tall White Ladies, with white petals and lemon centres, are inclined to flop and spoil in damp weather. These bulbs would have been dug up and thrown out in favour of the newer, more reliable and commercially viable blooms. Uphill, between banks thick with big clumps of primroses, bright dandelions and patches of vividly blue violets, ever-wider tractors, en route to manure and roll fields, have eroded the sides of narrow lanes. Near home, a herd of suckler cows bellows as each one is put through the crush, in a routine test for TB.

A walk across Wessex

October 2005

We walk from Streatley-on-Thames in west Berkshire to Maiden Newton in Dorset, mainly on the Ridgeway national trail, passing a succession of chalky horizons marked by knolls of trees, ancient forts and modern masts. Didcot power station, Harwell research establishment and spreading Swindon seem remote – background features for the play of light and shade below this rolling downland with its pale track. Sections of the way's surface have been modified recently with deep gutters and compacted chalk rubble, and signs prohibiting wheeled vehicles between November and May. In Oxfordshire, Uffington's prehistoric and dazzling white horse 'races' above its precipitous mangers (and the strange dragon hill), but it is no longer 'scoured' during ceremonial fairs. Days later in Wiltshire we pass above Westbury's white horse, now covered in painted cement. Turf on lynchets, escarpments, gallops and banks contrasts with the shallow flinty earth and deeper browner soils in coombes, all minimally cultivated, with furrows curving to the edge of large fields and tractors pulling two implements in one pass followed by seagull flocks. Big straw bales, scattered or in lines, appear small in this expansive landscape, adding to the incongruity of Silbury Hill peeping out of its site by Avebury (and the nearby sinuous course of the Wansdyke).

Apart from tractor drivers, very few people are out in the open countryside. Two couples are walking all the way from Lyme Regis to Hunstanton in Norfolk; a huntsman consults a man on a quad bike with an orange-eyed eagle owl in its cage; a party of pheasant shooters ride in a converted horse-box to a drive below marshals waving red flags; and a platoon of soldiers packs up guns on the Imber range.

We pass onwards through clayey woods on Cranborne Chase in Dorset and quiet picturesque villages with ponds. Ox droves and bridleways continue between hedges thick with berries and the fluffy golden orbs of ivy flowers, a magnet for red admirals and bees. Strong winds buffet the ridges above the Frome valley, and we descend overlooked by sheep spread over Cattistock's castle hill and a cluster of aerials on more distant

Rampisham Down. The thatched roof of our last B&B stop absorbs the sound of rain in the night, and by morning the river runs full and muddy.

Painting the mine

June 2006

Sometimes I accompany my sister, a painter, on her occasional forays away from the Tamar valley to the coast. Dizzard wood at bluebell time is buffeted by storms. Then comes a clear day when she can stand and paint without tying down the easel, set above a tangle of stunted oaks plunging towards the butterfly wing blue of Bude Bay. By late afternoon, encroaching mist blots out sea and land; swallows swooping up over the crest of this north-facing wood to fly low inland across an early cut silage field and cow poached pastures. More days of fog, rain and wind stall any attempt to paint cliffs at Botallack. Then, at the end of last week, we went to that exposed coastal belt, once noisy with mining machinery. At its peak, in the 1860s, there were 11 beam engines operating and 550 people working under and over ground at this mine alone. Victorian tourists went down into the submarine workings under the spectacular Crowns engine house, lowered down in a special wagon or gig (even after an accident when the gig chain broke, killing eight miners and a boy in 1863).

Now, ruins, stark chimneys and dumped reddish spoil are engulfed in flowery summer vegetation, including the precipitously set shaft where a granite plaque reminds of the

20 men drowned in 1893 after 'a holing engulfed the mine with water'. Ruined walls have been capped, shafts covered with grilles, stonework repointed and toxic arsenic removed so that these historic sites can be explored by visitors. Hart's tongue ferns and fresh ivy leaves shoot beneath brambles, with campions, sorrel, cocksfoot and bluebells growing in abandoned little fields. Pink thrift and white bladder campion thrive along the old tramway (now part of the coastal path) and colonise retaining banks of early tin-dressing floors.

The silver river

January 2007

Downriver from the Hooe meander, exposed Thorn Point is strewn with seaweed, the strand littered with driftwood, cabbage leaves, cans and plastic debris. Across choppy salt water, the old warehouse on Cargreen quay is now a dwelling but, within living memory, the agricultural merchant delivered supplies by boat across the tidal river to this isolated causeway. Cornish strawberries were also brought over and carted to Bere Ferrers railway station, a mile away through fields. Upstream, beyond saltings at the mouth of a wooded tributary – already spring-like with golden catkins, honeysuckle and elder leaves – sailing boats are moored off Weir quay. As early as the 13th century this berth served local silver mines, and in the 19th century the smelting works was an important centre for lead and silver, including ores imported from Spain, France and Newfoundland.

Lumps of slag with solidified runnel marks can still be found on the shore, and 28lb and 56lb ingots of Tamar tin were salvaged from the wreck of the steamship Cheerful, 110 years after it sank 25 miles north-east of the Longships, en route to Liverpool in 1885.

Beneath corrosion, ingots still bear the hot marks of the Tamar works – the lamb and flag symbol of purity and the name, Tamar Tin Smelting Company. Also included were ingots from Treloweth at St Erth, and Carvedras and Trethellan, both at Truro. The Tamar works closed in 1896 and was later reopened and adapted as a jam factory.

Across the peninsula, a path skirting the river Tavy's mud banks is edged with bright green cow parsley and alexanders leaves. Uphill, camellias flower in the specialist shrub nursery, and daffodils are out in hedgerows and a commercial bulb field.

Showing off the crops

March 2007

Pyramids and plastic face packs of creamy cauliflowers were interspersed with tiers of perfect camellia blooms at the 83rd West Cornwall Spring Show at Penzance, a week before the recent icy blast of weather. Effulgent magnolias and flamboyant Cornish Red rhododendrons contrasted with sprays of dark conifers. Children's miniature gardens, arranged on seed trays, included a unique self-sufficient version, complete with wind generator and rows of tiny seedling vegetables. Egg yolks were displayed alongside their broken shells, and there were simnel cakes, and honey and floral arrangements. Two boxes of de Caen anemones and another box of large violets bunched up with ivy leaves, made up the classes for packed exhibits grown in the open. This part of Cornwall is renowned for its early crops – the nearby golden mile continues to produce cauliflowers and potatoes. On the cliffs towards Lamorna, old terraced and stonewalled gardens, known as 'quillets', once grew flowers and potatoes. Hedges of fuchsia and privet further protected these pockets of cultivable ground, facing south-east and away from prevailing salty gales. The sheltering bushes have since amalgamated into thickets, sprawling among blackthorn and gorse, but old-fashioned narcissi survive, emerging ragged between brambles. These plots were laboriously created in the early 20th century when local quarries were still active. Picking flowers and sending them by rail to upcountry markets where these early flowers were appreciated as harbingers of spring was an important source of income. Now, celandines, succulent scurvy grass, three-cornered leek, campion and stitchwort are flowering along the coastal path, set high above blocky granite rocks battered by the swirling sea.

Boats with wheels

August 2007

Two miles upstream from Bude Haven a fisherman sits on the grassy wharf, overlooking water lilies and shielded by willows from the 'Atlantic Highway' – the A39. Close by, in a restored workshop, is displayed a surviving tub boat. This flat-bottomed craft, with its four little wheels, was dug out of preserving mud almost a hundred years after the Bude canal was abandoned in 1891. It took sea sand inland, its wheels allowing it to be dragged up and down the rails on incline planes between different levels of the narrow waterway. Underground water wheels powered the inclines and horses pulled the 20ft boats as they floated along the winding, shallow channel, each carrying four tonnes and working in trains of four or six. Sea sand with a high calcareous content was long valued as a fertiliser for sweetening acid soils. In the 15th century packhorses carried it to Werrington, on the upper Tamar, at an average cost of 1s/2d for 20 horse-loads. When the canal reached Launceston in 1825, prices for this essential commodity dropped by three-quarters. Such a hard-won local product and its integrated transport bear little resemblance to today's reliance on mechanically pulverised limestone and oil-based artificial manures, bulk manufactured and delivered to merchants and farms by lorries.

At the canal mouth the sea lock has been refurbished since 2000 with greenheart oak from South America, and gates and fitments made in Holland. Tourists, braced against the wind, stroll along the edge of the basin, gazing towards the breakwater and beyond, to the choppy, silver-streaked ocean. The adjoining beach, once the source of fertiliser, is thronged with people enjoying the sand and surf, while daring youngsters brave big waves washing over the outer wall of the sea-filled bathing pool.

CHAPTER

Ten

Half and Half

In just a few years' time it will be 100 years since Helena Swanwick became the first woman to write the Country Diary. If her spirit joins the celebrations, it will no longer be alone in a room full of chaps wearing cardigans and smoking pipes. For most of the century, there has only been one woman at a time in a team of half-a-dozen, but the 1990s brought change, on a large scale by the standards of this miniature world. There are four women now – in 2008 – out of 14 regular contributors, and those in charge want the ratio to carry on moving in the direction of equal balance.

The increase in women's numbers was started in the 1980s by a burly man with a beard, Chris Maclean, the section editor who pleased Enid Wilson by turning up at her home in the Lake District with the carapace of a dead freshwater shrimp. He enlisted Sarah Poyntz to keep Veronica Heath company, and was looking for others when internal changes at the paper moved him elsewhere. During a subsequent period of confusion for the column, when a wholesale redesign of the *Guardian* saw the diary vanish to the back of the new G2 section, Jeannette Page managed to hold things together and brought first Audrey Insch and then Virginia Spiers on board.

Page shares Spiers' view that warmth is a distinctive quality of the women diarists' writing, treating their mostly unknown readers like friends and encouraging them to feel involved in the gentle pottering and poking about. The work is characteristically accessible too; amateur observations are reported, as opposed to the confident tone of many of the male Country Diary writers who have worked professionally for wildlife and nature-related organisations. When news gets round of a space, the Country Diary editor can expect a grand total of 600 hopefuls (usually around a third are women) to write in, on top of the half-dozen or so who apply every month on spec. But the field then narrows dramatically when the test of merit is applied and the need for a geographical mix. Page was delighted when both worked in favour of Insch, who initially wrote from south-west London, where she was teaching. 'I had just been thinking that it would be a refreshing change to have an urban diary, and perhaps a metropolitan one,' says Page. Insch's address in Wimbledon hit the spot.

The current editor of the Country Diary, Celia Locks, has kept up the pace, looking particularly for female recruits on the rare occasions when one of the team retires or, as has happened with more than a third of all diary writers, dies in harness. She was an urban child herself, but lived just close enough to Epping Forest in east London to go for walks there, checking out plants and stalking the wildlife. Her father worked for a local newspaper group and the family had a walled garden behind their house, which provided a second world of nature on a smaller scale. One of Locks' favourite diaries is the miniaturist one by Enid Wilson referred to earlier in this book, written during ill health when the usual ramblings along the Lakeland valleys or to outlying farms had to be replaced by a simple survey of Wilson's garden. 'She discovered so much, from spiders and shrew-mice to chaffinches,' Locks says. In the same way, the Locks went frogspawning, learned about flowers from Celia's mother, who was a knowledgeable gardener, and watched ducks on Eagle Pond. 'I remember getting very excited when Canada geese arrived,' Locks remembers. 'They're everywhere now – an indication of the way that nature changes.'

When she took over editing the Country Diary after the millennium, she inherited an idiosyncratic rota, some columnists writing twice every three weeks, others fortnightly, a third group monthly and Virginia Spiers tenaciously sticking to one every three weeks. They seemed a settled lot, but then Insch moved to Edinburgh from Pembrokeshire, to which she had successfully transferred the diary after retiring from teaching in London. Scotland was already well-covered and so she bowed out. There was therefore a vacancy in Wales.

Locks would have appointed a woman if one had leapt out of the pile of applications; but none did. 'I was astonished how difficult it was to find one,' she says; instead the monthly contribution went to the distinguished mountain writer Jim Perrin, who lives in the beautiful Tanat valley running west into the mid-Wales hills from the Shropshire border. The men were creeping back into their old dominance; until in 2006 the chance came to make two appointments – in Celia's description of the column's curious schedule, 'each writing a column nearly once a fortnight'. One was from the Shetland islands and the other in east Yorkshire.

Both were new places to be chosen as long-term diary stations, although past writers had made occasional visits to Hull, the Yorkshire Wolds and the wartime seaplane station on Hornsea Mere. It was from this gentle farming area that Celia took a phone call in the spring of 2007 from a Mrs Rosemary Roach, whose adult son Darrell had recently started buying the *Guardian*. 'I borrowed it and read the Country Diary with interest, but I didn't see one for Yorkshire,' says Roach, showing the traditionally strong loyalties of her county. 'I plucked up courage to telephone and I spoke to Celia Locks and asked if they had anyone writing a diary for Yorkshire. She said: "No; are you offering?" so I replied: "Yes!"' She submitted a trial piece, Locks was pleased and Rosemary adds, in the time-honoured phrase used by Janet Case, Enid Wilson and Veronica Heath: 'I have been doing it ever since.'

Roach could be loosely called a housewife, but as is usually the case with that term, she does a great deal else besides. Darrell has three sisters and a brother, all of them aged between 23 and 33 and three still living at home with Roach and her husband, Tony, in the village of North Cave. The couple have a grandchild to babysit in the next village; and then there's the matter of three acres of heated greenhouses where they commercially grow cucumbers; Tony is in charge, but Rosemary plants, crops, grades, picks and packs. And, interestingly, carries out a regular wildlife survey of the nursery so that the cukes can qualify for Tesco's 'Nature's Choice' branding.

There is another side to her life, too. She was brought up on the far side of Hull in the pretty village of Winestead, birthplace of Andrew Marvell, whose poem The Garden matches Gilbert White as an inspiration for Country Diarists. It was a farming community and her mother had a smallholding where the children helped, so that learning about plants and wildlife was second nature. While her conventional career took her from school to secretarial college with no qualifications higher than a clutch of O-levels, including biology and English, she was busy seeking the company of other wildlife enthusiasts. She joined the Wolds and Riverbank Countryside Society and became secretary. She started keeping records of butterflies and moths and is now the membership secretary for Butterfly Conservation's Yorkshire branch. She has done bird surveys for the British Trust for Ornithology and the Royal Society for the Protection of Birds and contributed to the national survey of shieldbugs.

Quite a busy housewife, then. And her enthusiasm dovetails with that of the diary's second recent recruit, Christine Smith, who has been the column's most northerly outpost since 2006. From an old clifftop house in Shetland, Smith marches out daily on walks with a sense of freedom that she never quite felt in the north of England, where she was brought up. This has a modern relevance to the work of female naturalists and not a happy one, given that quiet observation is mostly best done alone. Smith says: 'Shetland is a place where a woman can walk on her own without any of the worry and wariness which you can't get away from in other parts of the country. You can simply relax here and let your mind take in the surroundings.' The freedom also encourages the mind to wander; there are endless sources of themes for the Country Diary in Shetland, and initial ideas for the column regularly change. One February week this year, Smith set out to look for frozen waterfalls and ended up writing about collecting driftwood. Strenuous solitary walking exercises the mind, she reckons, and leads to a meditative state which, in turn, creates a sense of connection with the landscape.

She discovered Shetland more than 20 years ago, on holiday with a friend whom she had met on the lower yardarm of the training schooner *Winston Churchill.* They shared a love of walking in the countryside, which had been much encouraged in Smith by her parents on summer outings with them and her younger brother, and by happy chance, the friend had a dog that had got old and lame. 'So we discovered the pleasures of walking slowly, which include seeing birds and then learning to watch them carefully,' says Smith. She and her friend lived 125 miles apart, but invested together in a shared first telescope. On the way back from another trip to Shetland, the hobby brought Smith together with her husband, Simon. 'We were the only two people on the deck in the rain, watching birds,' she says.

They got married on the same boat ten years later, and it was Simon who pushed her to have a go at writing a *Guardian* Country Diary. 'Go on,' he said, as she was humming and hawing about putting herself forward. Both have a love of living on islands and in 1994 they went for five years to the remote billet of Skomer, off Pembrokeshire, where Simon was warden of the island nature reserve while Christine carried out seabird research for Oxford University. By default, she also took over a column in the local newspaper called Skomer Diary, which was reckoned to be good publicity for the work on the reserve. It was her first crack at writing and she loved it. 'I got into the swing and it just got longer and longer,' she says. 'They didn't seem to mind how much you put in.'

The *Guardian* would be different, she knew, and when an envelope with the newspaper's franking arrived in Shetland, she was sure that it would be a polite rejection. Instead, she read a letter from Celia Locks saying: 'Let's do it,' and so another step towards gender equality in the column was taken. The whale at the end of Smith's garden and the otter with a taste for guillemots joined the Country Diary's long cast of characters. 'I was amazed by them,' she says in words that could stand for all her colleagues, going back to Helen Swanwick's debut. 'I wanted to share them that so that others could be amazed too.'

Christine Smith

Birds on the seacliffs

May 2006

A day of bright sunshine, a high blue sky streaked with white mares' tails. A brisk breeze – but now the damp ground smells of warmth and spring, the sea is a deep, rich, bright blue of the startling intensity that is characteristic of Shetland. From the cliff edge one of the pair of nesting ravens leans outward, throat feathers ruffling in the wind, and cronks out a warning call to its partner below. A skylark's song cascades from above, while on a knoll a mad-eyed oystercatcher repeatedly pipes its carrying two-note call.

Wheatears are everywhere, their white rumps catching the eye. A few weeks ago there were none; now on every other boulder and tussock there is a tail-flicking bird giving a brief burst of scratchy yet melodic song before taking flight again.

Down where the sea and the land meet in a jumble of boulders and stones is a rocky outcrop perfect for sheltering from the wind. A solitary guillemot idly swims on the calmer water. It dives and I wait for it to resurface, which it does in an explosion of wildly flapping wings. I grab my binoculars and am astonished to see the bird is clamped in the jaws of an otter, which is swimming strongly for the shore, ignoring the flailing blows from the guillemot's wings. Out of the water surges the otter, and there is one last flurry of wings before, with one or two snaps of the jaw, the struggle is ended. The otter takes some time to complete its meal before it slips back into the water. It dives, its sinuous body visible until it disappears into a tangle of weed.

A feast of sand eels

July 2006

After a fine summer day, the night time is little more than a period of deep twilight and near dark before sunrise. Vegetation has taken on luxuriant shades of yellows, whites, pinks and purples. In the short cliff-top grass below the house are the first

*Christine Smith's clifftop house in Shetland –
the most northerly outpost of the Country Diary*

creamy delicate flowers of Grass of Parnassus and shiny-leaved cushions of rich purple thyme. The cliffs are hanging gardens of variously hued pink thrift and sunshine-yellow bird's-foot trefoil. The nearby stony beach is out of bounds – a small group of Arctic terns are breeding there and even walking some distance behind the beach provokes diving attacks from the birds. Others are bringing silvery sand eels to feed the chicks.

The roadside verges and ditches show colourful abundance. There are floating cloud-like flower heads of hogweed, unknown whispering grasses, red clover scenting the air, the last of the orchids showing in purple spikes and yellow tormentil spangling the ditch banks. Any walk is filled with the sound of birds. The gulls swoop over the road adding their objections to your passing by. A pair of whimbrel added to the medley when they wandered, with their chick, from their breeding area to the end of our track. Until they moved on again their repeated piercing alarm calls were almost constant as they protested the movement of anything and everything – sometimes from the air, sometimes standing long-legged on a fence post, with curved bill agape.

Mice in the boot

December 2006

Another grey morning. Low cloud hides the hill behind the house, sits sullenly on the headland and hangs heavily over the sea. It's raining hard again and the burns running off the hills are full and peaty, spouting and splashing their way downhill on to already sodden land. A strong breeze drives the rain into diagonals and picks up the sea into white caps.

When the weather clears, it's a pleasure to be outdoors. A watery sun gleams over the sea and inland a towering grey and cream sky trails hail showers over the hills. Lapwing swoop overhead, and curlew call and take flight. Small flocks of turnstone rise silently from the fields, swirl briefly and resettle. The contact calls of the greylag geese precede their appearance in a wavering line over the crest of the hill. Coming nearer, they gradually lose height until in a rush of wings and clamour of musical calls they land on the slopes and begin to feed. The winds have brought rarer visitors too, both North American ducks. In the north of the isles a bufflehead appeared, while in the south a redhead was found on Spiggie loch. Birders cram visits into the short days.

Less welcome visitors are the mice, who find indoor life an inviting prospect in the cold. Having finally been blocked from every access to the house, one at least has found its way into the car boot, where it has set about the contents. The boot is now equipped with a live trap and the cheese has already been taken once – but the marauder is still at large.

The palette of dawn

January 2007

In south-easterly gales the sea hurls itself against the low cliffs below the house, flinging spray into the air. Seized by the wind, it is instantly reduced to a fine salty airborne mist, driven inland

and occasionally lifted over the kirk roof. Down on the rocky beach a layer of frothy off-white foam is built up; small globules are blown free, whirled briefly into the air or bowled across the road on to the fields, where they remain like unseasonal patches of cotton grass. The morning after a gale our windows are opaque with dried salt.

At this time of year the sun rises from the sea directly in front of the house. Rarely is there a clear sky, but the clouds and the state of the sea ensure that no two sunrises are alike. The reds, oranges and golds of the strengthening light, the changing silhouetted shapes of the clouds (their lilacs, greys and purples underlit with warmth before the sun even breaks the horizon) are glorious. The sea picks up the breaking light forming a complex shifting pattern of copper on steel.

Yesterday morning was a succession of showers, sunshine and rainbows intermittently bathing the hillside behind the house in light and warmth – perfect for seeing mountain hares, whose white winter coats render them startlingly visible in these conditions. Lying in little hollows or under overhanging peat edges were 14 individuals, the most I've ever seen at any one time here. One delightful addition to our garden has been the robin that has been present on and off since November. A rare winter visitor in Shetland, it's one of several small birds common elsewhere but of note here. That other favourite garden bird, the blue tit, turns up even more infrequently – two birds seen in 2005 were the first recorded in Shetland since 1999.

Wind in the winter

February 2007

In the dead of winter the sun rises so late and darkness falls so early in the afternoon that days are just brief intervals between the long nights. The winter hasn't yet passed, but already the days have lengthened considerably and there is a sense of change on the way. In summer, oystercatchers seem to be present everywhere, their far-carrying peep-peeping clear among the calls and songs of the other birds that are the constant background to any outside activity. In the winter the oystercatchers leave us. Shetland is not quiet in winter, but for me the sound of the weather is the major theme: the wind whistling and roaring around the house and clattering the roof slates, hail pinging off the windows, the sound of the sea crashing into the cliffs or the singing of the swell after a gale. But it took just one call from a returning oystercatcher this week to awaken an instant anticipation of the summer and its music – to signal the beginning of the end of winter.

Ravens hold territory all year, so the pair that breed in one of the two geos near the house are never too far away – now they are displaying with increasing frequency, their loud cronking calls alerting us to another precision performance. They fly almost wing tip to wing tip, matching each other's movements with effortless elegance until corvid exuberance takes over and one throws in a casual stall or a jaunty roll.

Fulmars also nest in the geos, coming and going throughout the winter. That morning, birds occupying ledges cackled in warning as others intruded into their space. A fulmar had taken possession of the nest used by the ravens for the last two seasons – not uncommon where they share cliffs. In the other geo, the remains of the older nest had disappeared: only time will tell if the fulmar occupancy is a bit of temporary cheek.

Life in the mist

April 2007

The morning started misty, with white swaths of fog drifting across the sea and blowing ghostlike past the house, while the white-hazed disc of the sun briefly appeared and then vanished as it lost the struggle to break through. The only sound in the mist-imposed stillness was the water trickling off the moor and the plaintive note of a distant golden plover, the only movement that of half-seen sheep picking their way over the grazing. Suddenly the hilltop emerged from the greyness as the mist settled into layers. Weak sunshine began to brighten the higher slopes and glimpses of blue sky appeared overhead. Within minutes the hills were clear, the coastal mist dispersed in rags and tatters, and the landscape was full of sound and movement.

On the heights, a party of bouncing, squabbling hooded crows appeared, their harsh cries a contrast to the song from the two skylarks starting their ascent into the newly cleared sky. A meadow pipit unwound its song as it floated downward, while a curlew passed in an elegant controlled glide, its bubbling song so evocative of a moorland spring. In the valley lapwing launched noisily into their aerial performance, climbing, swooping, rolling, tumbling, displaying aerobatic mastery with an air of abandon.

Other birds are already nest-building. Around the house two pairs of starlings were taking nest material into their chosen sites – one in the stone outbuilding and the other in the garden wall. The blackbirds' previous tactic of ground nesting has resulted in their eggs being plundered. Now they have opted for the wall, taking the further precaution of choosing a site behind a stunted fir tree. Described in the survey as 'little more than a dilapidated field dyke', the stone wall is desirable real estate in the bird world, and is also used by one or two pairs of wrens. Even the mossy top is plundered for lining material.

The crooning seals

December 2007

The ferocious winds of the past few days had died away to a fresh breeze and, though cold, the day was bright and invigorating. Setting off briskly, I was soon gazing southward to where the sun lit the open sea to undulating silver. Nearer the shore, from a raft of eiders came soft, suggestive calls as the males, with their unlikely pink breasts and green napes, indulged in a little out-of-season courting. Across the bay a more drawn-out crooning could just be heard, and then suddenly from below another voice answered. Skirting the crumbling wall that marks the unsafe cliff edge, I found a safe vantage point. Below was a seal hauled out on a rock. No! Three seals, two still so dark, wet and shiny that they merged all but perfectly with the rocks.

The largest and driest reclined gracefully on its side, hind flippers curving into the air. Sensing my presence, it turned a fore flipper, scratched idly; dark eyes regarded me assessingly. Then, dismissing me as being no danger, it returned its gaze to the bay and recommenced its singing, accompanied by a less melodious burst of cackling from the nearby fulmars. With the sun behind me the colours took on a new intensity in the clear light. A small fishing boat thumped along the sound, red hull glowing against the blue sea.

Further on, the sea lapped gently against the deep orange-yellow sand of the little enclosed beach. A single bird drifted into view. Cautiously, in the hope of getting closer, I picked my way along the little jetty as far as the exposed slippery seaweed. As the bird slowly paddled nearer, I saw it was a puffin. Not the instantly recognisable bright-billed creature of the summer, but a bird travelling incognito. Grey-faced, narrow-billed, it was a juvenile blown landwards by the earlier gales from the puffins' usual wintering grounds, well out to sea.

The Mirrie Dancers

December 2007

This is the time of year when we pay for the long days and brief nights of the Shetland summer. The seemingly endless light of the 'simmer dim' is both months behind us and still months in the future. Now the days are short and darkness comes early – on cloudy days daylight sometimes seems to have barely been here at all. The sea and the lochs reflect the greyness of the sky and the colours of the landscape are flat and dull. Some days the sun slices its way through narrow gaps in the cloud with great searchlight beams of warm orange, which light the land with welcome pools of colour. There are also sun-filled days of incredible beauty, from the red-gold blaze of pre-sunrise skies to the towering peach and steely lilac clouds as the day softens and fades, and when the light has gone there is the magnificence of the winter night sky. A sky that is filled with undimmed stars and sometimes lit by the wonder that is the Mirrie Dancers or Northern Lights.

Shetland, with its northerly location and lack of light pollution, is one of the best places in Britain to see this spectacle, and we keep a regular lookout. Consulting any of the useful websites that predict aurora activity doesn't seem a very exciting approach, so we opt for the low-tech option. On a very clear night we put on coats and hats, open the door, go outside, watch the sky and shiver. The Mirrie Dancers in the middle of a performance cannot be mistaken for anything else, but displays vary in form, colour and intensity, and sometimes the beginning and ending can be subtle, so a first glimpse of any unusual colour or brightness sparks hopeful anticipation. However, even without the Mirrie Dancers, the nights are striking. Out in the bay the moonlight strikes a clear path across the sea and silhouettes the skerries, guarded by their flashing light. On the headland and the stack beyond, a red and a white light blink their own regular rhythms and between them create a third.

From one side of the sky to the other the Milky Way is a silvery blur while the constellations stand out crisp and clear.

Orion, invisible earlier, has cleared the horizon and now strides across the sky, Sirius at his heels. We find the others which are as easily recognisable – the Plough, Cassiopeia, Ursa Minor and the Pleiades – and wonder how every year we manage to forget the new constellations we learned so carefully the previous winter.

Harvest of the beach

February 2008

Visiting the nearby small beaches to see what's been washed ashore after strong winds is always interesting. Sometimes it's not much more than the ubiquitous rubber-soled sandal but other times are much more rewarding. Maybe a couple of cowries discovered after searching through the pebbles. Once, we found an item like a giant dustpan with a long handle – we've no idea what it is, but it makes an efficient snow scoop. Then there was the large wooden frog. Our beachcombing usually has a practical aspect to it as we burn driftwood in the multi-fuel stove in our sitting room. Our most recent visit was to a nearby cove where a small stream has worn a slippery access route through otherwise steep cliffs. Down on the sheltered beach, it was treasure trove. A wren flitted from rock to rock feeding madly while, beach stones clinking and grinding underfoot, we scrambled gleefully about amassing a surprising quantity of wood. The waterlogged wood is heavy and the largest pieces cumbersome and difficult to manoeuvre, particularly uphill, so only some of our haul made it back to our wood store to dry out. The rest remains piled above the high-water line for later collection. Wood from the sea – wrack wood – left like this is sacrosanct in Shetland and no one would dream of removing wood from someone else's pile.

Other beach finds are part of the garden. Bright plastic fish boxes become planters and a prized old wooden fish box looks lovely filled with thrift and bronze grasses. Yellow, orange and green fishing floats piled against a stone wall provide a welcome splash of colour in the winter. On the island of Mousa my husband once found the great prize of beachcombing – the legendary message in a bottle – its words still legible despite its journey from the Faroe Islands.

Rosemary Roach

Return of the butterflies

May 2007

The countryside is coming alive, looking very lush and vibrant, with all the shades of fresh green. The oak is in full leaf but the ash is only just starting to break, and the saying 'oak before ash, we will just get a splash' is certainly ringing true this spring, although the garden would really welcome a good soaking. There has been a short, sharp shower of rain, but for it to be of any good we need more prolonged rainfall. The fields are a patchwork of colour, with the vivid yellow oil-seed rape dazzling us in the sunshine and assaulting our noses with its pungent smell. You either love it or loathe it: I like it from a

The Humber bridge linking the north
and south banks of the Humber estuary

distance, but the insects love it. A local beekeeper once told me that people with allergic reactions to oil-seed rape should, during winter, have in their diet some honey made from it, and it will alleviate their problem.

The sunny weather has brought out all the spring butterflies and, as a member of Butterfly Conservation (Yorkshire branch), I have been out in my garden recording them. I have been very pleased to see the brimstone, peacock, small tortoiseshell, comma and all the whites, including the orange tip, but just the male so far with the distinctive orange tip to its wing; however, the female can often be mistaken for the green-veined white when in flight, because it has a black tip to its wing, and its underwings are a mottled green. Also, it has been good to see again the speckled wood fluttering around my garden. This butterfly has moved beyond its traditional wood margins and only recently has extended its range to the east and to the north. I remember in 2002 travelling over to Brayton Barff, near Selby, to see them there, because it was as if there was a line east of which they were not recorded. Now they are on my doorstep! It is a promising start to the season.

The last of the sunshine

June 2007

Heading towards Hull, on the outskirts of the pretty village of North Cave, and just five minutes away from the busy M62/A63 junction, is the Yorkshire Wildlife Trust's North Cave Wetlands nature reserve. Once a commercial sand and gravel quarry, a successful campaign saved it from becoming a household tip, and it has now been transformed into a freshwater reserve. I stepped through the gate into tranquillity and took a leisurely stroll down the perimeter track. The lingering evening sun was still licking at the wild roses and bramble flowers and glossing the cherries that were starting to change colour. Enjoying this evening sun were a colony of the pretty brown and cream speckled wood butterflies, which seem to be getting everywhere now. There was also a painted lady, refreshing its energy in the dappled sun's rays. The painted lady is one of our migrant butterflies, and perhaps it had just arrived from the continent, flying in off the North Sea and making its way inland.

Migrant birds were in abundance too: I heard the plaintive call of the willow warbler, a family of blackcaps along the wooded walk were chucking at me to move on and sand martins were continually trawling over the lakes. Then there were swifts, squealing and circling around. The swift is one of the last of the migrants to arrive in May and among the first to leave in August. Swifts spend their whole life on the wing, apart from when they are on the nest they sleep in the air, circling to heights of 1,000 to 2,000 metres. Each time I see swifts I remember that the 18th-century writer Gilbert White thought swallows and swifts hibernated here in the winter cocooned in mud at the bottom of lakes! Of course we now know that they spend the winter in Africa, and return here each spring.

A trip back home

August 2007

We are in Winifred Holtby territory, seeking the tranquillity of the countryside immortalised in her novel *South Riding,* but on this rare summer's day the farmers are out in force, trying to get their harvest in. In one field, though, part of the barley has been left standing; huge muddy ruts in the stubble show that the ground is so wet for the heavy combine harvesters that they are unable to continue.

We drive on into Holderness, taking the country lane that leads through the pretty hamlet of Winestead, and as we pass the Old Rectory we think of the inspiration that the 17th-century poet Andrew Marvell must have gained from here when his father was rector. We soak in the view: in the distance, looking southwards, there is the Lincolnshire coast rising above the Humber, and on a good day you can see ships trawling down the river to the sea. Scanning eastwards there is the tall spire of St Patrick's church at Patrington, known as the Queen of Holderness, virtually unchanged since its completion in 1410. In contrast, further to the east at Out Newton, rows of wind turbines spin round.

The alarm call of a pheasant in a paddock close by breaks the stillness. A cock pheasant is prancing about as it is lobbed by swallows: it displays to them and has a merry old dance. Butterflies are dancing too, enjoying the sun. The seemingly black ringlets flutter in the grasses then move over to the bramble-clad hedgerow and back again, never tiring. As they settle on the bramble flowers to seek nectar, you can see the five small white rings on their wings, and how they got their name. Alas, this summer the rain is never far away, and looking skyward, dark shapes have moved in from the west, hiding the sun. In the field the ringlets are now nowhere to be seen as the first heavy drops of rain fall.

Traps in the grass

November 2007

Walking in the early-morning mist is like walking into a world in a different dimension, almost like entering Narnia, but it's not a winter wonderland, more a fairytale world of gossamer. Each bush, each shrub, each clump of grass, thistle and weed is covered with the most intricate spiders' webs. One after another, angled together, touching yet not touching, strands of silk run from one grass stalk to another, each circular web, each inner thread, glistening with tiny water droplets, like glittering jewels, highlighted by faint rays as the sun breaks through the mist. A fly, perhaps mesmerised by the glitter, stumbles into a web and a spider shoots forward and immobilises its victim. The spider rotates the fly, spinning a silken cocoon around it. It twirls and twirls it until it is covered and leaves it suspended by a thread, swinging, a pre-packed meal for it to relish later.

The spider in question is a garden diadem, grown quite large with a very bulbous abdomen. It is a beautiful shade of chocolate-brown, with its own jewelled crown of silver-white markings, but I cannot help smiling to myself because it looks as if it has striped football socks on, and I wonder which team it is playing for. Then, as I watch it, upside down now, surveying its web, I notice that the underside of its belly has two eye markings. Many insects have these false eye markings, no doubt to ward off predators. I feel very guilty as I walk on through the long grass, breaking webs as I go, for I know I am making work for the spiders. They do not just repair their web; they will reel in all the threads and spin another perfect web. Now the sun has burned away the mist, the jewels have all evaporated into thin air, and the fairyland world has disappeared. As I return home all I see now are the bushes, shrubs and grasses, all looking a little bedraggled, dull and damp.

Envoi

I wonder if you have noticed a final distinction of these women's writing as you have read through this collection: the way in which they generously compliment other women, whether fellow writers or thoughtful neighbours. I kept picking up on this as I went along, whether it was Audrey Insch enjoying Women's Institute mince pies or Sarah Poyntz warmly acknowledging the influence of Enid Wilson (as well as giving Virginia Spiers the confidence to send a sample diary to the *Guardian*).

They are a kindly band, who bear out the touching comment made to Sarah Poyntz by her father: 'Your mother and life itself have given me a very high opinion of women.' She significantly adds that 'the countryside filled him with happiness'. Here you have that same combination; and though it is certainly true that there are mean women and stupid ones, and that 'feminine' characteristics such as gentleness will be more common to both sexes as equality marches on (Hooray!), we have been lucky in the ones who brought, and continue to bring us news of nature in the *Guardian*.

Never imagine that it is all a doddle either, sauntering out of the front door and noting down flowers and birds like Fotherington-Thomas in Geoffrey Willans' books about the schoolboy Molesworth. We began with Enid Wilson, on blossom, and now we will end with her, on the hazards of getting to see it: the dangers of being a *Guardian* Country Diarist ...

July 1978

A lifetime in the Lake District and over a quarter of a century of writing Country Diaries makes me wonder if it is time to seek danger money – but from whom and for what? Most hazards are small if you respect the fells and watch your feet and the weather. There are sheep ticks if badger-watching in bracken, and deer ticks in scrub and once a usually quiet work-horse, having trodden in a wasps' nest, thundered down a steep fell and over a watched sett with all the impetus and abandon of a tank out of control.

Once a roebuck – generally self-effacing – turned nasty, menacing me with its head down, leading tines pointed forward, but then I had come on a 'roe-ring' in a thicket in July. One October dusk a red stag, with its hinds at its back and a younger stag down the wood, looked quite willing to add me to the snags for removal, roaring angrily and tossing clods in the air.

Now the menace looks very ordinary – cows. This summer I have been watching a pair of fox cubs where, two years ago, young cows shared the field and were quite content with the odd snort down my neck or a lick up the ear as I sat, stone-still, waiting. But now things are different. The cows are grown into massive black-and-white beasts and, currently, much given to rough cow-play. At first they just went in for a bit of barging and head-clashing amongst themselves but one full moon night lately (are cows affected by the moon?) they included me in their games, ending up with a kicking-up of back legs.

I left. Last night I could not – dare not – go near the earth. Am I getting soft? Victorian? I think not. A farmer I know, no small or timid man, says that in a like predicament he 'ran like hell'.

Select bibliography

Crookenden, Kate with Worlledge, Caroline and Willes, Margaret *The National Trust Book of Picnics* National Trust 1993

Heath, Veronica *A Taste of Northumberland* Powdene 2001

McBryde, Gwen (ed) *Letters to a Friend* Arnold 1955

Newman, Paul *The Tregerthen Horror* Abraxas Editions & DGR Books 2005

Page, Jeannette (ed) *A Country Diary* Fourth Estate 1994

Poyntz, Sarah *Memory Emancipated & Poems* Poyntz 2005

A Burren Journal Tir Eolas 2000

Spiers, Virginia *Burcombes, Queenies and Collogetts* West Brendon 1996

Swanwick, Helena *I Have Been Young* Victor Gollancz 1935

Thomas, Keith *Man and the Natural World* Allen Lane 1983

Wainwright, Martin (ed) *A Gleaming Landscape: A Hundred Years of the Guardian's Country Diary* Aurum/Guardian Books 2006

Wartime Country Diaries Guardian Books 2007

Wilson, Enid *Enid J Wilson's Country Diary* Hodder & Stoughton 1988

Woolf, Virginia *The Platform of Time* Hesperus 2007

Editor's biography

Martin Wainwright is the Northern editor of the *Guardian* and the husband of Penny Wainwright, who is a trustee of the Hepworth Gallery, Wakefield, and the Thackray Museum, Leeds. He is the son of Joyce Wainwright, a former nurse at Guy's Hospital in London and president of North West Leeds Liberal party. His younger sister, Tessa, teaches English as a Foreign Language in Bradford and their older sister, Hilary, is editor of *Red Pepper*.

First published in 2008 by Guardian Books
119 Farringdon Road, London EC1R 3ER
guardianbooks.co.uk

A catalogue record for this book is available from the British Library

ISBN: 978-0-85265-101-8

2 4 6 8 10 9 7 5 3 1

Designed by Two Associates
Typeset by seagulls.net
Printed and bound in Great Britain by MPG Books, Bodmin, Cornwall

PEFC
PEFC/16-33-111
CATG-PEFC-052
www.pefc.org

The policy of Guardian Books is to use papers that are natural, renewable
and recyclable products, made from wood grown in sustainable forests. In
the manufacturing process of our books, and to further support our policy,
preference is given to printers that have FSC and PEFC Chain of Custodt
certification. The FSC and/or PEFC logos will appear on those books where
full certification has been granted to the printer concerned.